ITCHY NIPPLES AND ANXIETY

My Life Is A Comedy Of Perils

BY VONDA MAXWELL NEWSOME

ISBN: 978-0-578-32194-3

contents

Acknowledgements v

Prologue: Clutziness With a 'C' ix

Introduction: There's My Little Rain Shower xiii

Chapter 1   The Great Crayon Incident 1

Chapter 2   If At First You Don't Succeed 21

Chapter 3   "Thank You, Miss Newkle!" 57

Chapter 4   Birthday Celebration at the Cornstalk Motel 87

Chapter 5   Regret 115

Chapter 6   "Hey Ruby!" 165

Chapter 7   Five Nice Ass Friends? 173

Chapter 8   Well...Why Not? 205

Chapter 9   What Dreams May Come 233

Chapter 10   Read The Plate and Figure It Out 241

Epilogue: It's OK Not To Be Perfect;
Completion is Better Than Perfection 285

ACKNOWLEDGEMENTS

This book simply could not have been written without the support, help, and love from so many amazing people. While I would love to write a novel's worth of specific good things about each and every one of you, I am afraid it would spiral out of control and become a book of its own!

So if you are on this list, please know that I could write volumes about how much you mean to me and how much I appreciate you.

And if you are not on the list but should be, please do a search in the book for all the places I talk about my ADD, and the reason will become obvious! But know that I appreciate you anyway, and will happily make it up to you somehow!

FAMILY

My parents James and Ada Maxwell (LORD, I don't know what to say here...) I think the stories will speak for themselves. I love and miss you both, always.

My husband, Greg, for putting up with me for nearly 20 years. I promised you, "It'll never be dull." I am a woman of my word and I dearly love my hot sexy testosterone pumpin' hunka mmmm. You truly deserve a medal.

My daughters, Amber and Cassandra, my stepson Matt, and our five grandchildren; Kyler, Hunter, Emily, Conner and Zachary. You've all provided me with so many wonderful experiences and countless funny stories. Stories the world will soon know...if not in this book, they'll be in the sequel. Ha!

My Aunt Sandy for being the first person to tell me my writing style resembled that of Erma Bombeck's and for encouraging me to pursue my dream of writing and publishing a book.

My talented niece, Rachael McNeill, for creating my book cover.

FRIENDS

My magical friend, Linda Cheek, for being the most supportive, encouraging, and at times like a fruit fly in my face, steadily and regularly checking on my progress and pushing me to go for it. You have been my link to the universe and my reminder to be patient (there's that "p" word again).

Duncan King-Williams, my Arthur Murray dance instructor for encouraging me to write about suicide, which I hadn't planned to include in this book. Duncan, thank you for that inspirational nudge and for dancing the polka with me! It always makes me so happy!

Aaron Orin, concert pianist and former Arthur Murray dance instructor for suggesting I contact The Carnegie Center for Literacy & Learning. Thank you, Aaron.

My therapist and life coach, Sheryl Woolverton, for without you saying, "*That* should be your book title," I wouldn't have added the *Itchy Nipples and Anxiety* part. You have helped me, and I know it's cliché, but more than words can say.

Nancy Forrest, my high school best friend and partner in crime. Oh, the things we got into (and out of) all those many moons ago. That poor bush.

Vickie Hinton, for reading my every blog post, sharing your reactions, and showering me with your loving support throughout my writing journey.

Elaine Sadlon, for believing in me and your lovely words of encouragement.

EDITORS

Leif Erickson, through the Carnegie Center for Literacy & Learning, for performing the in-depth organizing, tweaking, and final edits on my manuscript. It has been quite an adventure! When you put two ADD people together on a project, it's extremely entertaining, as well as—Look, squirrel! I knew right away that I'd found the right person and I could not have done this without you.

Dan Liebman, Owner of Staxx BBQ, Frankfort, KY, for doing a primary edit in 2019 when my book was in its infancy, its most raw draft form. Bless you for your patience.

STRUGGLES

Years ago, I saw a young girl with the phrase, "Trust your struggles" tattooed vertically up her arm in a lovely cursive font. That image stuck with me and I remembered it during my challenges. Now, I get it: Trust your struggles—for they are a necessary part of personal growth—they help lead you the right direction—one day you will realize they served a very important role in your journey.

EVERYONE

Writing this section was extremely difficult for me because the thought of inadvertently leaving someone out paralyzed me. I wanted to thank every single person who ever complimented my writing style via my blog, Facebook, everyone everywhere throughout my life. Well, to remember all those encounters would be a

Herculean task, and as I said, would probably fill another book! So, here I offer this global thank you:

To all of you who've crossed my life's path, offered a kind word of encouragement, a kudos, or a "You can do it," I sincerely thank each and every one of you, for you were all like little cobblestones gathering together, creating the path which inspired me to complete this book.

CLUTZINESS WITH a 'C'

1. Dedication

Back in 2010, when I'd been a nurse for less than two years, I had a patient, a wise and lovely elderly woman. She was witness to my extreme grace when I became tangled in the curtain between the two beds. While I was, well, untangling myself, I bumped into her bedside table, which spilled a cup of water all over the table and onto the floor. In the meantime, I dropped my pen and while bending over to pick it up, my glasses fell off.

"You are a comedy of perils!" she said while giggling.

I got the biggest kick out of that! She made my klutziness sound so elegant. By the way, I've always thought that word was spelled with a "c." You know, "clutziness." Learn something new every day! Anyway, I thought, "Yep, that's me!" I decided that if I ever wrote a book, that would be the title.

To my lovely patient, if you are reading this, I hereby dedicate this book title to you.

2. Fair Warning!

NOTE: Now, I must tell you, I do possess a bit of a warped sense of humor, which, at times, can be crude or naughty. I'm also guilty of using a curse word, or two. So, if you are one who is easily offended, appalled or otherwise insulted by such humor, crudity or words, I strongly advise you not to read beyond this note. I have now given you a fair warning.

Therefore, IF you choose to disregard said warning and IF you continue reading my book and become offended, appalled or otherwise insulted, please refrain from blasting me through horrible reviews. I am not responsible for your curiosity and/or lack of self-control. Thank you.

. . .

Being Me

People meet me
Each day I show them
This is who I am
The same as yesterday
I'm nice
I'm funny
I'm peaceful
That doesn't mean I am weak
It doesn't mean I am a pushover
I'm merely watching you show me who you are
You bully or try to control
It won't work
You will incite a fight
I can take care of myself
You won't be welcome in my life
Afterward I'll still be me
Just the same as I was when we met
I'm nice
I'm funny
I'm peaceful
I'm still being me

THERE'S MY LITTLE RAIN SHOWER

I hope that someday when I am gone, someone, somewhere, picks my soul up off of these pages and thinks, "I would have loved her."
— NICOLE LYONS

I owe a lot to COVID-19.

As we all know, in March 2020, COVID entered our world and ravaged it. However, for me personally, it was a blessing in many ways.

I had been an endoscopy recovery room nurse for about two years and was becoming burnt out. I secretly wished for "a few months off." As luck (or the universe) would have it, the caseload at work was so low, they put prn ("as needed") personnel on furlough. I ended up having four months off work and was able to receive Trump's unemployment. I cannot stress the huge impact this time off had on me, but I can explain how it changed the title of my book from *A Comedy of Perils* to *Itchy Nipples and Anxiety: My life is a comedy of perils.*

When you are given the gift of time, yet are required to stay home as much as possible due to a pandemic—the "stay busy" part of you and your life can feel extremely uncomfortable. When an anxious person slows down, activity-wise, there's nowhere to run from the anxiety. You're forced to face it, or over-indulge in drugs and alcohol to dull it (not an option for me).

I hadn't fully grieved the loss of my parents and with this time staring me in the face, I realized I needed help with the grieving process. For years, I felt I needed therapy, but when that thought would surface, I'd immediately counteract it with excuses: It costs too much. Telling one person all of my secrets is too risky—I can't have anyone knowing that much about me. It will be messy to finally deal with all of my emotions (those I shoved into a prover-bial "emotional junk closet," vowing to never let them out) and my eyes will be swollen for days. I felt the messy aftermath would outweigh the benefits.

However, I chose to see this time off work as a gift, an oppor-tunity to do something for me—to heal—at long last. I wanted to and needed to do something for myself and chose to seek ther-apy. My eldest daughter suggested a facility and I made my first appointment. Again, given the pandemic situation, no in-person sessions were allowed. I had my first session via online/Zoom on April 7, 2020.

I gave the therapist some of my personal history and told her my main reason for seeking therapy was to deal with my compli-cated grieving. I also mentioned that I did not want to take any type of medication because I felt "it is just a bandaid" and I wanted to deal with the true root of my issues. We met on a weekly basis.

In mid-June, my session led me to a real eye-opener. I'd been discussing my concern that I was suffering from paranoia because of my habit of keeping doors locked, keeping a watchful eye on oth-ers wherever I go, and the fact that I must lock the bedroom door while I shower (among others). As a child, I was alone a lot. I was a latchkey kid in grade school and by the time I was a preteen, my parents would leave me alone on weekends. I was scared a lot, but not paranoid. It taught me to be independent and rely on myself. My lack of feeling safe [I believe] came from an incident when I was 18 years old: Husband #1 (then boyfriend) and I were living in Elgin, Illinois, 40 miles from Chicago, where he worked. One evening, for whatever reason, I had to go to downtown Chicago to pick him up at the sewer repair company's headquarters. It was mid-January, extremely windy in the "Windy City" (appropriately named), very cold and dark outside. I'd exited from the freeway and was stopped at a red light. I remember looking around at the people walking across the street, noticing how differently they dressed, when I heard a loud crashing/bang noise to my right. I looked toward it and saw an arm reaching through the shattered passenger side window, snatching my purse from the seat. I screamed frantically and hit the gas to get the hell out of there!

Needless to say, we had a very chilly ride back to Elgin. I don't know which made me shake the most —the shock and terror I felt or the extreme cold wind swirling throughout the vehicle. For weeks after this "mugging," I would routinely check our entire apartment for intruders each time I entered it. *Like, what would I have done if I'd found someone? Really!*

During that first therapy session, I realized that I hadn't truly felt "safe" for a long time, or that my feelings of being safe were/ are short-lived. My therapist told me that she believed my "issues stem from anxiety." Nah, me? I knew I'd had anxiety for decades, but didn't think it was a huge deal and that I could "handle it."

She suggested that I take the Burns Anxiety Inventory. She didn't have it on hand, but I found it online, printed it, and began to answer the questions once our session ended. I added up my numbers, then turned to the last page to get my results. There are three categories: Anxious Feelings, Anxious Thoughts, and Physical

Symptoms. I was very surprised at how many items I checked in every category and realized I was oblivious to the fact that such physical and mental symptoms could be caused by anxiety. Still, I assumed that I'd score in the low to medium level of anxiety, feeling as though mine is the same as everyone else's in this world.

There were six categories:
0 - 4 Minimal or no anxiety
5 - 10 Borderline anxiety
11 - 20 Mild anxiety
21 - 30 Moderate anxiety
31 - 50 Severe anxiety
51 - 99 Extreme anxiety or panic
My score: 51?!

Seeing these results made my anxiety go through the roof as I realized just how much it has affected my whole life. About 20 minutes later, my stomach began to cramp and gurgle as if I would have diarrhea. It was like my body had become aware of the fact that I am now aware of what it's been doing and it freaked out as if to say, "HOLY SHIT! She knows!" Then, I felt a bit of comfort, knowing that this can be treated and worked through. Minutes later, I experienced chills and shivering all over my body. At about 4:30 [session was at 2:00], I was eating a keto pizza that I'd made and it was the BEST tasting one ever! It was like my taste buds suddenly woke all the way up!

• • •

One day, I was working hard in the flower bed behind our shed. I was determined to get all the weeds out of it because the moonflowers I had planted were trying to survive among the overgrown weeds. I had a thought and shared it with my friend, Linda. "It would be nice to have a little rain shower to water our garden." Just a little one, enough to keep them alive and growing. Well, about 10 minutes later, I noticed one, not very large, dark cloud up above. I felt that was hopeful. It didn't look like any others were around or on their way. I shrugged. Maybe. Then, it started to rain and I sat down on the covered shed porch. It rained hard for about 20 seconds and then seemed to stop. There's my little rain shower, I thought, and was about to resume my weed pulling. Then, it rained more, and more and harder and harder, and wind blew, and thunder rolled, and lightning flashed, and it rained harder and harder, for at least 30 minutes. I was reminded of how much I'd loved being outside, watching storms, when I was younger. As I sat there, I wouldn't say I'd forgotten how much I used to enjoy it, but I did underestimate how much I enjoyed it. There I sat, well, moving from time to time when the wind blew the rain on me, enjoying every minute of that storm. The trees blew wildly a few times and I felt I should probably run for the house, but I stayed. If there hadn't been any lightning, I may have run around in the yard, letting that rain thoroughly soak me. It was the BEST DAY of my summer, thus far.

Later, I realized that the constant negative chatter in my head, the rumination of regrets and guilt I felt from past events, that had been my companion for so long—it was basically gone that day. I was present, enjoying the moments as I was living them. Fully engaged, me and the rain, thunder, lightning and wind.

I didn't realize how much anxiety I'd actually suffered with—until it was gone. I felt bliss. It truly was the BEST DAY—yet!

In the next session with my therapist, I shared my score with her and explained how very surprised I was to have such a high one. In that session, she recommended that I be started on anti-anxiety medication, something which I'd been adamant about from the beginning: "I don't want to take any medication. It's just a bandaid." However, looking back at years of suffering and not wanting to continue, I relented, and upon her request, I made an appointment with my primary care provider (PCP).

It just so happened that during this time, my nipples began itching. I mean, it was intense itching. I had tried to see my gynecologist about it, but couldn't get an appointment for at least a month. Since I was going to my PCP for anxiety treatment, I decided to add my nipples to the mix. When I called to make the appointment, the receptionist asked what my reason was for being seen. I said, "This is going to sound weird, but—itchy nipples and anxiety." She remained composed and professional and got me scheduled.

My PCP explained that itchy nipples can be caused from anxiety—another shocker to me! It's not necessarily all the 19 horrible diseases that I found on the internet with the itchy symptoms listed. Amazing!

A low dose anti-anxiety medication was prescribed, I was instructed to use cream on my itchy nipples, and I was on my way.

Less than an hour after taking that first pill, I felt calmer. Psychosomatic? Maybe. But, relief is relief is relief. My therapist had told me that since I'd lived in such a high state of anxiety for so many years, it would be possible to feel almost immediate relief from the medication. That first week, I felt better, but it pingponged back and forth between panic and calm. Having felt that first blip of relief, I decided to keep taking it.

I've been taking Buspar for several months now, and, as is common, I've had to adjust my dosage a few times. It has been crucial in my therapy journey and I've learned coping skills that have changed my life. I am deeply grateful for a wonderful therapist. I thank COVID-19 for giving me the furlough from work that allowed me/forced me to accept that I have issues that need tending to by giving me nothing but time, slowed me down enough that I could no longer ignore it, and for giving me the courage to reach out for help. At last. I am grateful to my daughter, Amber, for recommending a facility and my reading the bios of all the therapists and finding Sheryl, whose bio most resonated with my needs. Thank you!! Thank you!! Thank you, ALL!

· · ·

So, what led me to write this collection of hilarious, true-to-life, you-can't-make-this-stuff-up stories, thoughts, quips and quotes, scattered throughout (and interspersed within) the traumatic experiences, tragedies and heartbreak? Well—life. My life is not so different from everyone else's because being human comes with inherent loss, heartbreak and trauma, etc. However, my life's story is unique, albeit a bit hard to believe that so much can happen in one lifetime. Writing my story has been instrumental to my healing process and I hope it will help others, with a few laughs along the journey.

CHAPTER ONE

THE GREAT CRAYON INCIDENT

"Up from the ashes grow the roses of success."
—FROM THE MOVIE, *ANGEL IN THE HOUSE*

Childhood

I'm the youngest of four children born to a unique couple who were truly living the American dream. My parents were born and raised in Ohio, 125 miles from each other. They met in 1948 while students at the same Illinois college. My father once told me, "She was easily the prettiest girl on campus." Married six months after their first date, their first home was a tiny trailer. My father said it was 18 feet long, 21 feet with the hitch. It was a blissful, little honeymoon nest and they were extremely happy.

OK, I must tell this story before we go any further. This clearly shows that much of my sense of humor comes from my father. One of his favorite tales to tell was about when he and my mother had gotten engaged and were in the process of purchasing their little trailer. I transcribed his words from a video I'd taken in 2012 during the celebration of Mom's 87th birthday:

"We had this little, 21-footer Superior Coach trailer, but it only had 18 feet inside for actual living space. I think we talked to the seller about getting the thing, and I'm not sure if we had even made the down payment at this point. It cost $1,000 and we had to take out a loan to cover it. We made payments for one year to pay this thing off. Anyway, up there at Kankakee, just south of Chicago, we had horrendous storms, mostly ice storms. The ice would blow and freeze. It was terrible. Anyway, this night, we were out on a date, if you can call it a date, all we did was walk around. We had had an ice storm and we decided we'd like to go back and see the trailer, to just look at it. I don't think we even had any keys to get in it. It wasn't hooked up. We didn't have any electric in it, no heat or anything. I mean this was a dumb idea.

"Anyway, we walked down behind the gym and there was a newly poured gravel path that had not been smoothed out. It was in a mound and that was the path that went back to the trailer park. We started going down the trail to see the trailer and I don't think we had gotten 15 feet from the gym. Grandma (as he referred to my mother) was on this trail and I was standing beside her, holding her hand, and the first thing I knew her feet shot out from under her and she went down. Of course, I reached over.

"I was a gentleman at that time. Now, I wouldn't do it. But, anyway, I reached over and tried to get her back up on her feet and by God my feet slipped out and she came down on top of me, and she said, 'Oh, I've peed my pants!! And, you'll have to marry me now.' Peed her pants on the blasted trail behind the gym, before I could even get her back on her feet again!"

After he finished telling us this story, I asked Dad, "How long were you married before you found out you didn't have to marry her?" He said, "I finally read it in Woman's Day magazine that you didn't have to marry a girl because she pees her pants. I think it was five years later. The kids have gotten a bang out of that, but that's actually the truth."

They got married on a blustery, cold, winter day and honeymooned in Chicago. Every day for several weeks after their wedding, Mom would prepare Dad's supper, placing each item in its own small container on the table before him. As she cooked and served the meal, my mother would vent to my father about how poorly her mother had treated her, what she'd done throughout her life, and how much it upset her. Then, one day, she was done talking about it. Reminds me of Forrest Gump, "That's all I have to say about that." Incidentally, my mother's mother did not approve of the union, at all. I'm not sure about her father, but neither attended the ceremony.

Two years later, my parents started having children, first two boys, then two girls. Their first-born son was a rambunctious boy, extremely hyper and into everything. My Uncle Joey once said of my eldest brother, "He is a restless spirit." (That was so very true throughout my eldest brother's short life of 49 years.)

I should mention here that Uncle Joey was often referred to as "Apple Joe." It all started because one of his nephew's couldn't pronounce the word "uncle," and would say "apple" instead.

Four years later, their second son was born. He was the exact opposite of their first. This little boy was, as my mother described him, gentle, loving and very sweet. "Even in the womb," she said, "he would just roll," while her first son would apparently dance the Irish jig on her ribs and internal organs.

Then, three years later, along came a girl. Not just a girl. She was an extremely beautiful baby with bright, sparkling blue eyes. She was also, I believe, the first granddaughter on either side of the family. She became the jewel of the family, or "princess" as I have called her.

This is, by my own theory, where brother number two stopped growing up. He was abruptly and effectively dethroned of the "family jewel" station and title. He still, to this day, resents our sister's existence, now 60+ years later. Then, three-and-a-half years after my beautiful, princess sister entered the world, you guessed it, along came Vonda—the surprise baby.

My father was a Methodist minister throughout my parents' child-producing years and he baptized all four of us kids. By the time I was four, they had moved into the house where they would finish raising their kids and spend the rest of their lives.

Around that time is when my Dad left the ministry and became a high school history teacher and worked with students who needed extra help. At that time my mother was an "Avon lady." With her natural, radiant beauty, this was a perfect fit for her and she did quite well with sales, receiving multiple awards throughout her career with the company.

I remember before I was school-aged, going with her on her Avon calls. Many of these ladies would give me candy. I loved candy! And, it loved me, apparently. By the time I was 6 or 7, I had 14 cavities—at one time. Later, my mother also went into teaching and worked with children that, back in the 1960s and '70s, were termed MR (mentally retarded) and TMR (trainable mentally retarded).

When I started school in the fall of 1967, I had just turned six that August. For whatever reason, I did not get to go to kindergarten and went directly into first grade. For a shy, naive and truly uneducated child, first grade was really traumatizing for me. I remember standing in the doorway to the classroom and looking around at all the other kids. Many of them were looking at books, some were actually reading words on the pages.

The room was filled with far too many children, as I recall, but later that day the group was divided into two classrooms. I was sent to Mrs. Bowling's class. She was a short, very round woman with dark hair, and maybe glasses.

This was 1967, you know, back in the days when teachers were allowed to paddle their students for wrongdoing or disruptive behavior. Well, Mrs. Bowling paddled me twice that year! And, I promise you I truly was innocent on both counts. Of course, Mrs. Bowling did not believe me. Today, I no longer remember one of my alleged crimes, but the one I do remember is what I call "The Great Crayon Incident."

We had those desks where the seats were attached and the chairs were that cold, gray metal. On the seat in front of me, there were crayon marks all over that metal chair back and I got blamed for it because I sat behind it and (this is the kicker) I had the "same color crayons" that were scribbled on this chair.

Well, NO SHIT lady! We're in first grade. We all have the SAME F'ING COLOR CRAYONS! Looking back, I think that Mrs. fat Bowling ball bitch hag targeted me and perhaps perceived me as a slow child. I truly knew nothing that a kindergarten graduate would/should know. And, my quiet, shy, unblemished demeanor made me (as it has always made me) a target for bullies.

I was always a quiet child. So much so, in fact, my father would say, "She's growing up and nobody's noticing." I was "the baby," "the caboose," of my parents' four children. I remember them referring to me as "the bonus baby" a time or two. Actually, I was the "Oops, I guess I really should've used my diaphragm, even though I just finished my period," baby.

I'm not whining or complaining about that fact. It is, quite simply, a fact. My Mom told me so. Ha! Ha! Mom would always introduce me as, "This is Vonda, our baby." When I was a young teen, I asked her to stop introducing me that way, and, surprisingly, she honored my request. Thereafter, she'd say, "This is Vonda, our youngest. She doesn't like to be called 'the baby.'" Yeah, that's much better, Mom. Thanks!

As a young girl, when someone would ask me, "What do you want to be when you grow up?" I would always answer, "An artist." I loved to draw, having inherited artistic ability from both sides of my family. My mother was a talented artist who could sketch, draw with charcoal, and paint beautiful pieces of art. My favorites were her country snow scenes with horse-drawn buggies. My father's youngest brother, Apple Joe, was an incredible painter, even though he was left a quadriplegic after being dragged 100 feet underneath a train at the age of sixteen. So art was a major presence in my life (more on this later).

In my childhood and adolescent years, my father was angry much of the time. I remember him yelling, slamming doors, and retreating to his bedroom, where he would remain for long periods of time. We learned to stay out of his way.

Perhaps he was dealing with his own childhood demons. Or, the fact that his teaching job, though he thoroughly enjoyed his classroom experiences, included an administration that royally pissed him off on a continual basis. Or, maybe it was the fact he taught the more special needs students, used up all of his patience throughout his work day, and when he came home to his "normal" children, he had higher expectations for our behavior? I don't know and I never asked him.

Growing up with a father whose temper was as fragile as a thin sheet of ice on a lake can be unnerving and may affect you for the rest of your life. Still today, if I hear an argument brewing, voices being raised, I'm out the door, going the opposite direction, hiding under a table, whatever it takes to get away from it.

In fact, there was a code at the hospital where I worked, called "Code Strong." This typically meant an unruly or violent person was causing a ruckus and they needed all hands on deck to help with the situation. Yeah, needless to say, whenever I heard that code being called, I remained steadfast in my current, safe, as-far-away-as-possible location. Once, when I was about 7 years old, I don't know how I managed to, but I knocked over our family Christmas tree. Now, today, I don't remember exactly how long I hid behind the bushes in our backyard, but when I re-entered the house it was very, very quiet.

This irritable behavior is what earned my father the nickname "Grumpy." At times, we could actually joke with him about it. If he was being particularly jovial and playful, I'd enthusiastically yell, "Daddy's in a good mood!!!!" He would unfailingly respond with a loud, authoritative, "NO, I'M NOT!!" Then we'd all laugh. During family gatherings he could only handle so much of the festivities, then he'd disappear to lock himself in the bedroom. He was so slick, with his stealthily unnoticed departures, it would take us several minutes to even notice his absence. This became a family joke as well. One year for "Operation Christmas," as he always referred to our family Christmases, I drew up the "Grumpy Watch Schedule." Each family member had a 30-minute rotation of duty, keeping a steady eye on Grumpy so that, for once, he wouldn't be able to escape the fun. Well, it didn't work! I swear, trying to catch Grumpy's departure was like trying to catch Santa Claus eating the milk and cookies!

There has been an internal sadness that has followed me throughout my entire life. There was a lot of loneliness, too. At times, it would become a bit overwhelming, and I had actually considered taking my own life, though I never had a plan and made no attempts to do so. It was just something that would surface now and then when the sadness became too heavy. I'm sure that's a shocking revelation to people who've ever met me. By the way, there is absolutely no need to call the suicide hotline!

Although I've always had a smiley, sunshiny type of personality and have been told countless times, "You're always in a good mood," still, there remained a deep, heavy sadness inside of me. I guess I've been a living oxymoron all my life—a sad-funny person. I'm reminded of Robin Williams at this moment; his death was such a tragic loss. He was one of my mother's favorite comedians. Regardless of my inner turmoil, however, I have always, I mean ALLLLWAYS, been able to laugh, often loud and heartily, at anything funny, or crack jokes myself to make others laugh. Over the years I've realized that laughter was my form of self-therapy, a friendly defense mechanism and means of survival. If I could still laugh, no matter what was going on in my personal life, no matter how miserable I was inside, everything was going to be OK. And, I LOVE to laugh. My favorite emotion is laughing…until I cry. That really helps you release your inner, private demons, thoroughly cleansing your soul. It is the most wonderful emotion.

My sister got married after she became pregnant at the age of 15. Her boyfriend was very nice, clean-cut, and so polite. That is, until he consumed alcohol. Then he was a complete and total asshole who spent the next seven years abusing my sister, both physically and emotionally, any time that he decided to indulge.

Our mother had always encouraged my big sister to live her life as an "example to your younger sister." Well, this example was frightening. I've seen her thrown over the back of a couch when she was five-and-a-half months pregnant. I saw her slammed against a wall after she'd just had her appendix removed. Countless other loud and violent fights, which sure didn't help me in the internal fear department. I saw her badly injured, with multiple facial lacerations, after she'd gone through the windshield in a bad car wreck. All this did was teach me a very valuable lesson. When I started high school at age 14, I thought of my sister and how her life choices led her to being 100% dependent on another human being: a man, a very bad man; a very mean man. I vowed to myself to not be put in that situation—ever in my lifetime.

To that end, when we signed up for our freshman classes, I chose those that would serve me in my quest for independence once I graduated. I took bookkeeping, typing, accounting, shorthand and, when it was offered my sophomore year, I got into the C.O.E. (Cooperative Office Education) program which allowed me to attend school in the morning and work at a school-provided secretarial-type job every afternoon.

By the time I was 15 (a *very* eventful year in my life) I didn't like my parents very much. That is a harsh thing to say, but it is the truth. It was so bad I had even decided to change my name. I was going to be Brenda Lee Cole. It sounded like a good name and a better life. I felt neglected, pushed aside, like they wanted to be finished raising their kids, and were ready to live and enjoy their own lives again, before they were too old to do so.

As they continued to pursue their outside interests, they would often leave me alone on weekends, which started not long after my sister had moved out with her new asshole husband (when I was 12). With my older siblings all moved out of the house, I was truly alone. While most teens would completely revel in the opportunity to have parties and live it up in absence of their parents, I felt abandoned much of the time. Lonely. And very often scared.

Now, that's not to say I didn't ever have friends over to party and sneak into my father's fully stocked bar. I mean, I was a teenager after all. In fact…funny story time.

When I was in high school, before heading to the bus stop in the morning, I would go to my father's bar and mix up the craziest concoction of a drink that I could create. Then, I'd take it to the bus stop so Nancy (my best friend throughout high school) could drink it. I don't remember ever drinking the monstrosities myself. I think I always allowed her to be the guinea pig in my haphazard bartending. I'm such a good best friend!

Anyway, this happened on many such mornings and when we'd see the bus coming, my bestie would toss any remaining beverage into a bush…the same bush. Every time. Later, we discovered that this bush had died. It's been 40-plus years and there is still an empty spot where that bush used to live—the end one in a row of about a dozen bushes. Yep, we did that.

Nancy and I also skipped school quite a few times. I'd always write my own excuse note to turn into the office the next morning. I was so skilled at writing just like my mother, it was never questioned—at least not to my knowledge. One time, we skipped school, and since we enjoyed walking the long winding creek that ran behind Nancy's house, that's exactly what we did on this day. It just so happened that this creek ran all the way to the high school, about five miles away. So, what did we do, with our muddy feet and having been absent from school all day? We got to the high school as the busses were loading for the students' return home, and we hopped right on that sucker like we'd been there all day. Curious eyes noticed our muddy shoes. I believe I told them, "We had a field trip today." We were such badasses!

During this time, I also lightly experimented with drugs. Yeah, I succumbed to some peer pressure and tried marijuana. I remember one such "partying" night with my friends. We were out "cruising" and smoked pot. Cruising—that's what you did as a teenager in the 70s. Just like "That 70s Show," we spent hours just riding around all the country roads we could find.

Anyway, I was high and can still remember, as I was watching the road ahead, how strangely it seemed we were moving in a slow, very jerky kind of motion. The trees all looked like paper. It was as if we had become miniaturized and were driving through a paper doll town or something. Could it be that that joint was laced with something? Could be. I'll never know. Sadly, that's the most enjoyable high I ever experienced with marijuana. All the other times, and there weren't that many, it made me restless, twitchy and severely paranoid. THAT is not a fun kind of high!

After a few more failed attempts in hopes of feeling the coveted mellow which all my friends seemed to enjoy so much, I refused to smoke the stuff any more. My friends would try, oh how they'd try to get me to partake again. "This pot's different," they'd say. Wasn't happening. They'd pass me that doobie, all their eyes fixed upon me, watching for me to give in—again, and I finally said, "Look. You can pass this to me but all I'm going to do is inhale it into my mouth and spit it back out. So you can either pass me up and smoke it yourself, or allow me to keep wasting your weed." They no longer pressured me after that.

Oooh, and I did try a black beauty once. That was considered "speed" or an "upper" back then. I was so wildly experimental! I tried a whole one pill ... er, capsule, and it truly was black. Anyway, all it did was make me laugh. I mean, I laughed hysterically for what seemed like a solid hour...during a class...in high school. That was it. My drug days were over by age 17. That is, other than alcohol.

I was 15 the first time I got drunk—on vodka and Wink. Remember that soda? It was a bit like Fresca, but tasted like carbonated grapefruit juice and came in a large green glass bottle with a screw top. My best friend made this drink in one of my parents' marigold yellow plastic tumblers...which I still own today, incidentally. After I'd gotten sufficiently inebriated, she and I went for a walk around the neighborhood and, for some reason, I was eating a cookie. Alcohol and dessert, that's always a good combo, right? Ha! Well, while we were walking, I dropped that cookie and I said in a very sad, almost tearful voice, "I dropped my cookie." You know, like those sad drunks you see on TV. My bestie could not stop laughing.

This type of partying continued and, I found out later, my parents thought I was an alcoholic when they took me to see a psychiatrist, Dr. Brady (who I'd done some babysitting for in the past). I always thought they took me because of my rebellious, depressive, distant, textbook teenage behavior. My parents' concerns were based on the amount of alcohol that was removed from my Dad's bar and sneakily replaced with water. I didn't think he ever noticed!

They had no idea that a good portion of that alcohol landed in that neighbor's bush leading to its demise. Another one of those things my parents and I never talked about.

They called the police once because the kitchen smelled like a "funny smoke." My friends and I were not smoking pot in the house, I assure you. We were (and I know this is something we were all told NOT to do as kids) playing with matches. We'd light them and immediately blow them out because we liked the sulphur smell created after they were swiped on the sandpaper side of the matchstick box.

Now, as a grown woman, I can better understand my parents' choice to leave me home alone. They had me relatively late in life. I was born when my mother was 36, so I can relate to the feeling of wanting to be out there enjoying life while you're still young and healthy enough to live it up. Especially when you've just entered your 50s.

However, when I was a teenager, I held onto that dislike, and for many years to follow. Now, I would still go home to visit for holidays, weekends, etc., and I'd enjoy being with them. Even so,

I never felt particularly close to either of my parents. I always felt like I was a baby assigned to these strangers who were charged with my upbringing. Although through the years it improved somewhat, I never felt I could truly open up and talk to either of my parents.

· · ·

You know the saying about first impressions being lasting impressions? Well, I beg to differ. First impressions of me are very often, almost always, wrong. Recently, I've had two people confess to me what their first impressions were. One was a co-worker who said her initial impression was that I "seemed a bit naive, innocent and unblemished." The second was a manager at a dance studio where I've been taking lessons. We were discussing my future lesson plan and, since we hadn't officially been introduced, he asked me to share a bit of my history. He told me he thought of me as "the nice, quiet, Lindy lady," because that's the dance I most enjoyed practicing. He no longer thinks of me as quiet, and after I'd shared some of the history that I'm about to share with you, his jaw —quite literally —fell open.

Me naïve. Me innocent. Me unblemished? Ha!

I lost my innocence to a perverted boy when I was 6. It took me 50 years to be able to share that truth—with anyone. For five decades I lived with it, in silence. Alone. It was his mistake, his crime. But, I carried that burden as my own secret shame.

Having endured such an experience myself, I can fully understand why people come out with their own accusations many years later, even when their abuser is a famous person. I don't believe it's always because they want to get rich and/or destroy the jerk's life. I think the building of their inner courage, to the point that they felt strong enough to face and confront their abuser about his/her wrongdoing, just happened to coincide with the a-hole's fame, or whatever.

For me, it took 50 years and it just happened to coincide with the day my father died. I was explaining to my abuser the reason for another affected female hating him and that it was "because of all the perverted shit you did when we were kids," to which he responded, "Nobody's perfect." Yeah.

He didn't deny it. Nor did he accuse me of lying. He simply offered an unemotional, unapologetic, non-remorseful admission of being a perverted asshole to other children.

Up until this point in my life, I'd been tormented with fragmented memories and uncomfortable images that would resurface over and over and over. I'd kept them locked up, er tried to keep them locked, in the very back of my mind, trying so hard not to see the vivid images when they'd resurface.

Maybe it didn't really happen. Maybe it was just a bad dream from when I was a child. Then, any time I'd see this male person, I would always wonder, "Does he remember? Does he feel bad? Does he wonder if I remember?" Now, since my confrontation, it has entered my mind much less often.

I should clarify: this abuser did not himself do anything to me physically. He did, however, put me in extremely inappropriate circumstances that allowed others to do physical things to me, as he watched.

While I confronted this male person after my father's death, I had not, until writing about these experiences in this book, ever shared the details of what actually happened to me—with anyone.

Two years later, I would share these particulars with my husband via a written letter. I had an appointment to see a hypnotherapist the next day in pursuit of achieving a deeper sense of peace and I truly hoped that by doing so, memories would resurface. Not memories of the incidents; I had no desire to relive any of that again. I hoped to uncover happy memories from that period of time which I remembered very little.

I remember being in a neighbor's tree-house with my pants pulled down and I was forced to lie down on my stomach, my private parts purposely lined up over a hole in the tree-house floor so the neighbor boy(s) could get a good look from the ground below. I remember standing up and screaming to an elderly neighbor man from the tree-house window, asking for help.

I also remember a warm summer night when I was under a tree, my pants pulled down, while a neighbor boy—who had obviously entered puberty—laid on top of me to show me, "This is how it feels when grownups..."

I can still feel his post-pubescent fuzz rubbing against my little girl's private parts. What I don't recall is any type of penetration being involved in any of these incidents. Actually, it became evident to me that there must not have been any when I had my first sexual experience in my teen years. I was 15 when I had intercourse for the first time. It was his first time, too. My boyfriend of seven months and four days (but who was counting) had confessed his love for me when we'd been together for about four months.

I knew enough about sex to know what parts went where. I knew the anatomy of it. However, I could never figure out what the big deal was about having sex. *OK, he sticks this here...then what? What's so great about that?*

So, when my first time happened and he began, you know, moving in and out of me, I was more than just a little bit confused. I thought, *WHAT is he doing? Can he NOT make up his mind?* Those were my actual thoughts. While this is very blunt, and embarrassing, it made me realize I apparently had not experienced intercourse prior to this "losing" of my "virginity"—voluntarily or otherwise.

That realization, which occurred well into mid-life, was actually comforting to me. I had always wondered if it'd happened and I had simply blocked it from my memory.

What happened to me is not as horrific, violent and/or disturbing as what has happened to countless other victims of childhood sexual abuse, to be sure. What I am not sure of is if those two memories are my only incidences of abuse. Other memories may resurface in time, and actually, I have a hazy memory of playing a game of strip poker. I'm not even sure I was old enough to be able to read the cards.

According to articles I've read on the subject, some childhood sex play or experimentation, with others or alone, is normal and healthy. However, when this play involves being forced to do things against your will, it's not play any more. It is sexual abuse and can cause lasting, even permanent damage.

A common characteristic, or residual effect, in those that have endured childhood sexual abuse, is that they have memory gaps— periods of time with no memories whatsoever. I have a very limited memory of first grade and no memories at all of second or third grade. Nothing. I do remember my teachers' names, perhaps because they're in my grade school yearbooks.

Writing about my experiences in this book has been quite therapeutic. Keeping such secrets locked away for decades can start to eat away at you. If you can relate, please know you're not alone. It DOES help to talk about it, to let it all out, so your soul can be free of the burden that you did something wrong, that you should remain ever shameful, that you should hide the experiences and their residue for the rest of your life.

Let it out. Let it go. Be free! After that comes forgiveness, so I have read/heard many times. And while at the time of writing this chapter, I have not forgiven him, I feel I will some day: for me; not for him.

That forgiveness, however, will not change the fact that he is no longer a welcome presence in my life.

• • •

During the summer that followed high school graduation, I left home at age 17 for a job in the proof department of a bank. For a while I lived at the YWCA. That's back when they rented rooms and you had to use communal bathrooms. It was a very old, dark and deeply depressing place. I stayed for about a month, at $40 a week. Thereafter, with my regular income, I was able to move into a one-bedroom apartment.

I remember going home to visit on my 18th birthday. My mother made me a cake and my sister was lighting the candles on it. I have a picture of it and when I look at it, I can still see and feel that I remained internally wounded and angry with my parents and still didn't like them very much.

Sometime during my early adulthood, however, I made a decision. "You know what," I thought to myself, "These are my parents. They did the best they could, based on what they knew, and they were a vast improvement over their parents. So, I'm going to love them anyway."

• • •

My mother grew up on a farm and my father grew up in a city, both in northern Ohio. Each of my parents had one very loving parent and one not so loving parent. For my mother, it was her father who was loving and gentle. From her stories of her mother, she was a cold, domineering, gossipy, selfish woman who was often mean to my mother.

On the positive side, Mom said her mother had quite a green thumb, could grow anything and had "the most beautiful flowers" in her garden. I never met my Mom's parents. They both died when I was quite young.

On my father's side, his mother was a loving presence and his father was, I think, a decent man, until he got drunk. Then, he'd come home cussing like a sailor and often beat his wife and kids. I never met my paternal grandfather, as he and my grandmother had been divorced for years prior to my birth.

When my father was a small boy, he'd run upstairs in their house and climb out the window onto a tree, his escape from the scary violence, then he'd run to a neighbor's house. An extremely nice lady lived there and would take him in until it was safe for him to return home.

My father would often say, referring to the upbringing he shared with his siblings, "We weren't raised up. We were dragged up."

I recently learned that my father's father, along with being an alcoholic, was suicidal: He once went into the kitchen, turned on the gas oven and stuck his head inside. My father, and his mother, pulled him to safety, saving his life.

I can't imagine what it was like for them, saving their abuser's life when they could have all been free if they let him succeed in his suicide attempt. My father always did the right thing. He instilled that in me by example. Regardless of inconvenience, cost or sacrifice —you do the right thing.

· · ·

Throughout my childhood, along with my drawing, I enjoyed writing, too. I wrote a few stories, but mostly I loved writing poems. I recently came across a poem I had written for my father. I'd painted it on a piece of leftover paneling from when my parents redecorated the room in the upstairs I inherited after my siblings left home. By the way, it was 1976, the bicentennial, and since I'd always been patriotic, tearing up during the National Anthem every morning throughout grade school, I chose to decorate my room in red, white and blue, with golden eagles in the wallpaper, no less.

My Daddy
My Daddy is quiet and doesn't say much
Except when he yells about dishes and such
He used to spank me when I was bad
And he would scold me when I made him mad
He's made me laugh and he's made me cry
I just don't know what I'd do if he'd die
I guess I should be happy for our time together
But, I'll tell you this, Daddy, I'll love you forever.
—WRITTEN FATHER'S DAY 1977

CHAPTER TWO

IF AT FIRST YOU DON'T SUCCEED...

*"If you imagine the worst case scenario and
it happens, you've lived it twice."*
—MICHAEL J. FOX

I am in my fourth and final marriage.

I don't say that in a negative way, like I wouldn't ever get married again because it's horribly miserable. I mean it in the sense that once you've had your best mate, the one who gets you, accepts your quirks and inconsistencies and continues to love you and be there for you, there is simply no one else after that. No way to ever top it or even duplicate it. I'm the mother of two beautiful daughters, Amber and Cassandra. I inherited a wonderful son, Matthew, through this marriage, and I am the proud grandmother of four boys, Kyler, Hunter, Conner, and Zachary, and one girl, my Emily.

Marriage #1

Yes, I've had three failed marriages. I am not proud of it, but it is what it is. I was trying to catch up with Elizabeth Taylor, OK? It's good to have goals in life.

I met my first husband when he was working with my brother and brother-in-law in my hometown, Fairfield, Ohio. It was December of 1979. I was eighteen years old and I had just graduated from high school that June. He was 600 miles away from his Wisconsin hometown and it was Christmastime. We invited him to my parents' house so he wouldn't be alone for the holiday and my heart went out to him. I felt so sorry for him, spending Christmas away from his family. I remember him phoning home and learning that he had a new baby sister. He didn't even know his step-mother was expecting another child. That blew my mind. How can you not know your mom's having another baby? Anyway, the company the guys worked for was a traveling sewer repair company and it was time for them to leave Fairfield. Next stop, West Monroe, Louisiana. He asked me to go with them. Being so suggestible, I agreed, packed up and joined the convoy south.

We married when I was 19. I like to say I was young and dumb and didn't fully comprehend what I was doing. Oh, and I should mention I was three-and-a-half months pregnant at the time of our wedding. We were married at the courthouse in a simple ceremony. His Catholic family funded our wedding reception which was a huge gathering. There was a polka band that played, and endless beer for all. I didn't do much dancing, other than being the Dutchman in the Flying Dutchman dance with my husband and his brother. They spun me around so fast, it's a wonder I could stay on my feet, but it was fun.

It was not a good marriage —we had many fights after he'd come home drunk in the middle of the night, or not return home until morning. Though he never struck me, I would go after him with a fierce anger and try to claw his face with my fingernails. Due to his strength and surprisingly quick reaction time, I didn't do any damage to his face and merely broke off my own fingernails (several times) down to the quick, leaving them bloody and sore for days. During one such fight, I picked up a wooden rectangular piggy bank and used it to pummel our bedroom door which was not made of real wood, was hollow, and cheaply made. We had no money to spare and couldn't risk losing our security deposit, so after I'd calmed down (a day or two later), I looked at replacing the door. That was too expensive. Eureka! *I'll buy some wood grain contact paper and cover the holes!* I quickly discovered that the paper didn't match the door, but, sly as I was, I covered both sides of it. *The landlord will never know.*

When I was nine months pregnant (one day before my due date), we had friends over for dinner. We all had a nice time and enjoyed some laughter. That is, until my husband decided to run his mouth in an attempt to stir me up and make me angry, which seemed to be one of his favorite pastimes. I asked him to stop. He didn't. I begged him to stop. He didn't. I warned him that he'd better stop. He didn't. Having all I could take of his bullshit, I grabbed the thing closest to my reach, a ceramic ashtray, and hurled it at him with all my might. It gashed his elbow which immediately started bleeding. In a whirlwind of activity, a frantic wife, and a stunned husband holding a bloody towel on his elbow, we got him to the emergency room. I was sobbing at the check-in desk when I told the receptionist, "I threw an ashtray at him." I was expecting the police to be called on me for domestic violence, or to be chastised for doing such a thing. However, the receptionist said, "Oh, honey. I've thrown worse things." My husband received seven stitches. Two days later, our first daughter was born and my husband stayed by my side in the delivery room. I have to give him credit for that. When I told family members what I'd done and how badly I felt about it, several of them said, "I would've aimed for his head."

By the time our daughter was 17 months old, I was still young, a little dumb and quite suggestible. So, when my husband attempted to get back into the Army to actually help support our little family and could not get the job he desired, he said to me, "Why don't you see what they'll give you." I willingly, albeit naively, agreed.

As luck would have it, with my good test scores, I was offered my choice of three different jobs. One was an administrative assistant, another one that I don't remember now, and the third job was a legal clerk. I thought being a legal clerk sounded like something I could turn into a career, and would allow me to support my family for years to come. "Sign me up, U.S. Army!"

Three months later, when our daughter was just 20 months old, I was shipped off to Ft. Jackson, S.C., for basic training where: I was awakened at 0430 each morning to do jumping jacks and pushups in the sand, where fire ants would crawl onto my hands, biting my fingers, then leave small, painful and itchy pus sacks; found myself in a gas chamber with 11 other female soldiers, one of whom totally lost her shit and we could NOT leave the chamber until SHE calmed herself down (we seriously wanted to take that bitch down); contracted a severe case of poison ivy on my arms while clearing grass and weeds from ditches with my bare hands (the military calls this type of cleanup "police call." Yeah, I don't know why either); and, I developed hemorrhoids because the food was so different I couldn't poop for almost three weeks and once I did, it turned me inside out. But none of that shit compares to how hard it was leaving my baby girl behind and knowing there was the possibility of not seeing her again for months.

One night, before lights out in the barracks, I could take it no more. I went to the female drill sergeant on duty and asked if I could speak with her. She allowed me to sit down in her office and I explained my heartache over leaving my daughter behind. As I said the words, "I'm afraid she'll forget who her mother is," the tears I had successfully contained up to that point came barreling down my face. While she attempted to maintain her butch and military-like, drill sergeant persona, she told me it just so happened, the company commander of our particular unit was a religious man. He did not believe in working on Sundays. Well, more like no "training" on Sundays. We still had to make our bunks, clean the barracks, etc. Then, she spoke the most beautiful words I could've imagined, "Our commander allows soldiers to have family visits on Sunday." My heart soared!

Thankfully, my husband and daughter were staying with his sister, a mere two-hour drive away, so we wouldn't have to spend money on rent while I was in basic training. I got to see my precious baby girl every Sunday up until graduation. I don't know how I would've made it through otherwise.

I spent three years in the Army on active duty, most of which was at Ft. Sill, Okla. We lived in a 2-bedroom duplex for about a year. It was there that I started waking up to the smell of semen. I'd go to the bathroom and while I sat there I'd wonder where the heck the smell was coming from —which became apparent when one night I was awakened by my husband ejaculating (after jerking himself off) in the crack of my butt. Yeah, I slept super hard and soundly while in the army. Needless to say, after that discovery, I wore shorts or pajama pants to bed every single night.

Later, we bought a mobile home and this is where our second daughter was born. Do you know how hot those tin cans can get during the summer, in Oklahoma, with no air-conditioning? 125 degrees! That's how hot it was inside our trailer when I'd get home. Husband #1 was such a tightwad, he refused to run the air-conditioner during the day. I'd turn it on every day when I got home and it would take several hours to cool the place down enough to be able to sleep.

Now, I'm not perfect. I made my share of mistakes throughout this horribly shitty marriage. I was a *very* bad girl —on that army post —and did a lot of bad things. Things which a young married woman should not be doing. Not sure I want to delve into the details here. Perhaps I will in this book's sequel? We'll see.

After I'd served my three-year active duty contract, we packed up and moved to Wisconsin, my husband's home state…the beginning of our end; not the state's fault.

Our marriage lasted six years. I grew up, but he didn't. He never changed. I wanted more out of life than spending it with a man who loved to play control/manipulation mind games and enjoyed being unemployed, allowing his wife to be the sole breadwinner. We were together a total of seven and a half years, of which he worked approximately two years, total. While he often espoused that being lazy was a sin, and I heard, "There could be more done in a day" after I'd cleaned our home, etc., he himself spent most of his days lounging on the couch watching TV (often soap operas). The hypocrite.

During what was to be our last year of marriage, I worked as a receptionist in an engineering office that included myself and one land surveyor who was out in the field a lot. That left me with a lot of idle time, and me with too much idle time —not a good thing. Maybe in this case, it was, however. I had gone from the hustle and bustle of military life, being around countless other soldiers on a daily basis, to working in a quiet office, in a town where I had no friends, all alone most of the time. As the days slipped by, I became more and more depressed with the realization of how utterly miserable I was in my current life situation. I was married to a lazy man who thrived on making me angry. It was seriously like crack cocaine to him. He loved to get under my skin. So much so that, to this day, I swear to you, if I'd have stayed with him, I would be in prison for murdering him, which would have resulted in both of my girls being without parents. I truly despised him.

Have you seen the movie War of the Roses? In one of the final scenes, the Roses had had a very long, drawn out, extremely violent fight in which they were both injured and ended up trapped on top of a giant chandelier, on which, coincidentally, Mrs. Rose had loosened the bolts earlier in an attempt to drop it on Mr. Rose. When the chandelier plummets to the tile floor beneath it with the Roses still clinging to it, Mr. Rose places his hand on Mrs. Rose's shoulder and at that moment, he takes his last breath. Mrs. Rose turns and raises her head slightly toward him, raises her arm and during her last breath pushes his hand off of her shoulder.

I related to that sentiment, as that's how much I hated my first husband during our last months of our marriage. Scary, huh? I actually tried to push him into the traffic on a busy four-lane highway once. I mean like, not his body. His body AND his car. He'd been following me as I was taking care of errands, or something, and I'd had enough. After I'd turned on a side road with him tailing me, I stopped, put my car in reverse and proceeded to hit the gas pedal. I gotta tell you, the look on his face in my rearview mirror literally made me laugh out loud!! No, I wasn't successful in causing a multi-car accident on the busy Ft Sill highway. But, I was successful in delivering a very powerful message to the SOB tailing me.

I needed to get out of this toxic marriage—for myself, and my girls—but I didn't know how. I knew I needed to get some help. Then one day, I noticed a bookstore across the street from where I worked. On my lunch hour, I went to check it out and headed right to the self-help section. With a lot of free time on the job, and the abundance of books to help me through my situation, I began my multi-month read-a-thon on how to be a stronger, more independent woman.

Finally, after a good 15-20 inspiring books, I mustered up the courage to talk to an attorney about divorce. His name was Kissinger. I wanted to pronounce it like that famous guy, Henry Kissinger, pronounced it. But, he pronounced his Kiss-ing-GER, not Kiss-ing-JER.

After I left Mr. Kiss-ing- GER's office, I had the overwhelming urge to run down the middle of the street screaming, "I did it! I DID IT!!!!" When our divorce was finalized a few months later, the girls and I packed up and headed back to my home state of Ohio. Incidentally, during our marriage, my then husband would always tell me if I left him, I would end up on welfare. Yeah. That makes sense. I'm the only one working full-time and supporting our family, but I'll end up on welfare the minute I leave you. OK. Dream on!

Now, though I have shared much negative information about my first husband, there are two positive things that I can say about this man:

1. He could make me laugh. Even sometimes when we'd be arguing, he'd do or say something so random and comical, my screaming would turn into a hearty laughter.

2. He could save money like nobody's business. I swear the man could work minimum wage and still amass a giant wad of cash. He knew how to survive on meager salaries, that's for sure.

Sadly, when I originally wrote this section of my history, he was in jail awaiting sentencing for first-degree murder. In December 2018, he received life in prison with no chance of parole.

• • •

After my parents' "caboose" and her two little girls arrived back home, I put all of our household items in storage and we stayed with my parents for about six months. Even though I was free of my tormenter, I was deeply depressed. Also, though I successfully maintained full-time work through a temp agency, I could not secure a permanent full-time job in the Cincinnati area. In the meantime, my sister, Becky, who had relocated from Ohio to Lexington, Ky., invited me to visit for a weekend. Thankfully, she had successfully gotten away from the alcoholic asshole and was now married to a nice man who spoiled her rotten...and still does today.

I accepted the invitation to visit and we had a great time. If memory serves, we visited several times and, while I was still in my suggestible frame of mind, my sister said, "You should apply for some jobs in Lexington and see what happens." "OK!!" I did, and in no time I had a full-time position as a legal secretary. I knew that legal clerk thing would come in handy!

We moved to Lexington and the three of us shared a one-bedroom apartment. Most mothers want their children to have a father, too, so during this time, my ex and I attempted to reconcile—once and very briefly. Seriously, what was I thinking?!

Interestingly, maybe even ironically, once I had established my own life in Kentucky, my sister and her family moved north—back to Ohio!

I'm still dealing with some residual damage done to me by this marriage. Throughout our time together, he would grab at my boobs or crotch any/every chance that he got and it didn't matter how hard I hit or punched him afterward —he kept doing it.

There are times when my forever husband moves in a way that transports me back in time to life with my tormentor and I'll swat his hands or quickly close my legs tightly. Sometimes when he playfully touches my butt, I turn around and smack his arm. I suppose it's time to speak with my therapist about this, too, huh?

Then, there are coats on the back of chairs. I cannot stand that! My ex would repeatedly put his heavy winter coat on the back of one or our flimsy, lightweight kitchen chairs and when I'd walk by, lightly grazing the jacket, it and the chair would fall to the floor. It got on my nerves —a lot. *Hang it up, dumbass!* Still today, I will remove any jacket placed on the back of one of our chairs and hang it up. I've even been known to do that at work, in our breakroom.

Marriage #2

About two-and-a half years later, during my midlife crisis at age 29, I entered my second marriage. I'm dead serious here. I turned 29. My life was over. I had nothing to look forward to and I was going to die alone. That's truly how I felt at the time. I had, after all, lived quite a bit of life in my almost 30 years on this earth.

At the time I met him, he was married. His marriage was not good and he later ended up leaving it. Then, the guilt I felt was palpable, constant and haunting. During our time together, I often had dreams about his ex-wife. She was on my mind a lot. How could I have done something so heartless? I have a vague memory of going to talk to her where she worked, and apologizing. She was gracious, seemed forgiving and openly admitted that her ex-husband "can be quite charming." Perhaps I'd done her a favor. Remember when I said I was young and dumb. Well…that followed me throughout my 20's.

It was during our flirtship/courtship that I tried one more time with my girls' father. I left him in my apartment when I moved in with the big-footed funny guy. He came to talk to me after I'd moved in with the stolen husband, Big-foot opened the door, saw who it was and screamed, "They're my family now," as he slammed the door. Though I hated husband #1, that event broke my heart and weighed heavily on it for years to come.

I did a hell of a job cleaning up my life, leaving a trail of chaos and drama! Didn't I? Sometimes, when you're running away from your past, your tormenting thoughts, your mistakes, you just end up making more blunders.

So, I married a really cute, quite charming, fun-to-be-around man. He was such a contrast to my first husband. He was so extroverted, had a heavy southern drawl of an accent and told really funny stories like someone on "Hee Haw." He was so friendly and charismatic, and much taller. I liked that he had bigger feet than my first husband—foolishly or naively thinking that would make him more of a man. He didn't seem to play mind games either, which was a major plus. However, he did possess a pretty mean temper.

I knew in my gut that marrying him would be a mistake. But, a mistake is better than being alone, right? Right! I knew I shouldn't do it. I knew it was wrong as I was walking down the aisle. Red flags popped up in my mind as I locked eyes with each of the many guests standing in the church, watching my father escort me to my future.

"Don't do this."

"MISTAKE!"

"Red flag! RED flag!! RED FLAG!!!!"

Five minutes later, "I do." Now, this marriage lasted a solid year, with us living together about half of that. The two positives about my second ex-husband? He was really, really funny! Um...I may have to think a bit on the second one. I'll get back to you.

Marriage #3

My third marriage lasted nine years. Our first date was a blind date set up by a dear friend of mine. We all three worked at the same place, but I hadn't talked to this guy much because he was extremely shy. He was also 10 years my junior. I had always said,

"I'd *never* date a younger guy." (*Never* say never). But, I went on this blind date and while we were enjoying our dinner at Friday's along with some lovely conversation, I realized I could tell this young fella anything. I'd never felt I could be so open with a male person in my life. It was amazing. I quickly and completely fell in love and we were soon engaged.

We were married on what was then labeled "the blizzard of the century," an extremely blustery, frigid day in March 1993. My parents were driving down from Ohio so Dad could give me away. Again. I seemed to keep coming back! However, the roads quickly became impassable as the snow piled up and was blown all over the roads. There were so many accidents littering the freeway, they had to turn around and go back home. In Dad's place, my brother-in-law graciously agreed to give me away.

It's a bit of a challenge when you're a 31-year-old woman with two kids and your spouse is a 21-year-old man who hadn't been on his own for very long and had been catered to by his mother and younger sisters throughout his life. But, we managed to work out those kinks, through time, and seemed content.

In 1998, the World Wide Web gained immense popularity within my family. My sister and her husband got a computer and "got online," and they encouraged my parents to do so as well. Now, for my parents this was quite a technological leap. Mind you, the last thing they had typed on was a manual typewriter.

I vividly remember watching my father as he typed a letter using the word processing program on his computer. When he would get to the end of the line where he was typing, he would hold down the space bar until the cursor showed up where he wanted to type the next paragraph. He was used to smacking that little silver handlebar on the manual typewriter. I giggled and said, "Dad, you don't have to do that. Just hit this return button," as I demonstrated for him. That amazed him and tickled me, a lot.

Well, of course, my husband and I had to get a computer and get online, too. Before long, I was chatting with my parents through a chat program called ICQ as well as through the chat feature on AOL. It was really cool being able to converse with them like that. And we did so often.

My father was very close to his youngest brother, Apple Joe, and went to great lengths to make sure that his quadriplegic little brother got to enjoy the normal pleasures of life as much as anyone else. Apple Joe could not sit upright without help, but Dad was going to make sure he enjoyed a ride on a boat in the pond located on their Indiana "farm." Dad fashioned a harness to keep Joe in the seat and used some kind of pulley system to lift Joe into the boat. Away they went. It was a beautifully touching scene like one from a sappy, feel-good movie, and the two brothers were so happy.

During this time, Apple Joe also ended up online, and we all enjoyed regular, usually very entertaining, group chats through ICQ. Apple Joe did not have full use of his hands or fingers. However, he had a pencil fashioned in such a way that it could be wedged between his fingers and he'd use his arm to raise it and hit each letter on his keyboard.

I had innumerable private chats with Joe and we became very close. Oh how I looked forward to chatting with him. He was very inspiring. In fact, it is because of Apple Joe that I became addicted to Starbucks coffee and became a nurse.

Joe sent me my first bag of Starbucks and when I first tried that stuff, it was sooooo incredibly strong, I didn't think I could drink it. But, since my dear uncle sent it to me, I adapted to it and got to the point where no other coffee would suffice. Apple Joe continued to send me more coffee when I'd run out. I once asked him in a chat, "What did I do to deserve you being so nice to me?"

He answered, "It's nothing that you did. I just feel sorry for your parents." He was so funny!

During one of my routine AOL chats with Apple Joe, he told me, "You would make a good nurse," and in a later chat, "With your personality, you should go into nursing." I said, "ME? A nurse?!!" If chats had sound effects, that would've been a very shrill sounding "ME?!!" Was he out of his mind? I was terrified of needles and I couldn't stand the mere thought of blood, much less the sight of it! It was extreme, to say the least. I mean to tell you, I would get grossed out and literally weak-kneed if I even thought about the blood in my feet and how when I stood up or walked, all those blood cells were being squeezed and squished between my foot bones and my skin. Yeah, it was that bad.

Five or 10 years prior to that, my sister-in-law had been going through nursing school and I remember seeing her study at their dining room table. She was reading one of those 20-pound nursing textbooks. They're both ridiculously heavy and expensive. Plus, they're usually "outdated" by the next academic year making hand-me-downs, in order to save a fellow student some money, quite infeasible.

I'd sit at the table and occasionally glance at her as she turned the pages, absorbing all the medical knowledge they contained. I really admired her determination to complete her degree with three young children at home. She went on to become an excellent nurse, too.

Every now and then, when she'd be studying, I'd catch a glimpse of something unpleasant on her current page. With my knees feeling weak, and my vision blurring, I would say to her, "I could *never* be a nurse," as well as, "I could *never* work in the medical field." This is just one of the many incidents where my use of the word "never" came back to bite me right in the buttocks. Hard.

Well, my sweet Uncle Joe, in all his wisdom, had successfully planted a tiny seed in my head. From time to time, I would mull over the idea of nursing but each time that mulling would be abruptly ceased by me. Never! Still, that little seed was determined to take root and persisted to the point that I was seriously thinking that, just maybe, perhaps there was a career in a medical field that did not require my exposure to needles or blood.

I know. I just heard you say it, too: "Yeah, right!!"

With that seed taking up more and more space in my noggin, I finally looked into degrees that I felt would be tolerable, safe from the gory inside the body stuff. Oddly enough, I really liked the thought of working in a hospital with lots of other people. There seemed to be a wide variety of jobs within the hustle and bustle of hospitals and that appealed to me as it was reminiscent of my army days.

Through my online search for a new career, I came across medical assisting. That didn't sound very scary. I spoke with a guidance counselor at a nearby college and signed up for the associate degree program. For my first 12-week semester, I registered for three classes—anatomy, medical terminology and a literature course. I made all As for that term and felt more confident I was doing the right thing pursuing this medical field sort of training.

The second semester rolls around, and I register for classes and—there it was—a clinical, hands-on class that required us to give shots and...draw blood! On each other! Needles?! Blood?! WHAT?! I didn't think medical assistants performed such tasks! I was mortified, petrified, and was no longer constipated, if you get my meaning.

The anxiety I experienced due to the looming poke-a-student-with-a-needle day was palpable, kind of like parachuting for the first time: You envision the outcome that you want, but there's always a chance of the opposite outcome! I considered dropping my classes, hanging up my school bag (way far back in a closet), changing my name, leaving town, the state, the country, and forgetting all about this short-lived medical training endeavor nonsense. I mean, *what* was I thinking, really?

However, I would think of my dear Uncle Joe and about how much he believed in me. He had encouraged me every step of the way regardless of my phobias. I surely did not want to disappoint him, prove him wrong for his belief in my abilities, or let him down. Deep breath. I persevered.

B-Day arrived. No, that's not a birthday, it's "Blood Day." On the day that we learned to draw blood, the instructor asked for a volunteer to go first. Surprisingly, I was the only one to raise a hand. I simply could not imagine waiting for my turn through the 20 or so other students and possibly being last. How agonizing that would have been for me. I wanted to get this over with—and as quickly as humanly possible.

My heart was racing. I think all my blood was in my face, but I was determined. The instructor slowly talked me through the steps. I tied the tourniquet snugly around my classmate's upper arm. I felt inside the bend of her arm for a suitable vein. I thoroughly cleansed the site with alcohol. Oh, please, can we just have a fire drill, like right freakin' now, please?! Deep breath in ... and exhale.

I had the needle in my hand and, with that vein in sight, I stuck that needle into my slightly hesitant classmate's arm. I wasn't successful at harpooning the vein so I didn't actually retrieve any blood. I think she closed them all due to the fear created when a visibly terrified, shaking, fellow student is coming at her with a needle, determined to jab her vein and remove a blood sample. But, I did it! I was so elated, I screamed, "I didn't get any blood, BUT, I POKED HER!!!"

The instructor hushed me and closed the classroom door. I must've been really loud. I actually did it. I left school that day feeling six-feet tall. I was going to say 10-feet tall, but when you're 5-foot-2, six feet is monumental. Surviving that experience was a turning point for me and I realized maybe, just maybe, I really could do this nurse type job thing after all.

Years later in 2003, once I'd obtained my associate's degree, I soon found that hospitals don't hire medical assistants. They're only used in clinics, doctors' offices, etc. That was a disappointment. However, I got hired by a small cardiology practice that was associated with my favorite hospital. My co-workers were great people and I enjoyed working there for a couple of years before boredom set in, along with my continued yearning to work in a hospital setting.

Since Apple Joe was confined to a wheelchair from the time he was 16 years old, he was susceptible to decubitus ulcers (bed sores). He'd been hospitalized several times for them. I remember him being in the ICU, and I drove 226 miles just to sit with him for a couple hours, and then drove back home. Not long after that, I'd completed an entire year of medical assisting school, a total of 12 classes, making all A's, and I was on the Dean's List. My Apple Joe was so proud of me.

Then, on an early April day, husband #3 came to where I was working as a legal secretary. Though he'd visited on multiple occasions, this was different. I don't remember if I was filling in for the receptionist at the front desk or if I'd been called to it when he arrived. He approached me, placed his hands on my shoulders, then said, "Apple Joe died." I knew Apple had been very sick, but never once thought it would lead to his demise. The tears formed immediately as I wailed, "Noooo..." and clung to my husband to keep from collapsing onto the hole I felt beneath me. My world was shattered.

I took this loss extremely hard. I'd lost my best friend; my inspiration to further my education; my confidante.

It was several weeks before I could even drink my Starbucks coffee again. It wouldn't have been the same if I couldn't sip it while enjoying a chat with one of my favorite people on this earth. Coincidentally, 21 years later, I still enjoy Starbucks coffee. This cup's for you, Apple Joe.

Things started changing in the last couple years of my third marriage. Again, I became depressed, but this time, I added a pretty good weight-gain to the mix. Even though I'd fallen in love with this younger man, in the back of my mind I'd always had the thought, "He's going to leave me one day." It was always there, softly whispering in the back of my mind from time to time.

Also, in this marriage, I was a bit of a control freak—I couldn't fathom the same things happening that I'd gone through with the others. He paid the price.

I do not remember exactly how the conversation started that led to our separation, but when we talked I knew something was wrong and pleaded with him to open up and just tell me what he wanted to tell me. Then, it happened. He proceeded to tell me that he thought he was gay and that he wanted to "try men." I was a very, very understanding woman and knew, innately, how diffi-cult that must've been for him to utter those words to me. I wasn't angry. I was a bit hurt, of course. There it was, and there we were. My husband is now gay. Not a whole lot I can do about that situ-ation, is there? I mean, short of donning a strap-on, that is...(not happening)! He got an apartment and moved out. I was devastated.

My despair and devastation, however, slowly started to churn until it grew into a bubbling, flaming, acidic pit of utter PISSED OFF-NESS. I WAS LIVID!!! Unless, of course, there is a word that means more pissed off than "livid." It became so intense I didn't know what to do. I felt like the bug in "Men in Black." You know, that alien bug man who's wearing the Edgar suit, but it's too small for him so he writhes and wriggles with every movement? Yeah, that was me, dealing with my now intense anger.

With my seething rage at its peak, I walked out into our garage, where all of his tools and other belongings remained until he'd had time to come clear them out. Then, I saw it; on his workbench. A hammer. I walked over, picked up that hammer and commenced to smashing every fucking thing I could reach in that garage.

Although it must've been incredibly loud in there, neither of my daughters heard it, thankfully. I smashed and cracked, whacked and smashed larger pieces into smaller pieces until I was both physically and emotionally exhausted. I just stood there, unable to move for a few minutes, and heavy tears began soaking my face. I looked around at the mess I'd created, as the hammer fell out of my hand and clunked into the garage floor. Then, I noticed the one thing I didn't even touch. It'd never even entered my mind to tamper with it. It was as though it were invisible to me during my fit of destruction. My soon-to-be ex's most prized possession—his metallic gold corvette.

I hate to disappoint you, but I didn't pick the hammer up and pummel the car into confetti. I'd gotten it all out of my system, I suppose. With each passing day following what I now call "my mass destruction," I felt a little bit better. Although I don't recommend dealing with anger in this manner, for me, it sure helped.

We were officially divorced a few months later.

The two positives about my third ex? He, too, was extremely funny. There was immense laughter throughout our nine years of marriage. He was very respectful of women and of me. During our time together, I don't think I had to open a door for myself more than two or three times. And, he was the first man I'd ever trusted.

OK, that's more than two, isn't it? Ironically, he remarried a few years later —to a woman.

Years later, I asked him if it were true he thought he was gay, or if it was simply an excuse to get out of the marriage. He said it was true and that he'd "tried" it.

• • •

Two of my ex-husbands were flat-out mistakes, in my eyes, but there again, it's all part of my past that makes me who I am today. Maybe they were all three mistakes. However, I do regret that one of my ex's spanked one of my daughters, leaving bruises on her thighs. The same thing had happened with my other daughter, due to a boyfriend I had after my first divorce. I will feel bad about these things, I believe, until the end of my time. The other husband/mistake, I later found out, while he did not do anything physically to my daughter, he tried to talk her into a sexual activity with him, more than once. Thankfully, due to her young age, she did not understand or agree to any such interaction. However, if I saw him today, I'm not so sure I wouldn't thrust my knee into his crotch.

I regret putting my children in these circumstances during that time in my life that I was continuing to grow up, pulling them along with me throughout the entire tumultuous process.

To my daughters, Amber and Cassandra, I am truly sorry for any negative childhood experiences you endured due to my life choices, causing you pain, injury or emotional damage/scarring. I did the best I could, based on what I knew at the time, but wish I could have done much better—for both of you. I can see how much better you both are as mothers to your own children; my beloved grandchildren. They are blessed. I love you, my dear daughters, with all of my heart.

Can I forgive myself? Well, I'm working on it. Writing about my regrets has given me a bit of relief, if only a smidgen. To confess such things—perhaps it's all necessary. Healthy. Therapeutic. Time will tell.

. . .

Enter husband #4, Greg

Greg is my "hot sexy testosterone pumpin hunka Mmmmm." That's for real his nickname. Well, one of them anyway.

After I'd healed from losing my previous husband to other men (Ahem!), I decided to pursue some kind of social life. NOT dating, just a social life. You know, with friends.

One weekend, my good friend, Dianne, invited me to go with her to a country western bar in Lexington called Cadillac Ranch. Sounded fun, though I was no fan of that type of music—at all. But, I met her there and it was, surprisingly, a lot of fun! They played more dance music than country western music and the live band was really good.

This quickly became a weekend ritual. We'd hang out, listen to music and watch people dance while we enjoyed our respective Coke and Diet Coke. I don't recall being asked to dance or having anyone offer to buy me a drink during this time. Hmm ... should I have been offended? Ha!

Anyway, one night she and I were at "The Ranch," as we called it, standing and looking around. I think we'd gotten there too late and all the tables were taken. Dianne pointed to this man sitting at a high-top table, alone I think, who was wearing a black cowboy hat. As she pointed, she said, "I always thought he was kinda cute." She was always looking for a man for me. Best friends are like that. Well, I looked at this man and said, "Oooooh, I think he's REALLLLY CUTE!"

Somehow, by fate I suppose (he he), we ended up near his table and he invited us to sit with him. Man, he was even cuter close up with his sexy blue eyes and snug-fitting bluejeans. Not long after I'd met this sexy man, he asked me three questions: How old are you? How long have you been divorced? Can you cook? I suppose that was the most important information to him, at that time. I told Dianne that he inquired about my cooking ability and she told him, "The first time I ate her cooking, I asked her to marry me." Ha ha!

Needless to say, my dear friend and I ended up sitting with this sexy cowboy every time we went to The Ranch thereafter. He seemed rough around the edges, like one of those cattle-driving cowboys in western movies. You know the ones who ride their horse into town, visit the "cathouse," then mosey over to the saloon? Even so, I instinctively knew, in his core, he was a good man.

Now, you'd think in a bar, a man wouldn't hesitate to try to pick up a woman, even the ones who pay them no attention whatsoever. I mean that's how bars have been portrayed in movies, etc., as "meat markets."

But, not this man, nope. I'd do my best flirting by trying to peek inside his double-breasted western shirt or tickling his knee through the hole in his sexy jeans. You'd think a guy would've asked me to come home with him right then and there, but it was a good three months before he asked for my phone number and he had to be drunk to do it. We were all leaving a few minutes before the bar was about to close and some guy asked Dianne for her phone number. I turned to my sexy cowboy and asked, "Do you want her number, too?" To my surprise and delight, he said, "I'd rather have yours." So, he got it!

The very next weekend, back at The Ranch, we're sitting at the sexy cowboy's table and he mentioned that he tried to call me. "You probably saw it was me and didn't wanna answer," he

said. "Ooooh, no! If I'd have seen it was you, I would've definitely answered," I assured him and explained that we had dialup
Internet and that my teenage daughter was always online, tying
up the phone. It was obvious he didn't believe me, but we had a
nice night anyway.

The following Monday, while I was at work, I looked up his
phone number on the Internet. *Yeah, I'll fix him.* That night, after
arm-wrestling my teenage daughter so I could use the telephone,
I called him. When he answered, "Hello," I said, "See, I told you I
would've answered the phone." We talked for a while and he told
me about where he lived. I said, "Oh, that sounds pretty. I'd love to
see it sometime." He said, "What are you doing right now?" That
was 19 years ago and we've been together since.

When I brought my youngest daughter, my constantly-tying-
up-the-phone teenager, over to sexy cowboy's house to meet him
for the first time, I jokingly suggested that we test him. You know,
based on our last husband/stepdad encounter and all. So, she asked
him, "Do these shoes go with this outfit?" and he responded, "How
the hell would I know?" We giggled and I said, "He passes!"

No offense to gay men intended here. By the way, if it's true
that you are all experts in fashion, then I have a fashion-illiterate
challenge for you right here. Me! Seriously, I do need fashion help.

Now, since we'd met in a country and western bar, when we
started to date we called it "court'n." After we courted for a few
months and he'd asked me to move in with him, then we were
"shack'n." Then, in a pile of sawdust during the construction of
his game room (now "man cave"), he asked me to marry him. I told
him, to keep the trend going, since we would be "gettin' hitched,"
we needed to do it at a hitchin' post. So, he built one.

We had a very western wedding, wore jeans, boots and hats,
the whole nine yards, and my father gave me away at the hitchin'

post. Again. For the last time—to my best husband. We still have that hitchin' post, too, in one of our flower beds.

Positives about my present and forever husband are numerous. He is and has always been the sexiest man I've ever known, a title previously held by a high school boyfriend, until the time I met my sexy cowboy. My husband never believes me when I tell him that, but it's the truth.

He is very hard-working. He spoils me rotten. He says he loves me, but that he doesn't know why. I giggle every time. We're complete opposites in a lot of ways, yet we fit together like the intricate gears inside a clock. I don't mean that in a sexual way. However ... never mind. Ha ha! We just click.

He's extremely patient. Patience is a character trait that I seem to repel. He regularly tells me, "Patience is a virtue," to which I inevitably respond, "Yeah, well, I never claimed to be virtuous!" We share the same core values and I was correct in my initial impression of him. He is a very good man and I feel extremely blessed to have met him (semi-stalked him) at The Ranch.

A major difference between me and my husband is that I absolutely love to travel, see new places, and experience different cultures. Hubby has little desire for such things; however, he does enjoy beach vacations! While he is happy to lie on a blanket in the sand, soaking up the sun, drinking his cold beer and listening to music through his earbuds, I'm either in the water swimming/floating on my pool noodle, walking along the shore searching for seashells, or riding a rented bike up and down the sidewalks enjoying the sites on the shoreline. If I'm sitting on the beach, it's only temporarily to watch the waves and listen to their sound as they come up on the shore. It's a wonderful sound, and thoroughly relaxes me. That is, until someone has their music blaring, thoroughly disrupting my mellow. I saw a meme once that said, "If you have to have music at the beach, you're missing the point." I completely agree and can relate to that sentiment.

The thought of lying in the sun does not appeal to me at all. I'll sit there for a while and visit with hubby for a bit, usually under an umbrella, but then I'm up and at it again. There is a term for children who play in the same room, near each other, but not with each other. It's called "parallel play." My husband and I sort of have parallel vacations. We don't try to convince or coerce the other into joining our respective activities; we do our own thing, and are content. It's much the same way when we are home. Hubby has a man cave. It's a real man cave, too! It's 1/2 of a 600 square foot pole barn. The other half is his garage. Now, his cave is the epitome of a "man cave," for sure. There is a sectional sofa, projection television with a 72-inch picture and an incredible sound system. There's a bar, a refrigerator, a pool table, lots of Budweiser decor, along with University of Kentucky Wildcats memorabilia, too. Man heaven up in there!

When he's working outside, he listens to music the whole time. I prefer quiet. If I'm working outdoors, or in the house, there's no music playing. The TV is not on at all during the day (unless there are grandkids here), and I carry out my tasks. While we're completely opposite in a lot of areas, we accept that in each other and live quite happily this way.

I recently told my husband, "You know, and I hope this comes out right. I feel like neither of us are truly marriage material, but we've found the one person we can live with for the rest of our lives," or something like that. I mean, between us, we *have* had five failed marriages. What I meant was that most women would likely pitch a fit about their husband spending so much alone time in their man cave, and most men would likely pitch a fit about their wife wanting to travel as much as possible and changing careers/

jobs often, as well as having a severe case of ADD (never knowing what they'll attempt next).

. . .

Marital Bliss

With super wicked and scary summer clouds among us, Greg and I scurried frantically to move all 16 chickies into the big coop with the old biddies and the butthead rooster so they'd be safer during the coming storms. Once they were all transferred and we were sufficiently covered with mud and chicken poop, I was in the laundry room shedding my filth and was down to my sexy black knee-high support socks, my bra and panties. With lustful eyes, Greg looked at me and said, "I like how your phone is in the top of your panties." I love this man!

. . .

Me: What'd I do to deserve you?

Hubby: I don't know, by god, but I deserve a medal.

YES, he certainly does!!

. . .

While I was out doing some shopping, I stopped at Lee's Famous Recipe for supper and brought a chicken dinner home for Greg. While Greg was on his way home, he stopped to get some supper. Guess what he got? You guessed it! Chicken dinner from Lee's Famous Recipe.

. . .

You'd think I'd have learned by now. Several years ago, I casually mentioned to Greg, "Sometime, in the future, no rush, I'd like a roof over the back porch so I can sit outside when it rains." I was expecting, you know, a simple wood and metal cover/roof. But, no! Three months later, we have the Taj Mahal of roofs over the back porch. Fast forward to late winter 2017. I say to Greg, "I really want a good garden this year," and mention the desire for a "real bumper crop!" Well, we only have six rows of green beans. We haven't even finished our first picking. There are blossoms galore on every single plant. I have, as of now, canned 52 quarts of beans (10 are from my mother-in-law's garden), and I expect that to triple by the end of summer. Note to self: Be careful what you ask of Greg Newsome. You just might get it! Lovin' it. Best garden we've ever had in my 19 years here! And, don't even get me started on the tomato plants that are massively full of green ones! My hot sexy testosterone pumpin hunka Mmmmm worked his butt off this spring so I could work my butt off this summer!

• • •

While hubby is toiling diligently, removing nails from our garage steps, remnants of the carpet he'd tacked on them years ago (long since removed), we have this conversation:

Me: Would staples have been easier to remove?

Hubby: Probably.

Me: Well, use staples for the next one you put down.

Hubby: Smartass!

• • •

Apparently, we're having two different conversations during this football game. I'm looking at the salt shakers in the restaurant and I wonder how they keep the salt from clumping up in this humid weather. So, I say to Greg, "I wonder how they keep the salt from clumping up." Still thinking about football, he says, "They drink Gatorade."

I'm crying!

. . .

I crept into the bathroom to try to scare Greg in the shower with my best "Psycho" impression, with sound effects and everything. I slowly opened the shower door. He turned around. Then, he shook his manhood at me. I said, "You win!"

. . .

Hubby: What's that red bowl with eggs in it doing beside the refrigerator out in the garage?

Me: Ooooh, I took it out of the fridge to do something, then forgot about it. Then, I saw it later and remembered I'd forgotten it, and then I forgot about it again.

Hubby: Why does that not surprise me?

. . .

During an average Saturday morning in the Newsome household, while I'm making my late breakfast/early lunch keto pizza, Greg walks in from the garage to fetch water for his routine second pot of man cave coffee. Ah, happy, content mutual enjoyment of married life. Ain't nothin' better. Well, I had a mischievous moment. Not me! So, while he was filling his coffee pot at the sink, I pants him. I mean, down to his ankles pants him. Shorts and boxers! I'm cracking up and it doesn't phase him one bit. After a good chuckle and a snort or two, I decide to do the decent thing and pull his pants up where they belong. As I'm walking back towards my pizza making, Greg turns around from the sink and faces me. While I thought I'd successfully covered up all of his parts, his digit was perkily poking out the top of his waistband! Giggles, snorts and after I peed a little later ... he goes about his business and I return to mine. Yup! Just another average day in the Newsome household.

. . .

I burst into the bathroom while Greg was taking a shower, with a roll of wrapping paper in my hand as a sword, and said, "Hello! My name is Indigo Montoya. You killed my father. Prepare to die." The look on his face as he opened the shower door was priceless.

. . .

One night, Greg was tucking me in for the night and I asked him to put my hearing aids on the sink in the bathroom. He said, "In the toilet?" I said, "Up your ass." Then he said, "You reckon I can hear a good fart that way?"

. . .

One morning, I spent over an hour creating a board on Pinterest to help promote my blog (https://acomedyofperils.blog). I followed the directions, saved it, and it supposedly exists in Pinterest land —somewhere. I'll be danged if I can find it. It doesn't show up in any search I've tried. It was probably posted on a secret government website! But, hey —long as they read it.

Keeping an eye out for a cavalcade of shiny black vehicles.

. . .

Tear down the wall!
My husband built our house a few years before we had gotten together. It's a beautiful home with a cathedral ceiling and a

walkaround brick fireplace located between the living and dining room areas. Near the front door, he constructed a half wall which essentially created an 8-foot wide walkway from that door into the living room. That was something I'd never seen before. This half wall was 15 feet long and stood at about waist level. Imagine, if you were to come in our front door, the half wall is on your left, you can walk with your hand gliding along its top, and to the right is the wall which includes the door to our bedroom. A really long living room couch backed up against this half wall and there were end tables with lamps on either end. Can you picture it?

Now, over time (not that much time, mind you), this half wall, *the great wall of clutter*, became a very irritating, anxiety-provoking, excruciatingly painful eye sore to me. I swear its primary evil purpose was to attract clutter. You know, crap like mail, newspapers, or anything else that could not find its way back to its proper home. My compulsive desire, er need, to keep it cleaned off at all times was repeatedly met with epic, catastrophic failure. Over time, my irritation bubbled into an intense loathing. I hated that damn wall and I'm convinced it could feel it, too!

One evening, my eldest daughter came to our house, opened the storm door and was knocking on the decorative, beveled glass windows of our front door. She would normally just come on in, but on this visit the door was locked. At any other time, I would rise up from my seat, walk all the way around the half wall, then walk all the way down the little hallway to the front door and unlock it. However, this time, not wanting to miss too much of whatever we'd been watching on TV, or perhaps I was simply too tired, I decided to take a little shortcut. I thought I'd save some time and effort by reaching the lock from the end of the couch nearest that front door.

I immediately discovered that reaching the door lock from the couch was a complete impossibility. Plan B ensued. I climbed up on the couch and commenced to straddling my body across the great wall of clutter. I strategically balanced my weight over it while successfully avoiding the lamp on the end table right beside me. Such grace and coordination I possessed. My rendition of the famous Dirty Dancing lift was done to perfection. Ha! Actually, it looked more like I was trying to give myself the Heimlich maneuver.

Now, reaching the door lock from this angle and position was not as simple as I had envisioned. I couldn't reach it enough to sufficiently grip the lock knob with my fingers. I can do this. *The great wall of clutter will not beat me!* I scooted my belly a tiny bit more across this wall and stretched my body toward the door as far as it would allow. Just as the sharp wood edges of the evil half wall are about to rupture my spleen, I achieved a firm grasp on the door lock. Yay! With the anticipation that my daughter will be able to enter our house in mere seconds, I began turning the door lock. At this same moment, however, I also felt my balance wavering and I knew, without a doubt, I would be tumbling over the wall onto the floor. A bit of panic washed over me and I was thinking, *OMG! I'm going to fall over this wall and hit the floor! This is going to hurt!* I swear to you, this all happened in super-slow motion, yet I was completely unable to stop the momentum already in full swing. My face was getting closer and closer to the floor *(Gee, I should really vaccuum over here...)*, I was doing the best I could to brace myself for the all-over body pain I was expecting upon my impact with the floor and my feet effectively knocked the lamp to the living room floor as I was doing a sloppy somersault to the other side.

My husband, who had witnessed the entire saga from his favorite seat in the living room, immediately jumped up to see if I was okay. He finds me lying there, my knees bent up towards my chest, barely breathing and laughing without emitting any sound. My daughter's raucous laughter could be heard from the other side of the still locked front door. The half wall was giggling and whispering to me, "How do you like me now?" Evil wall! It's been more than ten years since this happened and I have yet to see my husband laugh as hard as he did that day! And, he laughed for quite a long time, too.

Coincidentally, after we'd been married for a few years, I convinced my husband to tear down the wall in order to "open up the space into the living room." While he pounded holes into that half wall with a hammer, I stood there witnessing the painful demise of the great wall of clutter, wringing my hands with a contented evil grin on my face.

Mwah ha ha, how do you like ME now?!

· · ·

How to tell when a couple's been married for several years:

The wife...umm...successfully and quite thoroughly, clogs the toilet. Then, the husband, using every muscle in his body, toils vehemently to eradicate the blockage. That happened to a friend of mine!!

When he came out of the bathroom, he had sweat dripping from his face. That's what *she* said, anyway. LOL!!

· · ·

When Greg and I celebrated our 16th wedding anniversary, first on the agenda was getting our income taxes completed. An unusual way to celebrate our many years of marital bliss, but when has anything ever been "normal" with us? Ha ha! Anyway, we entered our accountant's office and saw an elderly gentleman seated in the lobby. I took a seat and Greg sat down beside me. I was giving Greg a hard time about something (imagine that), then he looked at the elderly gentleman, evidently hoping to find a sympathetic, commiserating man to be on his side, and said, "Does your wife do this to you?" The man said nothing, but locked his gaze with Greg's for a second, rolled his eyes then looked away. I thought that was the end of this interaction. A few seconds later, he turned back to Greg and said, "Women rule the world!" He explained that when they (women) want something, they will not stop until they get exactly what they want and that he has lived with such agony for 67 years. As he continued with his story, he mentioned that he had been in the Korean War and how truly horrific it was. He wasn't able to finish his story, as we were called into the accountant's office, so I said, "I want to hear more of your story!" I so hoped he'd still be there when we were finished.

We received good news about our refund and what a great anniversary present is that?! There had been some serious concern based on the new tax laws (which royally suck, by the way). We shook hands with our accountant and headed back out toward the lobby. I was pleasantly surprised to see the elderly gentleman still sitting there and said, "Now, I want to hear more of your story." He continued with graphic details about the Korean War and how visions of multiple deceased soldiers stacked in piles were permanently affixed to his memories. He and two of his buddies had voluntarily enlisted in the service, but he was the only one who returned home three years later. You see, there was no way to tell the difference between North Korean and South Korean soldiers, making it very difficult for others to survive this war. Then, he changed the subject to how he met his wife. He said that he was a senior and she was a freshman in high school. They were in a crowded hall at school and someone had pinched her on the backside. She turned around, saw him and walloped him upside the face! Stunned, he looked back at her and his immediate thought was,

"She is the prettiest little girl in this school. Where has she been hiding?" He was completely in love at that very moment. Love at first smack! They started dating and after his high school graduation, he and his buddies enlisted in the service. He said, "She went with other guys while I was gone, so I didn't know if I still had a girlfriend or not." When he returned after his three-year service obligation, he went to her and said, "I want to get married. Will you marry me?" Of course, she said, "Yes." It was the sweetest love story and I wished that I could've recorded the entire thing as he shared it with us. I was so moved, I hugged him and he kissed my cheek. Greg shook his hand and we left the office in smiles. I grabbed Greg's hand while we walked to our car, still smiling. It truly is the simple things that warm your heart.

Next on our anniversary celebration extravaganza: Longhorn Steakhouse! We walked inside and the manager greeted us and mentioned that he was very short-staffed this Friday night due to several call-ins from his employees. While the manager was gathering menus for us, he looked toward the door and said, "Here's my help now!" Apparently, he'd called several employees who were off that night and begged them to work. As this guy was walking through the door, I told him, "You are a good man!" He thanked me. We were seated and this good man ended up being our waiter. He was fantastic, quite possibly the best server we've ever had. As is our semi-newly adopted tradition, Greg got the Outlaw Ribeye and I got the Flo's Filet. We ordered an appetizer which is extremely rare, white cheddar stuffed mushrooms. OOOOOH MY GOOOOOOOSH, they were so delicious and I'm not even a mushroom fan! Since we'd asked to skip the bread, being true to our Keto lifestyles, our waiter asked the cook to omit the bread crumbs on our appetizer as well. He really was great! I seriously recommend that you try that appetizer. We could've made a meal of those mushrooms. Anyway...we enjoyed our perfectly cooked steaks and delightful conversation. Greg had a couple beers and I had a glass of wine, which I had never done during nights out to celebrate our marital bliss. New tradition? Maybe.

Then it was time for our next anniversary tradition. Well, it was a little different. You know, we gotta shake things up now and then to keep it interesting. Instead of going to Walmart, we went to Kroger for some shopping before heading home. The best anniversary ever—so far, that is. I've got lots more years of torture in store for you, Greg!

CHAPTER THREE

"THanK YOU, MISS NeWKLe!"

"If you follow the herd, you'll end up stepping in shit."
—DR. WAYNE W. DYER

In 2003, after I'd married my sexy cowboy and best husband, I worked as a medical assistant in a cardiology clinic until I became bored with it. I'd always envisioned myself working in a hospital, with lots of people and a wide variety of duties. You know, similar to my legal clerk days in the army. I came to the conclusion that, well, I'm just going to have to go school to become a registered nurse so I can work in a hospital.

By the way, nursing school is the hardest, most relentlessly stressful educational experience ever! I felt I had no life other than nursing school. I would sit through lectures, listening to and recording them on my mini cassette recorder, while I made hand-written notes. Then, at home, I would re-listen as I cleaned up and added to my notes, rewrite the notes into a study guide format and then study those notes over and over and over.

Friendships faded. I did some stress eating which led to a good amount of weight gain. I cried and threw books when I was sure I was going to fail. But, somehow, I made it through this torture and graduated with a 3.2 grade point average. Amazingly!

However, it was more than five years before the nightmares of nursing school relented. I'd dream I was late for class; couldn't find the class; didn't have proper attire; couldn't find the right building; we were taking a test that contained questions that had not been covered during class; I was failing the one exam that determined whether I'd be participating in graduation; and so on and so on, and so on.

. . .

Coffee vs. Sleep vs. Coffee

As a registered nurse, I worked prn (that's "as needed" for you non-medical folks). My schedule was flexible and varied week to week. Kind of like part-time but without a regular schedule.

One week, I worked more days than I usually do, and longer hours, too. By Thursday night, I was really hoping they wouldn't need me Friday and would call me off because I felt I was developing a cold and wanted nothing more than to sleep, sleep, sleep. Not receiving the coveted, you-can-be-off-tomorrow message Thursday evening, and determined to not call in and leave my co-workers short-staffed (I'm so conscientious that way), I plodded through the house to perform my routine preparations for the next work day. My scrub set, along with the required undergarments, was rolled up and placed on my dresser. My iWatch was placed on its charger on the kitchen counter next to all the things I put in my scrub pockets for work each day, as well as my car keys. I poured water into my coffee pot and scooped the precise amount of Starbucks mocha coffee grounds into the filter. Closed the lid. I was ready and could relax until bedtime. Contented sigh.

Friday morning rolls around and the first of my two iPhone alarms blasts away. I swear it was like 20 minutes after I'd closed my eyes. I get up, brush my teeth, then head to the kitchen to turn on my juice-of-life maker and get my travel mug in position to receive it. Shower, dress, makeup, briefly muss with the hair. Oy! Well, it looks good enough, I'm tired—just let that freakin' mega-huge cow lick show. I don't care! Put on shoes and head back to the kitchen to pour my coffee. What?! It didn't even brew?! I think, I must not have put the water in it, so I commence to filling up my plastic 2-cup measuring cup, which I use daily, with the proper amount of water and after about a third of that water was poured into the coffee maker, I realize the water had in fact already been in there. I'd just left the thing unplugged. I had precious little extra time to start from scratch, so I decided to let it brew and cut it off before it used the excess water. Making such good use of my time while my morning elixir is brewing, I go outside and feed the cats. (A group of cats is called a "clowder." Did you know that? I learned that from Sheldon Cooper on Big Bang Theory. I learn a lot from television.)

Anyway…having placed nine equal piles of dry cat food on the driveway, spaced very equally, too, by the way, I go back into the house to check the coffee process and decide it's brewed enough for my daily cup of life juice. Turn off the pot. Pour fresh, hot coffee into my mug, give it a taste test and discover it is not right. Too strong. So, I turn the coffee maker back on and let it spit out some more juice. Hmm…that looks about right. Nope, still too strong. Allow a bit more water spittage and pour part of it into my mug. That's good enough. Shut off the coffee maker and unplug it. Out the door and into my car. Every morning, once I've driven through the 6 miles of country road and turn on the main road, I start sipping my coffee and today's cup was just not right. Now, it's too weak. Oh well, I'm drinking this SOB'ing stuff anyway after all that extra effort. I don't care! I work all day, all the while hoping to be sent home early. You know, the coveted you-can-go-home-now verbiage. Nope. Lunch comes. Lunch ends. Back to work and I finish at my regularly scheduled time. It's all good. I survived and had a few good laughs with my co-workers. It was actually a pretty good day, despite my constant desire for slumber.

During my 25-mile drive home, I contemplate: Now, do I want to try to take a nap when I get home, or do I want to make a second cup of coffee? Three o'clock is kind of late to take a nap. On the other hand, three o'clock is also kind of late to be drinking coffee, too. I mull this over while twirling my hair with my left hand as I maneuver through the bustling Friday afternoon traffic. This sleep vs. coffee vs. sleep debate would continue until I was within 5 miles of home, and my drive to/from work is 30 minutes long, with good traffic. Finally, I reach a decision. ANOTHER CUP OF COFFEE IT IS! I might be up too late tonight, but I don't care!

The night before, my hubby and I had done some grocery shopping and, as luck would have it, Walmart was out of our favorite Starbucks mocha, "chocolatey and luscious" coffee. Great! Grr! But, I opted to give their vanilla-flavored ground coffee a try. What the heck is a vanilla anyway? So, after I got home from work on this sleepy, Friday, I thought it'd be a good time to try this vanilla stuff out. If it sucked, I wouldn't finish it, would still have ingested a little bit of caffeine to maybe help me stay awake a while longer AND I would still be able to sleep at bedtime. Sounds like a win-win to me. I fill my 2-cup measuring cup with water and pour it into coffee maker. Scoop precise amount of vanilla coffee grounds into filter. Plug in pot and turn it on. Several minutes later, I go back to the kitchen to pour my anticipated afternoon vanilla coffee treat and soon find that I have way more coffee than my very large coffee mug will hold. Yep! The coffee maker

STILL had unused water in it from the morning coffee fiasco, and, apparently, I'd left a bit of brewed coffee in the pot as well. I decide that, screw it, I'm drinking it anyway. It's not bad, just a bit weak. But, then I realized that what I'd been drinking was the morning's cold failure of brewed chocolate coffee that had been sitting in the pot all day which was now mixed with the fresh vanilla coffee. Nope. Couldn't do it. Down the sink. Rinse. Start over. From scratch!

Ugh! Rinse out my very large coffee mug, place it in the dish rack. Scoop out the freakin' vanilla, NOT CHOCOLATE—well, NOT MOCHA—ground coffee into another cotton-pickin' coffee filter. Fill up the cute lil 2-cup measuring cup with the precise amount of water, just over the 2-cup mark. Pour it into the [insert any irritated adjective—I can't think of another one and—I don't care] coffee maker! Flip the switch. Minutes later, a nice cup of aromatic vanilla coffee is brewing. I pour it into my big mug, add my precise amount of heavy whipping cream, give it a stir, then take a test sip. It's actually quite tasty and could, possibly, be my new coffee flavor, or at least an additional one. I'm enjoying it as I type out this heart-wrenching java saga to share it with you. I've only got about one-third of that coffee left in my mug so…I may be awake until 3:00 a.m. tomorrow. But, you know what? I don't care!!

• • •

Farewell, my friend…

I had to bid farewell to a very good friend today. A devoted friend who has been there for me every day, for many years. A faithful friend who offered me warmth and courage when I needed it the most. A friend who perked me up and made me happy when I was tired or feeling blue.

It was apparently a massive aneurysm that caused my friend's demise. It wasn't sudden, however. I noticed that my friend had been perking my coffee a little bit more slowly each day. I tried resuscitation by giving my friend a vinegar colonic, hoping it was merely clogged with hard water deposits. Alas, it didn't help. I had to face facts and accept that the end was imminent.

This morning, my friend was spitting and sputtering loudly and very little water made it through the coffee grounds. I poured two cups of water into the reservoir, but only one cup became coffee, which took several minutes. My dear friend, while fighting hard to be there for me, and making that one last cup of coffee with great heroism, spewed so much water and steam that the bottom of the cabinet was dripping. Yes. My Mr. coffee 5-cup coffee maker has crossed the caffeinated coffee filter bridge. I will always remember you, my dear friend. Tomorrow morning, when I use my new 5-cup Mr. Coffee mini for the first time, I will raise that mug toward heaven and say, "This cup's for you, my friend. This cup's for you."

· · ·

I thought I'd ask a question to the universe: Why do people argue over their opinions?

I have pondered this question numerous times and I'm convinced there is simply no answer to it. No single answer, anyway.

This may be a hot topic for many folks so I should note that comments to my posts are not automatically published on my blog —I have to approve them first. Therefore, negative, hateful or angry political stances will not be approved. There is more than enough of that on the news and blathered throughout social media. My sole purpose for writing is to entertain, make you think, bring a smile to your face or laughter to your day, if only for a moment, not to argue and fight. Thank you.

An opinion is an individual thing, much like fingerprints, DNA, etc. Right? So, what is it that makes humans argue about it? Really? This guy says that chocolate is the best ice cream flavor and this guy says it's rocky road. If we didn't all have our own opinion, if there was only one opinion for all of us, what would that even look like? There would be one religion, one political party, one type of cereal, one type of hot sauce, one country, one type of car, one type of…everything! Hey, Hollywood! You should make a movie about that and title it, There's Only One. I'd pay to see that.

We can't keep screaming that we are all equal and should be treated as such when at the same time we're all screaming about how different, or better than, we are when compared to others. It's a constant tug-of-war. Buffalo Springfield's song, "For What It's Worth," says it best: "Nobody's right if everybody's wrong." Think about that for a minute. This first guy is telling the second guy that he is wrong for feeling/believing the way he does and the second guy is saying the exact same thing right back to the first guy. It's dizzying! Who's right? Who's wrong? It's such a futile argument, yet so many people engage in it every single day. Don't believe me? Log into Facebook and feast your eyes.

With this COVID pandemic ruling our lives at present, there seems to be a constant barrage of one expert after another expressing his/her prediction, as if it is fact, regarding what will happen next, how many will die, and how it will ever go away. An expert opinion is still merely an opinion, is it not? No wonder people are anxious, restless and twitching!

Like I said, this is one of those questions which will not have one conclusive answer. Ever. That is, until the earth ends and then, at that point, we all will truly be equal. We'll all be right. All the same. Equally extinct.

. . .

The Story of Coffee and Cashews Coffee

My father LOVED Nescafé instant coffee, which he had been drinking since before he was 18 years old. Yes, 18. When my parents got married in 1949, Nescafé cost $.99 a jar. In today's market, $9.99/jar. Anyway, my parents moved to their Fairfield house in 1965, and at that time all the grocery stores carried Dad's favorite brew. Over the years, however, the number of stores to carry it have dwindled until finally there was only one left—Main Street Market. Sadly, and as an enormous shock to my father, Main Street Market closed one day. Being down to having a mere three jars in his stock, my Dad frantically searched for a distributor and found one online. He ordered a case of his treasured Nescafé and for his usual price, too. He was happy once more. In the meantime, I didn't know he'd found a supplier and I'd stumbled upon nine jars of Nescafé at our discount grocery store for $5.19/jar. I was so excited to surprise him with my bargain find. He now had 20-something jars of coffee.

My Mom loved cashews and always kept a can handy. When she could no longer eat them, dad kept buying them anyway and would give a daily handful to their bird, Kokie Poo (the big brat African Grey parrot). Well, I just happen to take after my mother and love cashews, too. So much so that I dug into dad's supply every time I was there. My brother, during a long visit, informed me that our dad had complained to him that, "Vonda eats all my cashews when she is here! Those are for the *bird*!" I thought, *Well I'll just fix him!* So, with every shopping trip I've made for him, I bought more cashews! I marked two cans in the bunch for human consumption only, just to irritate him. My dad was a hilarious nut with a side of mischievous little turd. He could be a real rascal at times. That night just happened to be one such time. He was picking on me about something and I was determined to say something to retaliate. And retaliate good! I shouted to him, "When you're gone, I'm putting your ashes in a cashew can!" Then, without hesitation or the mere blink of an eye, my father responded, "I prefer Nescafé."

• • •

One afternoon when I'd awakened to face my third work night in a row, I discovered that I was completely out of coffee. NOT GOOD! I scoured the cabinets and pantry three times. Nothing. This just CANNOT BE! Standing in the middle of the kitchen in total disbelief and despair, I think "Aha!" Maybe, just maybe, there's some coffee in the man cave! So, I put on some shoes, grab the key and head out there. Sure nuff, there in the back of the room by the coffee pot sits a little bag of coffee. SALVATION! I walk over, mouth salivating in anticipation of the sweet nectar of life, only to discover the bag of coffee is riddled with holes. Mice apparently have a caffeine addiction, too! I pick up the bag and look inside for critters or signs of "debris." Nothing visible. Studying the many holes in the bag I weigh the need for coffee against the thought of what's been in that coffee. Guess which won? You guessed it! I brought that lil bag of coffee in the house, ground it up to espresso and made a nice hot cup. Sometimes you just gotta have your coffee when you wake up.

Two weeks after this incident, I received a box full of Starbucks coffee—from my father.

• • •

So, during a stay at my parents' house one time, they got new cell phones. That evening, we're sitting around the kitchen table and dad inspects the contacts on his new phone. Realizing he hasn't made the first call on it yet, he selects a number to call. A few seconds later, the house phone rings and my Mom answers it. Then my Dad, who's sitting a few feet from her, says, "I'm gonna pull your panties down the first chance I get."

. . .

People get my name wrong all the time, especially on the telephone, but this has to be the best screw up ever. Dad wanted spaghetti, so I called the local Italian restaurant to order some for him. I gave them my name and my phone number. When I went to pick up my order, they had it under "Barbara Newkle." Yeah, that totally sounds like VON-dah NewSOME!! When I was leaving the guy said, "Thank you, Ms. Newkle." I replied, "Just call me Barbara."

. . .

I have long felt that every tragedy, heartbreak or loss contains within itself a blessing and that "Something good will come from it." The old every cloud has a silver lining thing. I truly believe it. Now, with this COVID-19 lockdown, quarantine, and don't-you-dare-touch-your-face pandemic, my belief hasn't changed. Yes, it sucks not being able to go where we want to go—a movie, out to dinner, to our jobs, to dance class, to see other human beings in person, etc. But, instead of viewing this as a punishment, sheer torture, or a cleverly plotted sinister plan against our country, maybe, just maybe, we can see it as a gift. An opportunity to make new choices every day, choices that will enrich our lives. Choices we will be proud we made when we look back on this lockdown years from now. Just maybe.

We often say, "If I had time, I'd…" or "I don't have time to…" Right? I think most of us have said that at least once in our lives, or perhaps even daily. If we are humbly honest with ourselves, we know that this excuse is a big fat lie. "I don't have time to read." Okay, but you didn't miss a single episode of The Walking Dead? You binge-watched that "Tiger" show currently on Netflix? Did you spend hours on Facebook today or yesterday? I'm not downing people who watch a lot of TV. I'm just as guilty of indulging in that time-sucker myself. We have the time to do the things we think we should do, we simply choose to do those things that we want to do. We are, after all, merely humans.

I have been complying with the social distancing thing for a month now and I've realized just how much of that time I've wasted. I could have sorted through the umpteen gazillion boxes I have sitting here just staring me in the face saying, "Start with me, I'm a small box!" I could have written thousands more words in my book. I could have posted a new blog every day, sharing something uplifting, funny or just plain silly to entertain and/or help others survive one more day of this madness. There's an idea! I could have been getting lots of dance practice or getting in shape with Zumba by watching Facebook or YouTube videos. I didn't do any of that. There are countless things I could've done, but by my own choice, I did other things. Time spent is gone. We will never get it back.

All we have is now—today. I am holding myself accountable for the way I choose to use this gift of time. What will you choose to do differently with your gift of time?

· · ·

What would you attempt to do...

I was at a friend's house enjoying a cup of coffee early this afternoon and noticed there was writing on my mug. I turned it around and read: What would you attempt to do if you knew you could not fail? I thought it was a fascinating question. I reread it. What would you attempt to do if you knew you could not fail? It echoed in my head as I contemplated my answer, the answer I knew I'd have immediately, if not sooner. However, my mind was, unexpectedly, a total blank. I was dumbfounded and had no idea how to answer the question because there are so many things that I'd like to accomplish and experience in this life. I have aspirations, dreams, and goals. So, why couldn't I answer the mug's question with one of them? I could have any of my dreams come true, just like that, and I can't choose one? It's just, well, none of them felt... right. Then, I questioned whether that means I don't desire those things after all. What the...?

It baffled me for several hours. I rehearsed the question and contemplated my answer, over and over. Surely, I thought, I can come up with one goal, one dream. Just one that I would like to be a guaranteed success. I had nothing. Nothing? Then, it hit me. That is my answer, "Nothing." This puzzling question revealed that I don't want my success to come to me effortlessly or instantaneously as if a genie grants my three wishes. Without experiencing the journey, the progressive realization of my dream, the prize loses its value. I want to earn it. While a smooth, guaranteed win would still be a win, it wouldn't be near as satisfying as the win I'll achieve through my blood, sweat, and tears, through overcoming obstacles, persevering in my pursuit, and risking possible failure.

I am mind-blown!

• • •

Puzzles!

During this COVID lockdown, shutdown, quarantine, or whatever you want to call it, I have discovered that I thoroughly enjoy putting jigsaw puzzles together. Up until about a month ago, I hadn't done a puzzle since I was a kid (when I thought they were boring).

These days, however, working a puzzle is very relaxing to me, I get lost in them and lose track of time. It's like a mini vacation. From myself. Sometimes that's necessary. I mean, wait 'til you read about the onion bludgeoning!

My most recent mini vacation lasted from about 7:00 to 10:00 p.m. this evening when I suddenly realized I hadn't posted my blog for the day. Oh, crap! What am I going to write about? I've done so well with my self-imposed 30-day challenge. I can't stop now! I sat in the living room contemplating what I could possibly write about as my anxiety revved up. Hmm. I was blog-blocked. I had nothing. Think think think!

I watched a few minutes of television, hoping something would inspire me to write. Then, my thoughts drifted back to puzzles and it hit me. I work puzzles the same way I write my blogs. When I do a puzzle, of course, I look for the edge pieces first. You've got to have your frame, for goodness sake. Then, I go about sorting the pieces into sections of "looks like" it goes here. Next step is putting it all together so it completes the picture.

When I write a blog post, the edge pieces are my main idea or story. Then, I'll have a sentence or a sub-idea and jot it down/type it, to be expanded upon or moved to its most appropriate place later. Next step is putting it all together so it reads easily, makes sense and is hopefully entertaining.

Anyway, I thought that was pretty cool and wanted to share it with you all. Eight more days until Day #30!! What will my edge pieces be for tomorrow's blog? I have no idea. Yet.

• • •

Donuts in a Blizzard

It's the great Kentucky blizzard of January 2016, and I have to go work my night shift at the hospital. It's a 30-minute drive in the daylight, with good roads and cooperative traffic. We already had 8 inches of snow on the ground, with the brutal wind blowing drifts high enough to thoroughly cover the roads. Lacking any confidence in my car's ability to trudge through the snow and get me to work safely, I ask my hubby to drive me to work in his four-wheel drive truck. I get myself ready an hour early in order to accommodate for the much longer commute we expected. We're in the truck nice and toasty warm and begin the trip down our long driveway through the heavily and very steadily falling snow. I text my work friend to let her know I was on my way. Away we went—dashing through the snow just as the sun was setting. At several points on the country road from our house to the main road, we literally could not see the road—at all. Just keep driving. Just keep driving. Hospitals don't close for inclement weather, and blizzards are no exception.

We were less than two miles from the hospital and, what's that I see? Starbucks is—is it open??!! "Pull in there," I shout to my hubby excitedly. I'm thrilled and so looking forward to a caramel latte to start my long night shift. It is so nice of them to be open for business in this horrid weather. Pull up to the order window, and…sadly, it isn't open. Apparently, they just leave their lights for no reason. No problem. Making the best of a disappointing situation, I notice the very empty parking lot in the shopping center beside the Starbucks, and I shout, "Do a donut in the parking lot!!" Well, no self-respecting redneck man would ignore that request. Hubby delivers and does the most perfect, full-spin, sliding donut in that snow-covered parking lot as I was woohooing the whole time. So much fun!! The moment the truck stopped spinning, we heard —sirens! What???! One donut and we get busted?!! No! It was only an ambulance heading to the hospital. Sigh of relief. On to work! We're about to pull into the hospital's entrance when I get a phone call from my work friend. "Vonda, uh, you're not on the schedule tonight. I thought I'd tell you before you got all the way here." Umm…ok. I reluctantly share this news tidbit with hubby. No words could describe the look on his face. As he's turning the truck around to head back home, he says, "I need a drink." Unable to contain it any longer, I burst out laughing, hysterically. There we are, dashing through the snow in a four-wheel drive truck, with me laughing all the way. Hubby is far less amused, which only intensifies my giggles.

My niece, Rachael McNeill, drew an illustration for this caper which is currently the cover photo on my *A Comedy of Perils* Facebook page. She's an amazing artist! I hope to use much more of her work within my blog and book(s). Thank you, Rachael!

• • •

When you gotta go, well…

I had an eventful commute home the morning after working a 12-hour night shift. It was a wintery, extremely cold January morning. There was snow on the ground and fresh snow was steadily falling with the wind blowing it fiercely. I was almost home when I noticed my car was nearly out of gas. The trip indicator showed less than ten miles were left on my tank. Even though the roads were becoming quite treacherous, I decided it would be a good idea to get some gas before I went home. To save what fuel I did have, I took a road that I would not normally take since it was the shortest route to the nearest gas station. The snow seemed to be falling more quickly as I moved along. Even though I had been driving slower and slower, when I came to a sharp curve and gently turned the steering wheel, my car insisted on going straight. I went right off that road, through a fence, bounced through a ditch and finally stopped in a field. There I sat, alone, with no houses in sight. I watched the snow falling and listened to the howling wind for a moment, contemplating my current predicament.

First thing I did was call my hubby and he arranged for a tow truck. A nice man pulled off the road and came to check on me. Apparently, he had been driving not far behind me and said that he nearly followed me into the same field. After I assured him I was okay and that help was on the way, he advised me to sit in the passenger seat of my car so I wouldn't be hurt should another driver run off the road in the same curve. There I was, sitting alone in the middle of the country in my booboo-covered car. Then, it hit me. I have to pee! What am I gonna do?!! There are no houses close enough for me to walk to and with my menopausal bladder, I wouldn't even make it 10 feet in that cold wind. There was nothing but snow and mud all around the car. Oh, that would be a sight—me squatting down beside my car and the wind blowing my stream sideways, likely all over my scrub pants and my shoes! I knew there was no way I'd make it until the tow truck arrived because it had another run scheduled before coming to rescue me.

So, desperate times, right? I look around inside my car. I guess I could pee in my travel coffee mug. No, that's gross. But, I realllly gotta go! There's got to be something that I can use! Aha! I spot empty McD's and Starbucks cups in the backseat. I double the two up (you know, just in case one is leaky), climb over onto the passenger seat, get up on my knees, manage to get my scrub pants down just enough to accommodate my makeshift female urinal and, yes, I peed in my cups!! Thankfully, I had some McD's napkins in the glove box, and I only dribbled a tiny bit on my car seat. Not long after that, the property owner came with a chainsaw to cut down fence posts and pull away the barbed wire fencing so the tow truck could pull me out without too much further damage. When the tow truck dropped me and the wreckage off at home, I was sore, but not severely hurt, and I was very thankful that my front seat adventure transpired without any witnesses.

Later that week, the insurance company declared that my car was completely totaled. The bright side? Well, when they towed that car away, it only had one mile left on the tank. At least we weren't out the money for filling it up, right?!

. . .

Next day, I woke up and found this message on AIM from my Dad: "How much are they charging you for the Prize Bull you hit?? Saw it on COPS!"

. . .

I'm all ready to leave for work, and guess what? I can't find the keys to my rental car. Shocking, I know. They're not in my coat pocket. Not hanging on the key rack. Not in the bedroom, living room, kitchen, bat cave, storm shelter, rubber room or lighthouse...Grrrrrrrrr!! So, I think they must still be in the rental car. I go out to check and don't see them on the driver's side. While I have the door open, I decide to "unlock" all the car doors so I can check around thoroughly. Close the driver's door and go to the other side to give a look around and the doors are locked. YEP! I LOCKED them ALL!! Breeeeathe! Go back inside, inform my prince of a husband what I've done—this time—and he proceeds to help me trace my steps in hopes of finding the blasted keys. Flashlight going through the yard, following my footprints in the snow from that morning when I fed the dogs. Check everything I wore, the laundry, the refrigerator, toilet, liquor cabinet (looking mighty good by this point). Nuttin'. Frustrated and beginning to utter words I didn't know I knew, I requested he give me a ride to work.

The plan:

- When I get off in the a.m., I'll hitch a ride with a kind co-worker to pick up Greg's truck at Wausau Paper;

- I'll call Hertz to see about getting a spare key to unlock the rental car.

- I'll unlock said car and find keys.

The world will be all good again. Like the old saying goes, sometimes even the best laid plans leave you frustrated, alone and constipated!

While I got a nap, Greg got someone from Hertz to come unlock the car. As soon as I found out, I went tearing out the door in my pajamas to search the car! Having two doors open at all times so as to not make the same mistake again, I removed everything except the upholstery and steering column, then grabbed my work bag, purse and winter coat that were in the back seat. Nuttin'! Come back inside in utter disbelief that I still HAVE NOT FOUND THEM SUMBITCHIN' KEYS!

· · ·

My wonderful hubby had been working very hard at finishing projects around our house. His man cave now has its own potty. Fabulous! Now, he's moved his productivity inside the house. This morning when I came home from work, I noticed that the door from the garage to the kitchen closed much smoother. FANTASTIC! Kitchen floor no longer has pops and creaks in it. Nice!

Then, I went about my normal routine of getting ready for bed and remembered I needed something out of my car. As is my normal routine, I went to the kitchen, opened the door to the garage, locked the doorknob and left it partially open so when I came inside all I had to do was slam it shut. Such a time saver! Well…not so much when the door now closes very easily—on its own!! As I take a couple steps into the garage, I hear the door latch. OOOOOH NO! Yep. It's locked.

No problem, I have the key for it in my car! But, guess what else is my "normal routine" when I get home? You guessed it. I LOCK my car! So…plan C. Maybe the back door is unlocked. Not this time! Front door? Nope. And, there I am, barefoot, wearing nothing but a T-shirt, sneaking around my house hoping to find entry. No such luck! I rang the doorbell several times hoping to wake my daughter or her hubby. NOPE! Go to the back door and bang on it til my hand hurts. Nothing. And, every time I walk through the yard, our dogs put their cold, wet noses on my bare legs. I really don't like that!

Anyway, I had to get back inside somehow. So…my last hope—on the front porch was an empty plastic flower pot. I grabbed it, leaned over towards my daughter's bedroom window and commenced to frantically banging and banging and banging. I thought the neighbors would've called the law by now. Still, I continued banging away. Nothing. Just as I began contemplating which window to break to get inside the house, my son-in-law came to the front door to be my salvation!! Worn out, feet covered with wet grass, I explained the situation to him. Yeah, go ahead, Chad. Laugh it up, buddy boy!!!

• • •

You seriously cannot make this stuff up!!

It was an unusually hot and humid day in July, 2017. My two daughters, four young grandchildren and I piled into my hubby's Ford F-150 truck, equipped with a 16-foot flatbed trailer and headed out for the 90-minute drive to my youngest daughter's ex home. She was going through a divorce and we were going to get her completely moved out. We stopped and got gas, had a bite to eat at Mickey D's, and got there without any real problems. Then, the heat index went through the roof. It was incredibly hot, humid, stagnant and miserable! The temperature inside the trailer was 96°. After I'd had all I could take, I went and started the truck and turned the AC on, then sat there for a while. Well, while I was sitting there waiting for Cassandra to finish packing and loading what she wanted to take, I noticed that the door lock button and the windows on the truck didn't work. Strange, yes, but I kind of just dismissed it as something electrical needing repair in hubby's truck.

Then, finally, with all seven of us loaded back into the truck, a full trailer, and a full covered truck bed, we headed down the road. We hadn't gotten very far when I noticed the truck was driving very sluggishly. I thought, well maybe it's just because of the heavy load. We continued on. Then, all the gauges on the dashboard all went to zero. The truck was still running, the air-conditioner was still on so I thought well I'll just keep going and try to make it home. About five minutes later, the A/C stopped working. The window controls would not work. There was no air coming into the truck and I'm about to flip the hell out because there are seven hot, tired and sweaty people trapped in this rolling oven of a death trap! I opened my window and tried to keep it cracked to allow air to at least come into the cab. Down the road, maybe a mile, the truck slowed way down. I could not get it above say 20 mph at the most. I went up around a curve, saw a gravel parking lot and pulled over into it just as the truck completely died. No lights. No sounds. No air.

We all got out to assess the predicament we were now facing and I called Greg while Cassandra called her soon-to-be ex father-in-law who said he'd come to our aid. Greg also said he was heading our way as Amber had called him. So, there we were, on a gravel lot, in the hot sun, waiting. Three women and four children. We got the folding chairs out of the trailer that Cassandra had packed and placed them in the minute shade created by the truck. Luckily, I'd packed a cooler with ice and bottled water, so we at least had some hydration…for now. Waiting. It looked like a mobile yard sale!

About 20 minutes later, this very nice couple stopped to see if they could assist us in any way. Having seen three women with four kids stranded on the side of the road in such heat, this man could not simply pass us by, so they turned around and came to our aid. I explained that we had two people in route to help us, but this sweet couple just couldn't leave us. Just after they had pulled up, so did Jason's Dad. The nice man stayed with us and the nice woman went on to their house, a mile further up the road to bring us back some large cups of ice water. Jason's Dad turned the AC on in his quad cab truck and let us cool off in there. While the men all brainstormed on what could possibly be wrong with the truck, we chilled and hydrated. The nice man called a friend of his who happened to be a mechanic and ran through all the symptoms the truck was displaying to try to figure out what to do next. Between the three men, they decided it was the battery and Jason's Dad offered to take the battery to a car part store to have it tested. I opted to go along so I could buy a new one, should that one be declared clinically dead. I left Amber and Cassandra with Hunter, Emily, Conner and Zachary and we headed out.

We had a nice chat during the drive to AutoZone and arrived in ten minutes or so. I texted the girls to make sure they were OK. Cassandra said she did not feel well. I thought, Ooooh great! Now, we're gonna have a heat stroke to add to the mix of this crazy day! I told her to stay out of the sun as much as possible. The battery, which was dated 2010, was officially DOA. I called Greg to discuss which battery he'd like to have: good, better or best; purchased his selection and we headed back to the truck. By the time we got there, Greg was there as well as the nice man who came to our aid and they were discussing the situation. A few minutes later, with the new battery installed, the lights inside the truck still did not work, although the truck started. A quick check of the fuse box revealed the one that had been removed during the diagnosis period had been put back in the wrong place. Greg consulted his owner's manual and figured this out and all was then working.

Meanwhile, the kids are all playing in the gravel and dirt like they're on a beach somewhere building sand castles. Zachary is covered with dirt from head to toe. When it's time to go, I wash him off as best I can with the leftover cups of water brought to us by the nice woman. Then, he looked like a mud man. So, we say our thank you's, give hugs to all and are on our way, at last, and with Greg following us in my car, we head toward our home. But, not without complications. About 15 minutes into our journey home, the sky opens and dumps an incredible amount of rain on us, the uncovered trailer and all of Cassandra's possessions that were riding in there. At one point, we could only go 35 miles per hour due to diminished visibility. We persevered. Thirty minutes later, the rain had cleared and we decided to stop for dinner since all the kids were starving. I pulled into the parking lot and took up three full spaces with the truck and trailer, since I am NOT skilled at maneuvering this rig in reverse. As I was getting out of the truck, Greg pointed to something on the trailer which he said had been there since we left the scene of the incident. A pair of black and white girl's tights had been flapping in the wind like a flag from our mobile yard sale. Perfect! They'd somehow gotten out of their box. At least it wasn't underwear or a bra! We enjoyed our meal, piled back into the truck and headed to the storage unit

Cassandra rented for her possessions while she stayed with us. Uh oh, where is Hunter? He's nowhere in sight. Don't look behind the storage buildings! He had to poop really bad and did what any salty outdoorsman would do—he pooped in the grass. We finished unloading what would fit in the storage unit, we all piled back into the truck and headed home, at last, when Zachary exclaimed, "This is the best day ever!!" We about fell out of the truck.

$$\cdot \; \cdot \; \cdot$$

A day in my life = birth of a new word

I sat down at my computer late yesterday afternoon. I suppose it was around 4:30. As I kept writing and tweaking my blog post, I realized that it was getting pretty dark outside. "Wow, I've been writing for a long time," I thought. My fingers continued clicking on the keyboard. "Hmm. This is pretty cool, actually, being so lost in my writing." Click click click, enter. "La la la..." then, BAM!! Oh my gosh! I totally forgot to take care of our chickens today! This was new. Not once had I forgotten to take them their daily treat, usually a scoop of dry cat food, and collect the 12-20 eggs they'd produced. Not once! I'd been so hyper-focused on my writing, it almost startled me when I snapped out of it. I have sometimes envied the people who are able to maintain their mental focus for long periods of time like that. With a touch of ADD, I tend to get—"Oh, look! Squirrel!"

Don't worry, the chickens are fine. I'd given them plenty of food and water the day before, plus I'll be checking on them much earlier today than I would normally.

Once I'd completed my blog entry, I walked into the living room to watch a little TV and relax for the remainder of the evening. I glanced at the clock on the living room wall. It was 8:30 p.m.??! I exclaimed, "OH MY GOSH! NO!!" This is just great! Not only did

I forget about our chickens, I'd also forgotten to go to my Tuesday night salsa class being taught at our local gym, which started only two hours ago! What?! I was disgusted with myself. Then, I was amused by the fact that I possessed the ability to zone out and be so completely engrossed in what I was doing. I sat down in my chair, staring into space. I was in a slight state of shock, of disbelief. How the heck could I have been so oblivious to what time it was that I missed these two activities which are both pretty important to me? Then, I felt all three emotions swirling around at the same time. These three different feelings inspired me to create a new word that would describe the trio occurring simultaneously. Welcome the birth of "befuckled."

Befuckled: When you are disgusted, amused and in disbelief at the same time. Created by Vonda Newsome on March 12, 2019.

Bright side—After reading my blogs for the first time, my husband told me, "You are a very good writer, by the way." Totally melted me.

The moral of my story—I will be using Siri reminders from now on! (Still shaking my head…)

· · ·

Communing with ducks

Since mid-winter, there has been a group of ducks that regularly visits our pond. The most we have seen at one time is seven. Would that qualify as a "flock" of ducks? Anyway, I think they were a neighbor's ducks, initially, but they like our pond, so we basically share joint custody now. I love it, too. I often admire them from afar as they paddle across the pond, flop their wings then shake their tail feathers upon leaving the water.

There were four ducks on our pond's dock today, all preening themselves after their swim. I was pulling a large tree branch to the fire pit in our field and, after I dropped it off, I decided to see just how close I could get to this herd of ducks. In the past, merely walking in their direction motivated them to get back in the water. I casually walked over to check my mother's memorial tree, which was roughly 30-40 feet from the band of ducks. They didn't move. I slowly stepped a few feet closer while pretending to look for 4-leaf clovers in the grass. They didn't move. This was getting exciting! I walked to the water's edge, still about 20 feet from the dock where the mob of ducks remained quite content, and they again didn't move. Every few minutes, I'd sidestep a foot or two closer to the dock, glance their way, then pretend I didn't see them.

After several minutes of this maneuver, I was close enough to the dock that I could touch it, and they weren't budging, but I waited a little longer. Sidestep once more, look at the troop of ducks who were still calm and happily sunning on the dock. Then, I went for it. I sat down on the dock, my back to the array of ducks, fully expecting that that would send them into the air, or into the pond. But, I didn't hear flapping wings or the splash of water. I slowly turned my body around toward them and was a mere 6 feet from this gaggle of ducks. They didn't fly away! I brought my legs up onto the dock, sat Indian style, and we communed with each other for 20-30 minutes, right there at our pond. The two largest ducks actually fell asleep, one perched on a single leg.

I enjoyed the interaction so much, this communing with the gang of ducks, but all the while I was thinking, *I really wish I had my camera. These would be some excellent photos.* Next time, duckies. Next time!

. . .

Chicken Coop Capers
A few years ago, my husband decided to build a coop and start raising chickens so we could have fresh eggs right here on our little

farm. To my amazement, chickens are a lot of fun! They've got personality and it's quite entertaining to sit and watch them. Of course this opened another chapter in my collection of humorous mishaps. It also, however, led me to the conclusion that roosters are major jerks!

• • •

How to freak out your chickens in five minutes or less: Give them their food scraps in a box instead of throwing them on the ground. One or two brave hens snagged a bite of food, then were immediately swarmed by their coop-mates. Eventually, they realized that the mysterious box was not a trap set there by KFC.

• • •

You want me to…WHAT?!

FYI: Raising chickens is not for the faint of heart!!

During Labor Day weekend, a friend of ours gave us their sole surviving chicken. Sadly, dogs had destroyed their other birds. She's a very pretty, fat and fluffy, black and white hen. We put her in her own coop area so that our flock could become acquainted with her through the fencing before making any attempts at integration. I would visit her multiple times every day, offer her treats, and talk sweetly to her. Regardless of my sweet talk, she would stay as far away from me as possible. I mean, she would spastically and frantically run circles inside the run—like I was chasing her with an axe and picturing her on our dinner table! This went on for about three weeks, along with a couple attempts to merge her with the group, which resulted in gang pecking and me breaking up the West Side Story street fight with a stick.

Then, surprisingly, one day last week, she was different. With her treat in hand, I entered her run area and she ran *towards* me!

This was new. Strangely, she stopped at my feet and hunkered down to the ground. I wondered if she was hurt or sick. When I bent down to check her, she let me pet her. Wow, I thought, she's really taming down and getting to like me. I was so excited, I had to run and tell hubby, "The new chicken let me pet her!" The next day, the same thing happened. Too cool! Then, it hit me. No other hen had ever behaved this way around me and I wondered if she could be, umm, you know—amorously motivated. I asked my husband, "Can hens get—horny? Is that possible?" He said he imagined that they could. I mean, why not? If a female praying mantis can devour her mate after sex, why couldn't a female chicken be horny? Seemed plausible.

Well, my brain couldn't stop questioning this possibility, so I consulted my friend, Google, for the true answer. My search led me to a discussion on the backyard chickens website titled: *Excuse me—horny hen?* As it turns out, hens *can* be horny! Who knew?! The obvious solution is, of course, allowing her access to a rooster so that he may service her, scratch her itch, and otherwise make her happy. It's only natural, right? I read further and learned of an alternative method to soothe a horny hen—without a rooster. I never would've imagined something like this: "If you cannot have a rooster where you live, move, get rid of the chickens, or reach down and put a finger and thumb on each side of her tail feathers and lightly squeeze and wiggle side to side—she will get up and shake it off just like the rooster was there. BUT, she will be back the next time you enter for more of the same. LOL." WHAT?! I've heard of animals receiving artificial insemination, but artificial sexual relations?! I'm not about to be a hen's surrogate lover! I mean, give a chicken a hand job?! Nuh uh. Not gonna happen.

Yesterday morning, as I was walking toward the coop with my daily treat delivery, and mentally preparing myself to receive another dance-with-the-feathered-pants from our horny hen, I discovered that she was not in her run area. What the...?! Did I leave the door open? No, it was still locked. Where in the heck could she—ahhh, I see. The little fence I'd placed between the two runs had been knocked down and she had escaped her safe haven. She must've been extremely motivated! Fearful that I was about to find her lifeless, hen-pecked, blood-soaked body, I ran to the main run to look for/rescue her. But she wasn't with the other chickens. She wasn't under the coop either. Curious. As I stood there pondering the possibilities, Frisky, that's her new name by the way, popped her head out the main coop's doorway. Well, look at that! I guess she decided it was time to integrate and was determined to make it happen.

Last night, just after sunset, I checked on Frisky and found her perched on top of her mini coop. I went inside, gathered her in my arms and while her claws nearly impaled my arms, I carried her to the main coop and placed her in one of the nesting boxes. I watched through the little window with my iPhone flashlight as she left the box and surveyed her possible sleeping spots. It took her a few minutes, but she finally claimed her place on the roost with the other hens. Yes, it would appear we have successful integration!

As of this morning, Frisky is mostly happily cohabitating with the others. There is definitely a pecking order with those old biddies and they certainly let her know it; however, she seems safe and content. I haven't witnessed any interaction with the rooster... yet. While I'm not hoping to watch such chicken porn, it might be kind of nice to know that she's being, umm, satisfactorily serviced by our rooster.

I tell ya, this farmin' stuff is BRUTAL!

. . .

The other day I had a heart-to-heart talk with our psycho rooster who hates me and tries his best to flog me any time I'm near the chicken run or coop. I knelt down beside the coop, looked him in the eyes through the chain link fence, and very tenderly said, "You know, we can eat you."

• • •

Raising baby chickens may traumatize you

It was late June 2018, a beautiful, warm, and sunny day. After getting home from work that afternoon, I had a little extra energy and decided to work on the little chicks' run and mini coop. The six adult hens and one cocky rooster enjoyed the show through the chicken wire between the two coops. I put lots of lovely, fluffy shaved pine bedding in the mini coop, then cleaned out the water bowl and filled it with fresh water.

Ahh, happy chickies! With a feeling of joyous accomplishment, I opened the door—uh, tried to open the door to get out, but it would not open. "Seriously?!" I exclaimed as I tried to open the door a second time. Nope. Nothing. Ordinarily, I would have my cell phone tucked into my waistband for just such emergencies (to which I seem to be awfully prone). This time, however, I had laid my phone on the outer window ledge on the big chickens' coop so I couldn't accidentally drop it in the muddy run. Smart, right? My phone was several feet away and out of my sight. Great! Hubby won't be home for at least four more hours. Great!! No one inside the house would be able to hear me yelling. Great!!! I'm freaking stuck in here, and I'm going to die. I can see the news story: Woman trapped in a chicken coop for hours suffers severe dehydration and numerous deep, life-threatening wounds from vicious pecking chickens! I tell ya, it's the modern-day version of that Alfred Hitchcock movie! You can't make this stuff up, folks!

There I was—trapped—left with 16 young, inquisitive chickens and my own wits and resourcefulness to get myself out of this mess. Okay, we're breaking out of this mother! The door to the run opens out into the yard, usually. I tried to pull it inside, against its normal flow, which got me nowhere. As luck would have it, the metal pipes I hammered into the ground to keep raccoons from digging under the fencing were now keeping ME from getting OUT. I'm sure the raccoons are having a good laugh right about now. Next, I pushed the door hard, in the right direction, hoping that whatever the SOB was catching on would be released. Of course, that didn't work either. Okay, let's try kicking the bottom of the door really hard. Yeah, that was futile. The next few minutes remained a blur to me as my panic from being trapped took over, and I basically beat the hell out of the door and bent the entire frame to the chicken run. However, to my surprise, my maniacal efforts paid off as I discovered a 6-inch gap through which I could possibly make my escape. I think I can. I think I can! I squeezed my body through the tiny and incredibly painful opening, effectively shaving inches off my hind-end and my breasts and finally got myself free! At that point, I had 23 birds standing there motionless, staring at me with a look that said, "What the cluck was her problem?"

CHAPTER FOUR

BIRTHDAY CELEBRATION AT THE CORNSTALK MOTEL

If you must look back, do so forgivingly. If you must look forward, do so prayerfully. However, the wisest thing you can do, is be present in the present...gratefully.
—MAYA ANGELOU

Growing up in the 60s and 70s

Lately, I've been a bit nostalgic. Perhaps it's due to this free time we seem to have since, as my grandchildren say, "Earth is closed." Or, maybe it's because when senior citizen status is flashing its high-beams right in your face, it could maybe, possibly cause one to do some reflecting on one's life.

Nevertheless, through my reflection, I've realized how very fortunate I was to have grown up in the 1960's and 1970's. It really was a great time to be a kid. We lived in a nice neighborhood where the streets were lined with little cape cod houses full of families, with sidewalks around every block. We left our doors unlocked and the windows open, weather permitting.

Our school year started after Labor Day and then we were out for summer, I believe it was just before just after Memorial Day.

Either way, we got a full three months for summer break every year. I walked to school from first grade through sixth. It was a block and a half from our "past the stop sign, seventh house on the right" residence. Every day after school I'd rush home so I could watch the Patty Duke Show and Larry Smith's puppet show, both mostly in black and white, if memory serves. Hattie the Witch was a funny puppet on Larry's show. After my brief TV time, I'd head outside to ride my bike and/or see what my friends were doing until it was suppertime. Mom would cook supper every night and she was a good cook, too! My absolute favorites were her vegetable stew made with hamburger, and her pork chops which she breaded and fried in an electric skillet. None since have compared to my mother's chops, but I've cooked her stew many, many times.

Mom would make chocolate chip cookies from scratch in that classic 60's green pyrex bowl that was white on the inside, and when she wasn't looking, my sister and I would sneak a finger full of that deliciousness and gobble it up, raw egg and all. I want to say that Mom caught us a time or two, lightly scolded us, and grinned to herself. Maybe. At least I don't recall ever getting in trouble for it. Ha ha.

Summertime was a fun time with lots of camping trips, swimming at the public pool which cost twenty-five cents, riding bikes, wading in the creek hunting for crawdads, and lemonade stands. I would eat breakfast and out the door I'd go. We didn't have to be home until the street lights started to come on in the evening, or until Mom would ring that big cow bell summoning us home for supper. By the way, we grew up calling it supper, not dinner. I think dinner might be a southern thing. I dunno.

Until I was in junior high school, our street dead-ended into a corn field. My friends and I would ride our bikes right between those tall corn stalks. It was a shortcut to our neighborhood park, which we frequented often. We'd come back to the house parched and drink cool water right from the garden hose. When he had a little money, we'd go to the King Kwik convenience store or Conrad's (I believe it was a cigar shop) and buy candy. Or, we'd ride our bikes across town to Bo Bo's for ice cream. Bo Bo's was awesome! There they'd give you a little dish of ice cream, then it was your job to go down the line and add all the toppings you wanted, which for me was always hot fudge, peanuts and sprinkles. Nowadays, it's a common thing, with all the frozen yogurt places, etc., to make your own ice cream sundae. But, back then, it was a super special treat. At night we'd catch lightning bugs, or hunt for nightcrawlers (big fat worms) with a flashlight. We'd often have sleepovers at each other's houses and sometimes pop a tent right in our backyard.

The movie Now and Then is an excellent example of how it was back then, riding our bikes everywhere between our town and the next. I realize I've mentioned bike riding a lot, but we really did do it a lot, basically every day, all summer long. That 70's Show is pretty accurate, too, with its portrayal of teenagers in the 70's, although I caught a blooper in one episode. Kitty made reference to a movie that didn't actually come out until the 80's. Still, it's a good example and reminds me a lot of my teen years and "cruising" the country roads with my group of friends, sometimes doing things teenagers ought not be doing, but…c'mon. It was the 70's.

Yeah, the 60's and 70's—what a great time to be a kid!!

• • •

I found some dance wax in my parents' basement and it took me back more than 40 years. Back then, my parents were big into having dance parties in their basement. I remember going down there and getting platefuls of whatever goodies Mom had prepared for their guests. Stick pretzels, lil pieces of salami and, of course, Mom's famous cheese ball on lil crackers were my favorites. Yummy! I can still hear the rhythmic sliding of feet all over that waxy dance floor, keeping perfect time with Glenn Miller playing on the stereo. I still love "big band music" to this day. Not sure how many trips I made downstairs for goodies, but it was a lot. I'd run down two flights of stairs, fill a plate, and then run two flights back up just in time for "The Brady Bunch" or "The Partridge Family" to return from commercial breaks on my 13-inch black and white television. Yeah, back in the early 1970s that was our Friday night prime-time television lineup along with "Love American Style." I'm not positive, but I think the fourth show at that time was "Mary Tyler Moore." What very special, treasured childhood memories.

· · ·

I am often revisited by childhood memories. I remember those chilly mornings during my grade school years. I'd be sitting at the table, barely awake, smelling the warm aroma of the hot chocolate Mom made me, swirled with the smell of freshly buttered toast. Dad would be sitting in his chair, making his routine cup of Nescafé instant coffee. He'd spoon the granules into his cup and stir it ever so gently. You could hear the light "tink, tink, tink" of the spoon hitting the sides of his cup. He'd be silent, often staring into space, apparently deep in thought. Such a very peaceful start to our mornings as the sun was just starting to light up the sky. "Tink, tink, tink." Ahhh, so peaceful. Then, out of nowhere— BAM!!!!! Dad's fist hits the table with fury, rattling everything on it and a loud "DAMMIT" flies out of his mouth! It was as if he'd suddenly remembered something that royally pissed him off! I can only assume it was a political issue, either the U.S. or within the school system where he was employed. I never asked. Needless to say, my eyes were then WIDE open and I was no longer barely awake!

• • •

When I started writing this book, I intended for it to contain only my humorous stories, many of which I've posted on my Facebook page, resulting in countless likes, LOLs, and comments like, "You really need to write a book," etc. But, while I thoroughly enjoy making people laugh, life isn't all chuckles and giggles, is it? My life is no exception.

I've witnessed horrible violence, I've had multiple failed marriages, endured the loss of dear loved ones including the deaths of my parents, buried two precious infant grandchildren after holding their precious, lifeless bodies, and a host of other traumatic, sometimes horrific experiences.

While I feel we have more than enough drama in the world— such as the constant barrage of bad news on TV and the overly dramatic "reality" shows —when you can laugh through your painful tears, well, there's just nothing better than that. We all endure and/or survive our own trials, tribulations and challenges, to be sure. You know, it's like in Steel Magnolias, when Dolly Parton's character says, "Laughter through tears is my favorite emotion." It certainly is in my life story.

• • •

It's hard to drive forward while looking in the rearview mirror.

It took me months to put this thought into the right words: Don't allow the person you are now to look back and bash the person you used to be. For, without the person you used to be, you wouldn't be the person you are now.

Continue moving forward, learning, and growing.

• • •

My Most Memorable Memorial Day

I wrote this story in 1993, and it got lost in my many floppy disks. At the probing of my daughter, I searched through the disks and found it. Here is my story, in its original format, errors and all. Preserved for all eternity. I hope you enjoy it!

I have two daughters, Amber age 11 and Cassandra age 7. Since Cassandra's birth, I had always suspected she had a hearing problem. Doctors would check her and find nothing then tell me she was too young for a hearing test. She wouldn't hear me when I talked to her unless she was facing me and it was impossible to get her to understand danger. When any door was opened, Cassandra would dart out of it and run right toward the street. I couldn't begin to count the near-misses this child has encountered.

Finally, during her kindergarten physical in the summer of 1991, her pediatrician found that she had a moderate hearing loss in both ears. Now, with hearing aids, she has marvelous hearing. My most memorable Memorial Day was nearly four years ago when Cassandra was three and a half, and more than two years before she obtained her hearing aids.

It was Memorial Day weekend of 1989. My daughters and I were spending the holiday with my parents at their cabin in rural Indiana. The cabin sits at the end of a one-half mile winding gravel driveway off of the main gravel lane and is surrounded by acres of dense woods. There is a serene pond which sits in a cove about one quarter mile down a gravel trail from the cabin. Normally, on warm sunny days we would swim or fish in the pond. On this particular weekend, it had been raining quite often, but we seemed to be having a good time in spite of it.

Late in the afternoon on Sunday, I happened to notice that my car had a flat tire. Knowing that there would be no garage open on Memorial Day, my mother and I took the tire to town in their van so that it could be fixed. My girls stayed at the cabin with my father. We must have been in town for about two hours and it was now pitch black outside. As we were driving back on the gravel lane that leads to the cabin's driveway, we found ourselves behind a slow moving jeep. It was my father. I wondered what he could possibly be doing out so late. I was looking for my girls in the beam of the van's headlights through the jeep. I remember casually saying to my mother, "Well, I see *one* head." I only saw Amber. We followed my dad just through the entrance of the driveway and he stopped. He got out of his jeep, came back to the van and said, "Cassandra has completely disappeared." I could feel my heart falling to my feet as a rush of panic consumed my body like a jolt of electricity. My father said that one minute she was playing with her Big Wheel tricycle and the next minute she was gone. Amber told me that Cassandra had said she wanted her mommy and was going to find her. I guess they didn't realize that she meant what she said, and knowing Cassandra as I did, I knew she could disappear before my father knew what had happened.

We then drove the one-half mile driveway to the cabin that couldn't have seemed any longer if it were a thousand miles. I felt as though we were traveling in slow motion and I could feel the bump of every piece of gravel under the van's tires. After what seemed an endless journey, we arrived at the cabin and we began our search for Cassandra. As my mother called the police, I grabbed the nearest flashlight and fled to the woods calling Cassandra's name with every step. I had the worst possible images going through my mind. Was she hopelessly lost in the woods? Was the brush scratching her delicate little legs? Is she close enough that she could see me if it were daylight; can she just not hear me calling to her now? I pictured her lost and crying for her mommy, or the worst, that someone had picked her up and was abusing her. I tried to maintain control of my emotions and told myself that we would find her.

The creek near the cabin was flowing steadily due to all the rain we had received and I feared that she had been swept away by the water. I pictured her little body lying somewhere downstream on the creek's edge, entwined in branches and rocks. I could feel my heart beating harder with every step I took and I kept repeating to myself "You'll find her. You'll find her." As I walked closer to the creek, the sound of the rushing water became louder and louder. An eerie chill rushed through me and it was almost as though the creek was whispering to me. Perhaps trying to tell me where Cassandra could be found. I shined the flashlight up and down stream while trying not to fall into the water myself.

Through the rustling of the water I thought I heard Cassandra crying, but she was nowhere to be found. My next thought was, "Oh my God. The pond!" How could I have forgotten the pond? I climbed up the creek bank as quickly as I could in the muddy earth below me and after reaching the top, made a bolt for my car. I drove frantically to the pond hoping to find her and being terrified that I would. Had she drowned? If I would have thought about the pond one minute sooner, could I have saved her? It seemed as though everything was constraining me and I couldn't move at the speed I so desperately needed. I kept repeating, "Lord, please just let me find Cassandra safe and sound." It was dark and a heavy fog was resting above the pond. A feeling of dread and despair weighed heavy on my chest. Even with the flashlight, I couldn't see a thing. I felt utterly helpless and as though I might collapse. I knew I had to find my little girl. "I just have to find her," I thought. With a deep breath and quick prayer, I continued searching near the pond and then worked my way back toward the cabin. On my way, I met my dad who was on his tractor moving toward the pond. My heart pounded harder as we neared each other and I imagined him telling me that Cassandra had been found lifeless in the woods; in the creek; on the road. I was terrified to hear what he might have to say but still I kept walking faster and faster. As I approached him, anticipation filling every fiber of my being, my father leaned over toward me and said the words I will never forget. "They have her at the sheriff's station." The relief I felt was so intense it was as though someone had just drained all the blood out of my body. I was nervously laughing and crying at the same time. We then drove back to the cabin so that we could call the Sheriff's station.

Mrs. Curzy, who lives one-half mile from the entrance to the cabin, had heard a continuous string of squealing brakes outside her house that afternoon. Curious as to what the problem could be, she looked out her front door only to see a little girl walking down the lane carrying a Big Wheel tricycle. Of course, this little bundle was Cassandra. Concerned for her safety, Mrs. Curzy brought Cassandra into her home. She tried to get information from Cassandra that would help to locate her parents. Unable to do so, she took Cassandra to the Sheriff's office. When we called, she and Cassandra were still there. Mrs. Curzy said that she would take Cassandra back to her house and that we could pick her up there instead of having to drive the eight miles to town. I felt another surge of relief and my knees nearly gave out. The drive to Mrs. Curzy's house is now a blur. I just wanted my little girl.

It seemed as though they had just pulled into the driveway when I arrived. Cassandra was asleep in the front seat of the car and her Big Wheel resting safely in the back seat. I was so numbed by the whole ordeal I could only stand there and look at the sweet sleeping child. I was amazed that she didn't have a scratch on her anywhere. I thought how lucky this child was that someone hadn't run her over in the street. This beautiful slumbering angel had no idea what she put her mother through. I then scooped her up in my arms and squeezed her as tight as she could stand it and she only slightly awakened. She was, understandably, quite exhausted from her mile long hike in search of her mommy. Feeling so relieved that my baby was now safe, I laid her in the seat beside me, and we started back to the cabin.

During the drive, I battled with the feelings of wanting to either hold her and cry or spank her bottom for running off like that. When we arrived at the cabin I took her inside and laid her on the bed. Within seconds she was again sound asleep. All my parents and I could do for hours was talk about the ordeal we had all survived. I believe my father may have been more shaken up than any of us as I am sure he felt a great deal of responsibility. If I remember correctly, it was about a fifth of Jim Beam that finally calmed his nerves.

Nearly four years have passed now and we still talk about the day Cassandra ran away and she herself remembers it. She simply says, "I just wanted to find you, Mommy." Looking back, I realize that this experience taught me of the boundless strength which radiates from a mother's love for her children. It's that strength that allowed me to remain relatively calm throughout the crisis. It may not be until Cassandra has children of her own, however, that she realizes the effect of this most memorable Memorial Day. For only a mother could truly understand the utter horror that this mother has survived.

. . .

A word of encouragement for parents of two kids

Do your children seem to fight nonstop and constantly accuse you of favoring their sibling? Well, congratulations. That means you are doing a fantastic job! My theory is that if both kids have the same complaint about the other, that means they're both getting the same treatment, right? You're welcome. Now, have a beer or a glass of wine and relax with your favorite Netflix series. You got this.

The same goes for families of three or more children. That is, if they are each pointing to a different sibling. Now, if you're the parent of two or more children and all fingers are pointing toward the same child as being the favorite, golden child–well...you're screwed. I don't know how to help you feel better about that. I tried. No beer or wine for you. [I'm kidding, of course.]

· · ·

A very dear friend once said to me, "Thankfully, your parents taught special ed children, so it made it easier to raise you."

· · ·

Remembering my mother on Mother's Day

When I was a small child and could fit in her chair with her, I would crawl up and wiggle my butt between my mother's butt and the arm rest, then I'd lay my head on her lap. Mom would always start stroking my hair, so gently. I can still feel her warm hand softly moving my hair from my cheek and placing it behind my ear—over and over, as we all as a family watched television. She would stroke my hair as long as I sat there with her. Mom, I wish you could do that today, one more time.

I remember the day when my mother got her very own piano. She was thrilled! Dad had one end of a heavy rope tied around the upright 1920's Euphona piano and the other end tied to the bumper of his VW beetle which he ever so slowly and inch by inch, eased backward as the piano was lowered into our basement. I can still hear Mom playing Nola, as she'd played countless times during my childhood. Mom, I wish I could hear you play your piano today, one more time.

My mother loved to laugh. Many times, she'd get to laughing so hard there would be no sound coming from her. We'd all say, "There she goes!" which only served to make her laugh that much harder until the tears started to flow. Mom, I wish I could see you laughing hysterically today, one more time.

But, there won't be one more time, not today. That's simply the facts of life. I will always miss my mother. Until we meet again, the memories of you will keep me company. Happy Mother's Day, Mom. I love you.

. . .

My Mother

My mother is like no other
She is unique beyond belief
At 60 she was taking karate lessons
And had braces on her teeth

She's just a little woman
Stands five feet and one inch
And if you were to walk pass her
You're sure to get a pinch

She's sure a sweet little lady
With a heart as good as gold
She still call me her "baby"
And I'm almost thirty years old

She's a real bird lover
And loves to hear them sing
She doesn't mind cleaning the poopy they make
She says, "See, it doesn't stick to a thing"

She has ten or twenty birds
And says she won't get any more
But the next time you visit, she'll have a new one
Of this you can be sure

She has a few nicknames
One of which is "Dumpy"
But, that seems to suit her fine
Because her husband is nicknamed "Grumpy"

When I go out for the evening
She says, "Have a good time..."
And I know before she finishes
There is a "But be careful" following behind

It doesn't matter how old you are
She worries about us just the same
And on a real good day, if we're lucky
It only takes her three times to guess our name

She smells things that aren't even there
And scrambles the words she tries to say
But, we've learned to live with all of this
And we just love her anyway

Happy Mother's Day 1990
Love, Vonda

• • •

Dammit—Where's the map—Damn Wind!

With both of our parents being teachers and having every glorious summer off, the crown jewel of teaching benefits, they took us kids on countless summer camping trips. On one trip, we brought along a very pregnant cat named Tilly. Mom was worried that Tilly would give birth while we were gone, so she insisted we bring her with us. We kept her in a box with the top open to keep her safe and comfortable during our trip, and in hopes that that's where she would have her babies. After we'd arrived at our camp site and all the tents were set up, Tilly decided it was time to give birth and she did just that, on the floor of one of our pup tents. My brother, my sister and I watched as she gave birth to four tiny kittens. That was pretty cool.

One of my favorite camping memories is when my sister, Becky, and I had constructed a trap near our campsite so we could catch chipmunks. I'm not even sure what we used now, but we propped up the basket or box with a stick which had a long rope tied to it. We'd lure the little chipmunks into the trap with some bread or breakfast cereal, pull the rope from where we were hiding, keeping a close watch, and we'd catch it. We did this for hours and caught several of those little critters, too. My sister was actually able to hold one of those chipmunks in her hands. It was so exciting for both of us since that was our main goal in catching them in the first place. However, the chipmunk wasn't having it and soon darted right out of Becky's grip, leaving its tail right there in her hand. It was hilariously entertaining, although I think Becky felt horribly about the tailless rodent.

Our father was nuts for "the old west," and in the summer of 1970, I believe it was, that is exactly where we were headed. Dad built onto a wooden utility trailer modifying it into the perfect tag-along for transporting all of our camping gear and our luggage, etc., and we began our westward journey. I can still remember how bored I was through Indiana and Illinois. It was nothing, I mean nothing but corn! Throughout this trip, whenever it was time to fill up with gas, we would hear Dad exclaim, "There's my price! Twenty-nine point nine." Can you imagine gas being 29.9 cents a gallon?

It seemed that the further west we traveled, the stronger the winds became. Perhaps it's due to all the flat open land out there. Dad did most, if not all of the driving and fighting those strong winds really irked him. He'd yell, "Damn wind!" And, if he and Mom were having difficulty finding a route he'd yell, "Dammit," followed by, "Where's the map?!" He'd get so frustrated. "Damn wind!" Ooooooh, how many times we heard that as we traveled further west. We must've heard him say, "Dammit" a hundred times along the way, too.

Now, with three kids in the backseat of a small VW car, well, it gets a lil bit tense back there. Due to my being the smallest child, I was sitting in the middle seat, "the hump," of that VW squareback, and in *every* VW vehicle my parents *ever* owned. Always on the freakin' hump! It is NOT fun sitting in the middle, on a hump, between two of your older siblings. If you are one who likes to sit comfortably in your own space, without your arms touching the skin of another human being, especially on very long car rides, well...you couldn't have endured the hump seat. I barely did it myself.

With no air-conditioning in the car, the windows were always open and the breeze was kind of nice, at times. However, with that lovely breeze also came my sister's very long hair which liked to blow across my face, tickling my nose and basically just getting on my nerves. All of them. "Get your hair out my face," I'd say. She'd retort with, "Move over!!" Our brother would shout out, "Mind your own business!" As you can imagine, after a few choruses of

"Move over," "Mind your own business," and "Get your hair out of my face," Dad would chime in with, "Get the switch!" That was Mom's cue to grab the fly swatter, turn around in her seat, glare at each of us with her deep, dark, brown eyes, and threaten us with the butt-swatting of our lives if we didn't "simmer down" back there. If memory serves, it usually worked, too.

We made it to the big state of Missouri and finally saw something interesting in the distance. Our parents simply had to check it out. Looking back, I wonder if they'd known all along that we'd be stopping to see the St. Louis Arch and were just making it more exciting by letting us imagine and guess what it was when we saw it in the distance. Once there, all five of us piled into one of those tiny elevator cars and enjoyed the bumpy, rickety, noisy ride to the top of the arch so we could look out the observation windows. Definitely more interesting than miles and miles and miles of corn.

Mom would always keep a dampened wash cloth handy, which she kept in a plastic baggy stored in the glove compartment. She'd use it to wash our hands and our faces as needed while we were on the road. I can still feel the warmth of that damp cloth on my cheeks. We didn't do much restaurant dining on our trips. Our meals were cooked by our mother either on a Coleman gas stove or we'd roast hotdogs over a campfire followed by the roasting of marshmallows, of course. For those long car rides, Mom would make sure to pack snacks for everyone, too. My favorite was the Underwood deviled ham on saltine crackers. She would pop that little can open, get a knife and she'd start spreading that deviled ham on crackers and be handing them out one at a time to her hungry crew as quickly as she could. I thought it was the best snack ever and could barely wait until it was my turn to get another one.

At one of the campsites on this westerly trek, my sister and I had had a fight wherein I viciously scratched her arms. That tended to be my fighting tactic, my only tactic, since she was much bigger than me and I didn't stand a chance physically. I believe I'd yelled and screamed at her, scratched her, then cried myself to sleep that night. When I awoke the next morning, all my fingernails had been clipped off. Every last one was clipped to the nub. Can you guess who did it? I'm sure you can.

We continued our journey and saw all the major tourist attractions along the way: The Grand Canyon, cave ruins, Mount Rushmore, Old Faithful, Bear Butte in South Dakota, old abandoned western towns, the Pacific Ocean, the steep streets of San Francisco, the Golden Gate Bridge, the painted desert, the petrified forest, Yellowstone National Park with its bubbling (boiling) mud, the actual Salt Lake and Salt Lake City, and I'm sure many more. It truly was a remarkable summer adventure. We even drove through Hollywood and saw the sign way up on that hill. I remember spotting the sign for Rodeo Drive, which I pronounced like the horse and cowboy event, not the proper way of "Roe-day-oh." We didn't see any movie stars, that I recall, but the Hollywood Walk of Fame was something worth seeing.

We arrived at the Rocky Mountains in Colorado where Dad was determined to drive way up as close to the top as he could muster. We were on a road that seemed to go in constant loops and turns which Dad called "hairpin turns." If I was to ever experience motion sickness, it would have been on this drive up the mountains. Thankfully, that wasn't an issue for me. We reached a high enough elevation to actually see snow. All of us in our shorts and tank tops and we were playing in the snow. So fun! My father's initial goal for his first trip to "the old west" was to drive across the U.S. to California, and then on up to Alaska. We went as far west as California and as far north as Montana before my parents felt the need to head back home based on their travel funds.

I don't remember if it was on our way out west or on our way back home, but for one night we got to stay in a motel. This was a very big deal for us because I don't think any of us kids had ever stayed in a motel. It was after dark, our parents were tired from the miles we'd spent on the road that day and they just wanted to go to bed without fussing with tent poles, pottying in the woods and such. There up ahead, shining in the beams of our headlights was the Cornstalk Motel. I kid you not, that was the name of it. It had a bright yellow, very shiny cornstalk right on the sign. Although we all had enjoyed camping, it was a nice treat to sleep inside, on beds. Oh, the memories.

In 1976, when I was 14, and the only kid left at home, I went out west with my parents for the last time. For this trip, we were traveling in my mother's butterscotch yellow Vega, with air-conditioning! I had my own pup tent and would set it up and break it down by myself at every campsite. We returned to Bear Butte in South Dakota and we all liked that campground so much, I think we spent two, or three, full weeks there. We would gaze up at the stars each night which were so incredibly bright and clear out west. When I wasn't gazing at the stars, I was watching the park ranger whom I'd had a serious crush on at the time. At night, I'd lie on my stomach with my head facing out the tent opening, my chin in my hands, watching him as he sat under a light pole looking through his log book or whatever it was he was doing.

On my fifteenth birthday, we were traveling on a long, straight highway somewhere in Arizona. The day before I told Dad that all I wanted for my birthday was for him to not say "Dammit" the entire day. Well, that worked out really well. Along that hot, dusty Arizona highway, with the temperature about 119 degrees in the shade (if you could find any), was where, as luck would have it, the Vega up and died. I don't think my father said "Dammit" as many times in one day in his entire life as he said it that day, my birthday. My parents ended up buying a used Jeep Wagoneer for $500.00 and towed the broken down Vega behind it for the rest of our trip. (Funny, after we returned home, the Vega was sent to a mechanic for diagnosis and treatment where it was discovered that a $10.00 part would have fixed it.) Since we'd already had an exhausting day with the heat, the dust and being stranded on a road somewhere in Arizona, my parents decided it might be a good idea to get a hotel for the night and take it easy. Wouldn't you know it—we came across the Cornstalk Motel again. The same place we'd stayed for one night during our first trip out west!

Earlier that day, my mother had purchased a Pepperidge Farm frozen chocolate cake for celebrating my birthday. Oh, but it was completely thawed out by the time we checked into the motel, all the icing having melted off the cake part and sufficiently pooled in the corners of the box. Mom had also gotten some fresh hamburger to cook for our supper which, by the time she got it out of the cooler (where there had been no ice for hours) had turned to a lovely, brownish color. Determined not to waste food, Mom proceeded to cook our hamburger supper on a hot plate right there in our motel room.

Although I'd been a bit concerned with the burger having that brownish tint and all, it was the yummiest hamburger I'd ever had. The cake too, even with its melted icing, was absolutely and incredibly delicious. I really enjoyed my 15th birthday celebration in the Cornstalk Motel! Dammit, anyway!

. . .

The things that really surprise me...
The subject of this section comes to you via the suggestion of a very sweet man named John S. Thompson. One day my eldest

daughter asked John what I should write about. John answered, "The things that really surprise me." I thought about this for a while and couldn't come up with a single thing. I had no monumental answers, nothing that wouldn't be on most people's list of life's surprises such as having twins when only one child was expected, winning an award, or a surprise party on a milestone birthday. But, I'll share a couple of mine anyway.

The first thing that surprises me is that no matter how old you are, you don't feel any differently just because you've had another birthday. It doesn't matter if you're 20, 41, or 58. People may ask me, "What's it feel like to be fifty-eight years old?" Well, the truth is, it feels just like it did at 57, 56, 55…23. That's exactly what my mother told me many years ago when I'd asked her how it felt to be her age. As it turns out, you bring you along with you through every birthday. It's not like you go to bed one age and wake up in the morning a year older with a whole new perspective. It seems that chronological age does not directly affect your core self. You still feel like—well, you. That is unless you have a midlife crisis at 29 years old like I did (not a joke), then you feel like somebody else, temporarily.

The second thing that surprises me is that the love you will feel for your grandchildren is immense, powerful and defies description. It's not that you love them more than your children, it's that the love you feel for your children is multiplied exponentially and heaped onto the grandchildren. It's not easily explained, though anyone who's been a grandparent will surely understand. It is an exceptionally, very special relationship.

Thanks to a funny photo shared by my magical friend, Linda, I became inspired to answer John's question by my dearly departed father's immortal words. The photo Linda shared was of a candle with a naughty word on it and the scent of this candle was

Go-Ask-Your-Dad Vanilla. I giggled and messaged back, "My father's candle would be named Peace-and-Quiet Chocolate!" Let me explain.

As far back as I can remember, whenever any of us asked Dad what he wanted for Christmas, or his birthday, or Father's Day, he would inevitably shout, "PEACE AND QUIET!" I always took it as a joke or that it was just our Dad being our Dad. Maybe he said it because he didn't even know what he wanted. We just adopted it as a family joke and blamed it on him being a cantankerous and grumpy father at times, not that we kids were loud and obnoxious— ever. Now, I wish I would've asked him what exactly he meant by it.

Now…What really surprises me is how I've come to understand Dad's statement and how I wish for the same things. It's not a joke, or me being cantankerous or grumpy. I truly, in my soul, desire these things in my life.

As my head hits the pillow every night, I wish for peace in knowing that I'd done all I could that day, that I did my best, and to quiet that squeaky inner voice that points out what I could've done and how much better I could have done it. I wish for peace in the awareness that I can handle anything that life throws at me, just as I have done thus far, and to quiet the tenuous, staticky, underlying feeling of impending doom and waiting for the other shoe to drop that ever so subtly attempts to erode that peace. I wish for peace in the realization that my husband, our children and their children are all healthy, happy and well taken care of, and to quiet that logical realist who whispers, "But, anything can happen to anyone at any time." I wish for peace in knowing that it's all going to be okay, that it is what it is and we will get through it, and to quiet, stifle and successfully gag that annoying Doubting Thomas who doesn't believe that to be the case. Thomas just needs to shut the hell up.

Tonight, as your head hits the pillow, I wish you peace. You did all you can do today. You are doing the best that you can. And, I wish you quiet. Take a deep breath and release it slowly, along with your worries. Repeat. Your weary mind needs to rest now. Tomorrow is another day and it's going to be okay.

. . .

One night, I told Dad the story of a patient I'd had at the VA when I was working nights as a nurse aide. Every time I'd go into this man's room, he'd ask me, "Am I dead yet? Am I dead yet?" I'd say, "If you were dead, how could you be talking to me?" He'd answer, "I don't know. Am I dead yet?" He literally asked me this every time I entered his room. Later that night, this patient's nurse and I had to clean him up as he had soiled himself. Once we had him all cleaned and cozy, we had to pull him up toward the top of the bed so his head would be on his pillow. As we were lifting and pulling him with the draw sheet, his eyes rolled back in his head, his body went limp, and he died. Light's out. Game over. Dead. During this same week, the same nurse and I pulled another patient up in bed, and that patient also died, but not immediately. It was later that night. Due to these events, my co-workers gave me the lovely nickname of—you guessed it, "The Grim Reaper."

Evidently, Dad had given my story some thought, and the next morning he asked me why those events had earned me such a nickname. I told him, "Because both patients died after we'd pulled them up in the bed." After a brief pause, Dad asked, "Did you pull them up by their necks?"

. . .

For whosoever does not believe that a full moon affects people, I invite you to come and take my place at work tonight. You WILL have a different opinion when you clock out in the morning. Guaranteed!!

. . .

QUESTIONS FROM THE KIDDOS!

A question by one of our grandsons:
"What were you like as a kid?"

As a child, I was extremely shy and very quiet. No, really. I was! I was so quiet in fact, my father would say, "She's growing up and nobody's noticing." I loved playing with my small group of neighborhood friends, riding my bike or walking around the block with our basset hound named Casper. Regardless of the weather, I wanted to be outside. Mom used to tell me, "You always liked bad weather." It was true, too. If it was snowing, I was outside trying to build a snowman. If it was storming, I was on the front porch swing watching it. While I really liked playing with Barbie dolls and Dawn dolls (you may have to Google that one since they don't make them any more), I equally enjoyed playing with my Hotwheels cars under our big tree in the backyard. I had that orange track and everything which I placed over rocks and logs to make ramps and hills. My favorite car was the Chevy Impala—that big ole boxy behemoth of an automobile. Not the Corvette. Not the Camaro. I preferred the big, old-lady sedan. Still do today! If memory serves, I believe it was green, Army green. I've not once in my life desired to own or even drive a sports car. My dream car is a red 2004 Jaguar. Don't get excited, it's a 4-door sedan.

2 QUESTIONS FROM MY NIECE. SHE IS SO INQUISITIVE!

Q1: "What made you join the reserves (Army)?"

Well, going into the military wasn't a life goal, or even an inkling of an idea in my mind at all. When my first child was about 18 months old, my husband at the time was trying to get back into the army. He was only offered the same job he had when he was enlisted years before and was not interested in that option. He said to me, "Why don't you see what they'll give you." Being super suggestible (which is what happens when you don't know what you want to be when you grow up), I said, "Okay!" I went through the testing, physical, all that, then was offered my choice of 3 military occupational specialties (MOS). I chose Legal Clerk. After my training, I spent the remainder of my 3-year contract at Ft. Sill, Oklahoma where my second child was born. About a year after my discharge, I entered the reserves and stayed for nine years.

Q2: *"What are your favorite memories of your Grandma?"*

I always felt I had only one grandparent, my father's mother. My mother's parents both died when I was very young, so of course I have no memory of them. My father's parents divorced, possibly before I was born, and his mother remarried, so I never met my paternal grandfather either. That left me with one grandma, Isabella, and her second husband, Tom, who I swear was 95 years old every time we visited. I don't recall having much interaction with him, only his presence in Grandma's house and me sitting at the kitchen table watching him sprinkle vinegar on everything he ate. I guess it's the only way he could taste his food? I don't know. Grandpa Tom died when I was between 5 and 7 years old, maybe. I remember going to his funeral. Now, at that young age, I knew that people died, so I understood what was going on there. What I didn't know was that when you go to a funeral, there is a dead body there and you get to look at it. When I caught a glimpse of Grandpa Tom's body lying in that casket, I froze in my tracks. I don't remember anything else until after the funeral, back at Grandma's house. I could see the sadness in her eyes and I said, "You miss him...don't you?" She said, "No," as tears soaked her cheeks.

My favorite memories of my Grandma are plentiful. She was a short and semi-round little Scottish woman, with long gray hair that almost reached the floor and she kept in a braided bun on the back of her head. She always wore a thin house dress and an apron which she kept damp by drying her hands on it. She lived in an old two-story, green house in a neighborhood very near railroad tracks, which were plentiful in Lima, Ohio. I remember it with all of my senses. The smell of her gas furnace as we entered the house along with the popping sound it made and the heat on my face when I stood close to it. The crackling of the old green linoleum when it was walked upon. The stairway in the middle of the house which seemed to ascend into darkness. I didn't spend much time up there, there never seemed to be any lights on. The screened back door with the wooden frame that would smack the house any time we went through it. The arbor in the yard where grapes grew. The taste of her cabbage ham and potato dinners which I thought was the best stuff ever. I loved it when that was our dinner when we'd visit. Come to think of it, I don't recall any other meals she prepared. I'm sure there were others, but I suppose we hold onto our favorite memories through the decades. Oh, how I still miss that meal today. Grandma died in 1976, the winter before my 15th birthday, and I still haven't had cabbage, ham and potatoes. One person made it for me back in the 1980's, and it tasted good (not like Grandma's though), and for some reason, it came back up later that evening. I guess Grandma didn't like me eating anyone else's cooking but hers and I have not tried that again. The smell and warmth of her freshly baked scones. Truthfully, I wasn't the biggest fan of those because they weren't sweet enough for me. Though I wanted them to taste more like cookies or donuts and they were more like bread,

I still ate them. Hearing the train whistles throughout the day and on special nights when we could stay a day or two. Sweet memories.

Grandma always had Tootsie pops in the bottom cabinets of her china hutch. I remember one time that I was upset with her—could've been because she wouldn't give me a Tootsie pop before dinner. I have no idea now. But, I ran to the huge back room which was a bedroom and bathroom combined and always smelled of Dove face soap, then climbed up on the bed to sulk and feel sorry for myself. It wasn't long before Grandma came to check on me, Tootsie pop in hand. She was a softy and gave in to my tantrum. She handed me that sucker and I felt so guilty for manipulating her with my spoiled brat behavior.

Grandma would just light up when we'd come to visit her and the first thing I would do when we'd get to her house was run inside and hug her tight. Then we would compare our heights to see how much I'd grown. I remember vividly the day that I finally exceeded her 4'10" stature, which didn't take that much time, and I felt like a giant. I was probably ten or eleven years old.

In that tiny package was also a mighty temper. Grandma always sat in a wooden, black rocking chair which sits in our living room today. One summer, I got to spend a few weeks with her and my wacky aunt, Mary. Grandma got really pissed off about something they were discussing and she was fuming, brows furrowed and cheeks bright red! I'd never seen her angry. Grandma was flat out done talking to my aunt and to prove it she gripped each of her rocking chair's arm rests, lifted that chair up close to her bum and spun around like a top, effectively closing out my aunt with the back of her chair. It was a little bit frightening and hilarious at the same time.

Oh, a funny memory of Grandma comes to mind! She had a little patch of whiskers on each side of her mouth. On one of our visits, she was standing in the dining room with an electric razor, happily shaving those patches. It was so funny, and she thought it was the coolest invention ever. I can still see that big smile and her contorting her lips all around the razor to make sure she was thoroughly removing those pesky whiskers.

Like clockwork, when our visits came to a close and it was time for the 2-hour ride back home, Grandma would stand in the doorway of her house waving goodbye, tears streaming down her face, and wouldn't stop waving until our car was out of her view. I would watch her every time, until I could see her no more. I felt so sad seeing her like that and hoped it wouldn't be too long til we could go see her again.

My Grandma was like my own personal, human divining rod. No, she didn't lead me to water, but she did lead me away from doing naughty things. When I would think about doing something bad, I would immediately think how it would make Grandma feel, and not wanting to disappoint her in any way, I wouldn't do the bad thing I had been tempted to execute. I felt a great loss when she died that winter of 1976, and when I turned 15 that summer, all hell broke loose. It was like I had no one to be a good girl for any more. The very shy and quiet little me was a full-out rebellious unruly teenager—from hell.

It's been more than 40 years, yet every time I hear train whistles, I'm transported back in time to Grandma's house and for a moment, I'm filled with a warm sense of peace and love as though she's hugging me from Heaven. I love that sound. I miss her hugs.

• • •

Memorial Day

The day our nation set aside
A time to honor all who've died
They gave all for you and me
Home of the brave, land of the free
Countless battles and many wars
Bodies sent home by the scores
Flag-draped coffins brought heroes home
Yet some of them remain unknown
Let us give thanks to each and all
They that answered our nation's call
For every conflict that was fought in
May they never be forgotten

Written 5-24-2020

CHAPTER FIVE

REGRET

*"You can't get something out of a person's head using reason
if it did not go in their head with reason in the first place."*
—MY FATHER

Is your loved one telling you goodbye?

When a loved one starts saying things like, "I don't think I'm going to be around much longer," listen. Especially the elderly, for they tend to know when their hourglass is close to empty. My mother said that 88 was her "last birthday." It was her last birthday. My father said he had "no aspirations to see ninety." He died at 89. Even though the world was in the turmoil of a pandemic, my mother-in-law insisted on cooking Thanksgiving dinner for her family because she "might not be here next Thanksgiving." She contracted COVID-19, and her little body simply couldn't stop it from destroying what was left of her kidney function. Although losing her was, and is, devastating for her family, many friends and her church community, I am grateful that my mother-in-law had the gumption and tenacity to cook that Thanksgiving dinner for us, her last one.

While it is human nature to think there is more time, or "always tomorrow," please do not dismiss the cues from the people you love!! Their words are not trivial statements in search of attention, or sympathy. And, even if they are, the time you give to them is never wasted. You must do what you can live with for the rest of your life, regardless of your fatigue from a grueling work week, or the favorite TV show that you might miss. That's what a DVR is for, use it!

I cannot stress this enough: LISTEN, when loved ones are telling you that they are running out of time, precious time!! Don't say, "I'll go over and see them this weekend, I'm just too tired." Go. Now! There isn't always tomorrow, or later, and that's the biggest regret of those surviving the loss of a loved one—the I should'ves that will consume your conscience when they've died and you realize all the time you could have/should have spent with them, but didn't.

You'll never regret spending that precious time with your loved one, even if it's only 30 minutes, for it will serve as a warm, comforting hug to your broken heart when they leave you with only your memories. Listen!

· · ·

Late in December 2020, I was having a text chat with my dance instructor. My mother-in-law had been in the hospital for two weeks with the COVID virus and I was keeping him updated on her condition. She had coded three days prior and was still on a ventilator. He asked if my father-in-law was in the picture. I told him, "Unfortunately, no. He committed suicide in 2011." I shared many of the details regarding his suicide, and he told me that "sharing the experience in your book could help so many, because so many people would shy from such a thing." The next day, I began composing this essay.

Suicide. We all know what it is. We probably all know someone whose family has been affected by it or have lost family members to it. Most of us have probably thought about it ourselves, during the lowest points of our lives. Yet, no one seems to share the whole story. The truth and the horrific aftermath.

It was August 25, 2011. I was working the night shift on a medical/surgical floor. I'd just gotten into bed at about 5:30 that morning when my cell phone started ringing. Normally, I would ignore it and go on to sleep, but something made me check it. It was my husband. I thought it was odd, he knew I had to work that night and that I would be sleeping. I answered and he said, "Get over to Mom's! Dad shot himself!"

"WHAAAAAT?!"

I jumped up, got dressed and headed to their house. It's normally a 10 minute drive, but I'm not sure my tires were even on the road. On my way, I called my closest work friend and told her what was going on. We talked until I got to my in-laws' house. I was the first person to arrive. I hurried out of my car and put my phone in the pocket of my red, cotton, Faded Glory shorts and went into the house. My heart was racing as I walked down the hallway to the bedroom. When I entered, I saw my father-in-law lying on the bed, his legs hanging off the side. I wailed, "WHYYYYY?!!!!! We loved you!!!" I was so angry for what he'd done! He wasn't conscious, was panting rapidly and gurgling.

In a flash, the paramedics came in the back/outside door to their bedroom and began assessing him, with my husband following right behind them. He'd seen the paramedics walking toward the back door as he pulled in the driveway. I went to my father-in-law, knelt on the bed beside him and grabbed his hand with both of mine. As I held it tight, I cried, "He can't die alone. He can't die alone." (Some time later, my closest work friend revealed to me that she heard this entire interaction. When I put my phone in my pocket, I hadn't ended the call.) The paramedics tried to calm me and made me leave my father-in-law's side so they could "try to help him." I didn't want to let go of his hand. Onto the gurney they placed him, and out they went through the double doors of their bedroom into the backyard. He was still alive when they moved him into the ambulance, and my husband was with him. By the time I reached the ambulance, my father-in-law was dead. They allowed us to sit in the ambulance with him and say goodbye. It was my husband, me, and I think my sister-in-law sitting with him. I don't recall when she and her family had arrived.

The paramedics had positioned his body so we wouldn't see the hole in his head left by the gunshot. But, blood was pooling under his head. As I sat there grappling with swirling emotions, the indescribable strong smell of the blood got to me, my stomach churned. I couldn't take it and had to get out.

They drove away with his lifeless body, and there we were. Left with nothing but questions. Questions that would never be answered. A bloody bed and bedroom floor. And, the bullet lodged in the wall having ping-ponged through my father-in-law's brain before exiting his skull.

I think we all suffered some PTSD from that day. We will never know why he did it. Not really.

At his funeral, our then four-year old grandson asked, "How did G-pa crack his head?" Although the funeral home did an amazing job covering the wound, that little boy could see it. I was the last one to leave Don's gravesite. I couldn't walk away until I saw every bit of dirt dropped onto his casket.

Why did he do it? Why did he shoot himself in the head while his lovely bride lay sleeping beside him?

Earlier that year, he had surgery to remove a cancerous tumor from his colon. His PET scan revealed that they got it all out. But, to be sure, they started him on chemotherapy. He took one round and decided he wasn't going to finish. They put him in hospice for pain management due to residual effects from the reconstruction of his aorta he'd undergone months before. At the time of his suicide, he was nowhere near dying, not from his diagnoses. He had to use oxygen due to some emphysema, but overall, he was doing pretty well.

He'd always been a cantankerous, often grumpy, man who liked to fuss about the news, politics, the world and such. When he'd get on one of his tangents, I'd cut him to the quick by saying, "I love you, Don Newsome." He would routinely reply with, "Sure nuff?" I'd say, "Sure nuff." During his last weeks, he was less grumpy and actually quite jovial. It was a pleasure to visit with him. Then, bam! He's gone. The thing about suicide is, you may never find out "Why?" He left no note. He didn't talk about it. He sat up in the bed, grabbed the pistol and fired it into his head, while his wife lay sleeping beside him. She told me she had heard the pop, knew what it was, and yelled, "No, Don!!"

Curiously, I don't recall a lot of interaction with my mother-in-law that day. I remember hugging her somewhere around the time I arrived, but not much else. What I do recall, and vividly, is the cleanup.

My husband is a remarkable man. He was the one who began the cleanup of the bloody scene so his mother would not have to deal with it. Others helped him. I don't think I did, at least I don't remember it. His parents had two adjustable beds which were flush up against each other so it looked like one king-size bed. The blood had run down between the two and onto the carpet. Imagine your husband removing bloody bedding and mattresses from his parents' home, laying them out on the driveway then spraying all of it with a power washer as blood clots and pieces of brain matter washed across the concrete, into the grass.

Later that night, well after dark, some of us laid down on the driveway and watched the clear sky full of bright stars. We saw multiple shooting stars—Heaven's celebration for receiving a new angel, is what I've always thought.

The evening after the funeral, several of our family members and close friends went out to dinner at Eddie Montgomery's steakhouse. Grief is an unpredictable thing. You think you're doing fine, then...you're not. While sitting at that table, looking at all the love around me, I began sobbing uncontrollably. Not only did my father-in-law leave a hole in his skull, he left a hole in all those he left behind. One that will never be filled. I love you, Don Newsome! Sure nuff.

If this harrowing story helps one person, if it stops one person from attempting suicide, if it gives you the courage to seek help, then it was worth my writing it. And, if you have endured an event such as mine, please talk to someone about it.

I'm thankful for my dance instructor who encouraged me to write about it.

• • •

A fact about motherhood that no one ever tells you. I will tell you.

When you become a mother, the first thing you learn is: You never knew just how much you could love another human being. This new little creature becomes the most important being in your life. You live for it. You'd die for it. You can't even remember how your life was before you became a mother. When you have another child, you don't give them half the love that you gave the first one. Not at all! Your love doubles. Your heart becomes larger. And, like a balloon filling with air, the more it's filled the more fragile it becomes. Yet, it still grows. When they hurt, you hurt for them double because two hearts are hurting. A mother's love is exponential. No one ever tells you that. Now, introduce a grandchild to your life. Your heart grows larger still. More fragile. As your family grows, you're holding more and more love in your heart. It expands more than you ever dreamed was possible. You literally want to wrap your heart around each of them and keep them safe—always. Because, when they hurt, you hurt with them—double. When a grandchild is hurt, you not only feel their hurt, but also their mother's hurt—because now you know what they're feeling. When I was little, my mother told me, "Motherhood is a heartbreaking job." At the time, I just looked at her with a blank, uncomprehending stare. Now I know—SHE WAS RIGHT!!

Now, I'm in no way trying to discourage women from having children. Not in the least. I just feel we should all know what we're really signing up for from the start. What my mother didn't tell me is that this job is permanent. It has no end. It doesn't stop on your child's 18th birthday. You can't retire or take a vacation from it. It's with you every day. Twenty-four hours. Seven days a week. Motherhood is a lifelong, continual, non-stop, exponentially expanding, heartbreaking and heart-filling job. It grows in your heart—and I wouldn't trade it for anything.

. . .

I feel I have been a good mother. Not perfect, but good. I did the best I could with what I knew then and know now. I corrected (went a different direction) than my parents did with me and tried to give my children what I didn't get from my parents: guidance. I remember asking my father if I should leave my hometown at 18 years old, with a man I barely knew, and move to Louisiana.

Perhaps my life would've turned out better if he'd spoken up...? I could see concern in his eyes, and he obviously struggled with whether or not to tell me what I "should" do. He didn't. I moved.

Of course, we cannot change the past. Even if we could, it would drastically alter our current reality. Yes, it *could* maybe be better, but it could also go the other direction. We will never know the answer to that.

If I hadn't moved to Louisiana, I wouldn't have had my beautiful daughters. When I asked my father for his direction/advice, he said, "I think it will be a good experience for you." Maybe he knew how easily teenagers listen to and follow the advice of their sage parents—not at all, usually. They're going to do what they're going to do. The parents are left there gritting their teeth, praying, and hoping that their offspring made the best decision and that everything will be okay. Looking back on my life, I realize just how many times I left my parents in that condition.

I suppose it's the whole "don't help the butterfly out of the cocoon for that is how the wings build enough strength to fly" thing. It's extremely difficult watching the butterfly struggle to gain that strength. You want to help them so badly! You see an easier way. You can help!

And when your butterflies are adults and you know in your soul, your heart and everything in your being that they are making a mistake and try to reason with them, guide them, show them in every way possible that it is a mistake, one that will cost them dearly, but they don't listen, or believe you, and continue on their path—all you're left with is a saddened, sickened heart— you did all you could do to save them, spare them, but it didn't work. You did all you could do, and you continue loving them, no matter what, period. You always have and always will. That's all a mother can do.

When my mother said, "Motherhood is a heartbreaking job," those were the truest words she ever muttered.

· · ·

My Mother was 88 years old when she died. If you Google Parkinson's disease, you will likely learn that the disease itself is not considered terminal, and/or that Parkinson's patients die because of its "complications." In my thinking, that's like claiming that the bullet didn't kill the murder victim, it was merely complications stemming from the bullet piercing through the victim's body that killed them.

My mother had Parkinson's, and she died with it, but I want to say "from it." It took six years from her first symptom to her final breath. I remember walking with her through the Atlanta airport and noticing she was shuffling her feet a bit. I asked, "Mom, why are you walking funny?" She said, "I don't know." Coincidentally, I learned about Parkinson's in nursing school just a few weeks before this trip to Florida for my uncle's funeral, and sadly, I knew exactly what I was witnessing.

Then came the tremors in her hands. Dad purchased weighted silverware for her to use, which significantly reduced the shaking of her hands during her meals. However, she complained that they were "too heavy" and refused to use them most of the time. Her face adopted the classic mask-like appearance, her cheeks drooped, and her mouth turned downward. It resembled the face of a sad clown. Mother had always had a lovely smile. My father often said, "She was easily the prettiest woman" at the college where they'd met.

Slowly, one-by-one, she stopped doing her favorite things. It's been several years, and I no longer remember the order in which she gave up her routine activities and hobbies. My mother had always been a classy lady; she wore pretty shoes and clothes with a precise amount of jewelry accessorizing everything. Whether she wore a formal dress or a leisure suit, her hair was styled, and her makeup was beautifully done. Mom's classy appearance faded. She turned into a frumpy-looking woman with baggy clothes, often mismatched, shoes with no socks, hair barely combed, no makeup, and no accessorizing jewelry. One day, out of the blue, she decided to do her eyebrows and walked into the kitchen sporting eyebrows that looked like she'd drawn them on with a melted black crayon. I was stunned but didn't say a word. She tried.

Mom loved playing her 1920's Euphona upright piano. Parkinson's caused her to quit that activity that gave her so much joy. She also loved her African Grey parrot named Kokie Poo. Mom worked around Kokie's cage every day, sweeping and laying down fresh newspaper underneath. Then, one day, she just stopped doing all that. Time went on, and eventually, Mom didn't interact with Kokie at all.

As Mom's swallowing ability was dwindling, she constantly drooled and kept a washcloth in her hand. Her medicines had to be crushed and given to her in a spoonful of pudding. Once it was evident that Mom was no longer able to nourish herself with food, a feeding tube was placed in her stomach. Before the procedure, I asked my mother, "Are you doing this for you or for us?" She pointed to herself, and I told her that it was good. I didn't want her to undergo any type of invasive procedure just for us.

Mom spent the last year of her life getting her liquid meals and medications through that tube directly linked to her stomach. She was admitted to hospice and was cared for in her home. Her hospital bed was in the living room, my father sat right beside her in a recliner, holding her hand. I spent most of my time on the loveseat directly across from them. Even though I'd been a nurse for several years, I had never witnessed Cheyne-Stokes breathing, until I saw my mother doing it. We stopped her tube feedings. She was receiving sublingual liquid morphine to keep her comfortable. My mother's doctor cited "pneumonia" as her cause of death, but she didn't struggle to breathe. There was no cough. She merely fell asleep, and several days later, her spirit took flight.

• • •

After giving my mother her tube feeding:
Me: Her belly is really bloated. I don't like that.

Dad: Yeah, I know. It pushes me out of bed.

Me: If she ever gets hiccups in bed, you're in for a ride and a half!

• • •

I'll never forget the day Mom died. It was in early October 2013. As I was standing outside my parents' house watching the hearse carry her worn-out little body away, a strong gust of wind swept through, and I could feel her presence. My mother was free.

The day before the funeral, I wrote this poem to be read graveside:

Goodbye for now, Mom
We watched your body slowly rob you
Of doing the things you enjoy
It was hard to witness this sweet life
That Parkinson's did destroy
Day after day we felt helpless
As we saw you fading away
Our hearts so tightly held you
But in this world, you could not stay
And now you are at peace, Mom
In a place where you can run

You can sing and play the piano
And dance around in the sun
Mother, I will deeply miss you
For into Heaven you've been cast
You were there for my first breath
And I was there for your last
There's nothing you can't do now
Your spirit is truly free
And I know deep in my heart
You will always be with me
Until we meet on the other side...
I love you, Mom

. . .

We ordered a red granite bench in Mom's honor, and the burial park said that it would be under the tree we requested, but would have to be slightly angled to avoid sitters having their feet on another person's marker. I explained this to Dad, and he retorted, "Well, can't they just move the people who're already there?"

. . .

After my mother died, and Dad had been alone for a year, I decided to go into travel nursing so I could, perhaps, be assigned to a hospital closer to him. That way, I could divide my time between my home and his and help take care of him. Well, this didn't work out very well. My first assignment was in Tennessee, seven hours from my father. The second assignment was in Ohio, but still two hours from him. However, I did get to spend more time with him if I had a day off in between. It was a lot of driving, but I felt better about being there for him. My last travel nursing assignment was in Louisville, an hour from my home. While it didn't really help me with being at Dad's more, it sure did pay well, and I signed additional contracts for almost nine months.

• • •

An hour drive to work can be a long time for an old lady bladder that's full of coffee, and by the time I got there one particular night, I really had to go. I parked in the parking garage and hurried toward the nearest restroom, knocking people out of my path. I swung the restroom door open like a western outlaw skipping out on his bar tab and hurled my bag up on the sink while sprinting into a stall. As I'm sitting there experiencing sweet relief, and reveling in the fact that my panties were still dry, I heard the rhythm of the automatic soap dispenser—dispensing soap repeatedly. I'm thinking, "Oh, no." But, oh yes, you guessed it! I'd thrown my bag right up under that sucker! When I was done, I had a giant puddle of soap lying on my bag.

• • •

The roads were VERY SLICK the last 10-15 miles of my trip one morning. If my sphincter got sucked up any more, I'd have been burping farts!!

• • •

On one fun night shift, it seemed like somebody opened the gate and said, "All the bat-crap crazy and annoying people, come right this way." For the love of…TAKE THEM ALL BACK AND SHUT THE DAMN GATE!!! It may have been a full moon.

• • •

I got to work early one morning so I had breakfast in the cafeteria. There was a sweet lil bitty old lady sitting at a table with a man who I presumed was her son. She reminded me so much of my dearly departed Mother that I just kept smiling at her. When I got up, I asked the man if she was his mother to which he answered affirmatively. I said, "Well, I just have an irresistible urge to hug her…she reminds me of my Mom." So I did and kissed her forehead. As I walked away I could hear her say, "Wasn't that nice."

• • •

Tiring of the massive number of miles I was packing onto my car and my life, and given the fact that I could not secure regular employment in Ohio, I decided to give up travel nursing and get a job closer to home. Back on a medical/surgical floor, night shift. Little did I know, this would be my last medical/surgical nursing job.

• • •

I'll just say it. Medical/surgical nursing is the armpit of the entire nursing profession. But I wanted to learn all that I could while working as a floor nurse, so my goal was to spend at least five years in "the trenches."

While medical/surgical is a great place to learn more skills and hone those you already possess, it is an extremely challenging and demanding area. One that is notoriously understaffed. One that has the very real potential of sucking away your soul, piece by piece, one shift at a time, like a leech with an insatiable hunger and a bottomless pit of stomach.

Not descriptive enough? You can have as many as seven, even eight or nine, patients at one time. You feel pulled 15 different directions at any given time and your patients can feel forgotten, neglected and uncared for under your watch. When you clock out, at the end of most shifts, you leave feeling as though you've cheated your patients because there is precious little, often no, one-on-one time to actually connect with them as human beings. The patients, who had entrusted their care to you, a trudging, overworked registered nurse, become a mere name on your to-do list of the many tasks you have to complete in your 12-hour shift. It's not fair to them; it's not fair to you.

Regardless of the nurses' collective complaints regarding being over-worked, over-stressed and ready to throw in the towel on their chosen career, this remains the common practice on most medical/surgical floors today. Needless to say the rate of nurse burnout is through the roof.

I suppose management sees all the work getting done and it looks good on paper, so why change anything? Because very valuable, wonderful nurses keep leaving those floors, and sometimes leave nursing altogether, that's why!

During my last year of being a floor nurse, I would literally clock in and immediately start counting down the hours and minutes until it was time to clock out again, with that time clock eating a piece of my soul each time. However, I did the best that I could for my patients and tried to stay positive during my shifts. As our 12-hour shift progressed, I'd very enthusiastically announce to my co-workers, "We're 15 minutes in, woo hoo!!" Yeah, it was like that.

While I wasn't exactly thrilled about my medical/surgical nursing career, I did make some wonderful and lasting friendships. I learned a lot. I had some fun along the way and had the privilege of taking care of some very special patients. Oh, and my 5-year goal in medical/surgical nursing? I made it a total of eight years. Go, me!

• • •

My last medical/surgical patient, December, 2016:
I'd worked on this medical/surgical floor for almost a year, despising the majority of it. I was miserable. Because of this, I had been

looking into home health nursing and had applied at several agencies. It was mid-December and I was working hard to finish up the paperwork for my new career as an agency nurse. I was elated to be getting out of floor nursing, at last, and planned to start taking assignments in the new year.

My last medical/surgical patient had been independent since she'd been in the hospital. She got up to use the bathroom by herself, etc. Everything. I spent a good amount of my last shift with this patient. To protect her privacy, her name will not be included in this story. We'll call her Destiny. That's a fitting name because I feel I was destined to be her nurse that day. We thought Destiny was having a heart attack early in the shift. Many calls and many meds later, she was doing OK. She rested well through the rest of the night. I gave her morning meds and she was fine. Five minutes later, she's laying in her doorway and someone yells, "WE NEED A NURSE! NOW!!"

I had just passed her room not five minutes before that and she was walking and taking care of herself without issue. I ran down there, as well as others, and she had somehow twisted the bottom of her leg and it broke! Her bone was exposed—about six inches of it, and her foot was lying beside, almost behind it! I thought I was going to faint.

She, like so many other people in my life, had shared her life story with me throughout the shift and said, "You're my therapist," at one point. Anyway, I called her doc and said, "Please get up here as quickly as you can. Destiny has fallen and broken her leg and the bone is exposed." He said, "She broke her leg?! Jesus Christ!!"

They called a code so people from every area would respond. It was a whirlwind! The super nurses dove in and did what needed to be done about getting her an IV, which coincidentally, was not achieved. Lab couldn't even get blood out of her that morning.

Several nurses tried. The ortho doc was called in and he basically put her parts back together and wrapped her leg for stability and we had to get her 400-pound body up on bed. She kept crying and apologizing...I kept patting her cheek and reassuring her, reminding her to breathe..."we don't want your heart to act up again..." etc. She just cried and cried and said, "I can't deal with this right now ... " (related to her life at the moment), "so many people rely on me."

I said, "Destiny, look at me." I had my hand on her cheek and said, "Yes, but right now, we have to deal with what is happening. I need you to be calm and breathe."

She said, "Is it broken?" I confirmed that it was.

She said, "Is the bone sticking out?"

I said, "It's very broken and you do not need to see it."

I'm in NO WAY a trauma nurse as far as the medical/urgent type shit. But, what I was able to do helped her and as they were wheeling her away, she said, "I love you."

Before clocking out that morning, I told my coworkers, "I'm done. This is it for me." Thankfully though, after this incident, I had 11 days off and planned to use them to rest and work through my leftover feelings regarding my last shift. However, two days before I was to return to work, I called the house supervisor to let them know I would not be returning. I truly was done.

While in the hospital, her chronic heart condition caught up with her and Destiny took a bad turn. All of her organs failed and she was to receive end of life/palliative care. Due to the pain meds she was getting continually, she had to stay in the ICU. I visited her in the ICU on my way home from Ohio. She would open her eyes when I said her name, but that was it. Then, when I was getting ready to leave, I said her name, and she opened her eyes and looked at me. I asked if she remembered me and she nodded with a smile. Then she was out again. Destiny died in the wee hours of Christmas morning.

I believe it was the next day, I was back in Ohio with my Dad and we were watching our evening movie. I got a notification on my phone from a co-worker. She told me Destiny had passed away. Now, in my eight years of medical/surgical nursing, I had only cried on the job twice. Both times it was because I was upset over pediatric patients. I'd never cried at home for patients either. But, when I read that message that Destiny had passed, I sobbed. Quietly and uncontrollably. Why did she have to have such a rough life? She had expressed to me that her mother died at her age.

I knew I was done with medical/surgical nursing and needed a change, but felt imprisoned because it's the only area where I had experience. I suppose I can think of Destiny as an answered prayer, because from our paths crossing, I gained the strength and/or courage to leave medical/surgical nursing.

For weeks after Destiny's death, I would scour the online obituaries in search of hers. Having failed to find one, I basically succumbed to the fact that she simply was not going to have one. Then, a couple months later, I was awakened by someone shouting, "HEY, VONDA!!!" I shot out of bed, ran downstairs to check on Dad and he was in bed. Sound asleep. Then, while I was having my coffee, Destiny popped into my head and I once again searched online for an obituary fully expecting the search to result in nothing. Per usual. To my surprise, THERE IT WAS. Her life had been acknowledged, at last!

· · ·

After my mother's passing in 2013, my father remained in their home and he managed quite well by himself, the vast majority of the time. I lived 141 miles south of my parents, yet I was the most logical offspring to care for either of them in their times of need. Thus, I was there to help them through any serious illness or major surgeries.

During a small, family style New Year's Eve 2016 party here at our house, I received a call from my brother-in-law, Gary, urging me to come to Ohio right away. Dad had become quite ill and Gary expressed his deep concerns. He and Dad had become besties and Gary would visit him daily and they'd share a cup of Nescafe coffee. I told Gary I'd be there as soon as I could, we ended our conversation, and I explained to my family what was happening. I told my husband, "I think I'm going to be gone for a long time, this time." In a flurry of activity, I packed my bags with everything I would need for an extended stay, gave my hubby an early Happy New Year kiss, and was on the road heading north by about 10:30 p.m. Little did I know, I would not return home until the following June.

When I arrived at Dad's, he was resting peacefully in his bed. The next day, as I assessed his every breath and move, I could see just why my brother-in-law called me to come up. Dad was having a difficult time breathing, looked pale and was extremely weak. Hours later, I finally convinced him to let me take him to the ER to be checked out. He stayed in the hospital three-to-five days for congestive heart failure.

We'd had him back home for 11 days and things were looking up. He was regaining his strength, had a better color and was back to his usual activities of watching the news, reading his emails and researching things online, and we'd resumed watching a movie every evening. I thought he was almost to the point where he could manage by himself again and I could return home.

Then, one morning while I was sitting in the kitchen having my coffee, Dad began his morning ritual of going into the garage to unlock the outside door to allow visitors to have easy access into the house. I was about 10 feet from him and watched him like a hawk as he went down the two steps, his hand securely grasping the handrail. OK, he's doing fine. Breathe. It is, after all, a delicate balance with the elderly—allowing them their independence and/or guarding their every move.

He reached over and unlocked the door. Success. Keep breathing. He was still holding on to the rail. Since those handrails were installed, he'd always been very careful to use them. Then, for whatever reason, as he turned to come back up the steps into the kitchen, he let go of the handrail before he grasped the one next to the door with his other hand. In the split second he reached for the rail, his oxygen level must've plummeted because he did not grab the handrail. He fell straight backwards into the garage.

I rocketed out of my chair and found him lying face down in the garage with blood around his head. I immediately called 9-1-1 and the ambulance was there within five minutes. Thankfully, my parents' house was a mile from the fire department. Although Dad was conscious and spoke to me during this episode, he never remembered any of our conversation afterward. It was after this fall that I began seeing a downward trend to his health and knew I could not return home—that I'd be with him until—the end.

• • •

After dinner one evening, Dad decided to get into his "banana cake" for dessert. He picks up the plastic cake container and begins to pry the base apart from the domed top with his fingers. As he turns it around and around and crinkles the plastic container repeatedly, he doesn't seem to be making any progress. He sets the cake back on the table and gets a butter knife. Watching him as he's prying the knife down around the seal of the stubborn container, it's apparent that it has a secret combination for entrance. It's also very apparent that Dad's blood pressure is beginning to rise. In a frustrated huff, along with some choice obscenities being muttered, he turns the whole cake container on its side. For a split second, I think he must've gotten the thing to gap enough to finally pry it open all the way. But, no!! In a maniacally frustrated grunt, he proceeds to pound his fist directly into the side of the blasted cake container. With that single blow, the cake lay open and nary a crumb was lost! My father then very politely sits back down and proceeds to calmly cut himself a piece of what is now referred to as "the pound cake." I just sit there staring at him. Speechless. Streams of tears going down my cheeks. Finally, I say, "Well, that's one way to do it!"

• • •

We are all in this together

While listening to the news in my father's kitchen, two things occurred to me simultaneously. One, how extremely divided this country is right now. Two, how We the People are ALL in this mess TOGETHER. Then, I thought, if you take away the different religions, races, sexual orientations, and levels of wealth, we are all the same. Just people doing the best we know how in this crazy world. Yet, when given the chance to band together as one, it seems the opposite course is the one that is chosen. I think that if we are truly honest with ourselves, we would see that we all harbor a little bit of prejudice and/or judgment against a particular religion, group, race, etc. If we are honest. But, my question to you is this: In your lifetime, have you or any of your loved ones received blood in a life or death situation? When that gift of life was transfused into the vein of the recipient, did anyone care what race the donor was, what religion they practiced, about their sexual orientation, or what political party they supported? I imagine that all you desired was that your loved one continued to live. When it came down to living or dying, no one asked what kind of person donated the blood. It didn't matter in the least, did it? That's what I want you to think about. We the People are ALL in this together and one day it may just be you and that one person who supports what you condemn. Just you. Just them. Your only hope of survival may be that one person. The one person who represents everything that you feel contempt toward—just like that donated blood was the only hope for you or your loved one. So, if when it comes down to facing the bitter end you would choose acceptance, compassion, and unity over hatred and segregation, why can't we choose that now? Like it or not, we are all in this mess together.

Today, more than ever, we need to band together. Coronavirus has literally taken the world by storm. It's the headline of the day—every single day. It's constantly blasting through Facebook (on which I have drastically decreased my "scrolling" time; although, the memes that have been created are pretty amusing). My parents lived 89 and 88 years on this earth and never experienced a mass shutdown. I wonder what they'd have to say about this situation and if they'd deem it worse than The Great Depression.

The fact is, no one's life is more important than another's life in this world. Everyone is someone's mother, father, brother, sister, cousin, friend, husband, wife, daughter, son, partner, or someone's sole source of support, etc. Earlier this spring, I read a headline that claimed gun and ammo sales had increased in the U.S. with larger than usual numbers of Asian-Americans making such purchases. These, our fellow Asian-Americans, neighbors, co-workers, and friends fear that they will experience retaliation due to the virus coming from China. It is no more our Asian citizens' fault that coronavirus exists than it is the gay's fault that HIV began in their community. These viruses could have happened anywhere and to anyone. Hate the disease, not our fellow human beings for getting it first.

Every time something horrific happens in our world, the number one priority seems to be the urgency to place blame. Who is responsible? Blame must certainly be assigned, posthaste! Press conferences and special reports are aired regarding, "It's the fault of…(blah blah blah)," and we are blindly placated, albeit temporarily, because it looks like our government officials are doing something about the current disastrous event. This current crisis may have started in China, okay. So…what? What now? Are we going to hate China and all of its people? Are we going to shun every Asian-American in the USA? Are we going to cuss the media and blame them for their current round of sensationalism? Sure, we can do it all, and sometimes it feels really good to vent, blame and cuss a bit. But, the fact remains, we have a health crisis in our midst and how is any of that going to help us get through THIS mess—you know, the one that we the people of Earth remain IN IT TOGETHER?!

I've long thought that the world was spinning way too fast, changing too rapidly, too many distractions and too much busy, busy, busy in our lives, and that something was going to "jerk a knot in its tail." This may be that knot being jerked. "This too shall pass," my mother told me many times. The fact is, human beings are being lost, and more will follow. All we can do is our individual and collective best. Blaming, hatred and mass hoarding is not a solution. It's simply a knee-jerk response to fear.

The news is rife with the catastrophe of the day and a good portion of the population watches, listens, and gobbles it all up day after day, like shoveling in popcorn during a scary movie. Not me. I do not watch any of the news channels, the nightly or local news, period. I've been instructed many times, "You need to stay current on what's happening in the world." Trust me! When there is a big news story, I hear all I need to hear about it from everyone else's conversations. At times, I treasure my hearing impairment.

I honestly don't know how anyone can watch the news all day, every day, TV on from sun-up to way past bedtime and not be suicidal. It's a constant flow of negativity, fear-mongering and… I'm about to have a panic attack just thinking/writing about it! I wish we could do a sociological experiment: that no one would seek out the news, in any form or medium, for 30 days. 15 days. Hell, even 7 days could have a direct positive impact on the mental health of our population and may even decrease the level of depression and anxiety currently rampant in our country. Yes, we need to be informed, sure. But, not inundated and overloaded. Imagine what the world would be like if for every negative news story broadcast, a positive and uplifting one was also shared. Can you imagine? Sadly, good or happy news doesn't raise the ratings, does it? We can tip the scale though, ourselves. Cut your news-watching in half and replace the other half with entertaining and/or funny YouTube videos. You do have a choice of what you subject your mind to every day. It sounds like another sociological experiment, doesn't it? Oh well. My calling in this life is to increase the number of smiles, spread a little joy and spark a chuckle or two. While there are no chuckles in this particular blog post, there are plenty in my other posts. Hey!! The positive outweighs the negative—nice! Go, me!

In my heart, I truly believe that something good will arise from this pandemic. Hopefully, we will be stronger, more united, wiser, and more appreciative of our daily lives, mundane as they may be on occasion. With the widespread panic and fear, doesn't mundane sound really good about now? Sigh.

• • •

As far back as I can remember, Dad loved to watch the news, and my visits home were no exception. He'd watch it every day, many times a day and, most often, very very loudly. Now and then, he'd mute the sound and just read the closed-captioning in silence. I truly cherished those breaks in the media noise, since one could have a difficult time ignoring the sound coming from a bright and blaring TV screen a mere 4.5 feet from one's face. That one was me, as that is where I sat with him in that kitchen, most times, in that little blue recliner that had been my mother's and was positioned in front of the television. This television remained on from the time Dad woke up in the morning until he went to bed at night.

I possess a very sensitive soul and it simply cannot endure the horrific, often graphic, worldly news that's splattered all over the TV, internet, etc. So, in order to survive my extended stay by avoiding the news details that, quite literally, have caused me to lose sleep, I purchased a single bluetooth earbud and started listening to music through my Pandora app. I opted for a single earbud so I'd have one ear available to focus on my father's activity. He required a lot of supervision, the rascal.

Along with my father's television being on all-day, he also had a small boombox in the living room on which he'd play the local classical music channel, also all day every day. Another of his morning routines was turning on that little box. Now, I've personally never been much of a classical music fan. Many of the pieces coming from that radio station would irritate me—a lot, actually, almost to the point of banging my head on the wall. So frantic and unorganized. Eek.

However, when a waltz, any waltz, would start to play, I would immediately feel my spirits being lifted, it'd make my heart smile and fill me with the urge to glide all through the house along with the music like Julie Andrews on that mountain top in The Sound of Music. I especially looked forward to catching Sleeping Beauty by Tchaikovsky on that radio since it became and remains my favorite waltz of all time. I suppose, mainly because it reminds me of being with Dad.

I don't remember what type of music I listened to first on Pandora, but once I started this courtship, I spent a lot of time listening to 1940's and 1950's music as well as waltzes. I do love the sound of a waltz, have I mentioned that? While I sat just 54 inches from the distracting news screen, I could play Candy Crush, or any other game, on my iPhone, successfully avoiding eye contact with the bad news box, while being swept away by the beautiful 1-2-3 melodies playing in my ear.

I'd often close my eyes and envision a large ballroom filled with couples in their lovely formal wear, music wafting through the air as they dance ever so gracefully and effortlessly around the ballroom. Then, I'd see myself out there twirling around the vast openness in a totally fabulous full-length ball gown. Oooh, it's so wonderful to dream. (Sometimes, when I was only listening to Dad's boombox, the triumphant part of the music would coincide with me winning a level in my game. I loved it when that happened! It's the little things, isn't it? Ha ha.) When I'm dreaming of waltzing, I keep seeing myself in an ivory-colored dress. That is most definitely NOT my color. It makes me look like I have jaundice, for real. Some of you may think the proper word is "jaundiced," but I looked it up. Jaundice is a disease, so it is a noun. Jaundiced is an adjective, so, I suppose I could've said I appeared jaundiced? I dunno. I like "have jaundice" better. On that note, I'll be right back...I'm closing my eyes and changing the color of my dress so I don't look jaundiced.

That took a little longer than I expected. Almost took a nap! I was going to say white, but that'd make me look like a bride. While I kept my eyes closed, holding the image of my gown steadily in my mind, the color of the gown changed continually, as if I were using a fashion app, until I landed on my very favorite color—red, of course. Not an orangey red, no. A deep, rich, luxurious, true red. Yes, that's the gown. Now, I can continue writing/typing.

Return to me sitting in my mother's blue kitchen recliner. Since I'd been imagining myself dancing to the songs, I had a brilliant idea. I could check YouTube for videos of actual people dancing to the actual song which had currently resonated with me. Insert lightbulb above my head! Voila!! I watched countless videos of people dancing to songs I'd heard through my earbud. I'd watch couples dance the jitterbug, foxtrot and the Lindy hop, among others, and that is where my long-time dream of learning to dance intensified. It looked like so much fun. Along with my favorite waltz of all time, I quickly acquired my favorite waltz videos, which were promptly saved in my favorites.

· · ·

Dance with fear

Since my teen years, I've always wanted to learn to dance, you know, like club dancing, out there doing your own thing. But, I was always too shy to get out on a dance floor, or any floor, and shake my groove thing. Yeah, I'm a product of being a teenager in the 70's. For a brief period of time, when I was about 17, I did go to a local discotech. They had specific, alcohol-free hours just for teens. I believe the age-range permitted to enter was 15-17 years old. I was dragged there by a very persistent friend and to this very day that friend remains the only person to ever get me to dance in public. But, oh how others have tried and tried, and failed and failed. Heck, I wouldn't even dance when I was home alone, with all the curtains drawn, doors locked, and the lights off. Regardless of my persistent friend's belief that I, too, possessed the ability to cut loose under the sparkling mirrored ball hanging from the ceiling of this disco tech, I would only mimic someone else's moves, mostly hers. I had no moves of my own. Nothing original. No "dancing with" or "feeling the music," like they always tell you.

Now fast forward a couple decades or so, the year is 2002, I was 41 years old and had been divorced for several months. It was then that I started going to a country-western bar with my very good friend, Dianne. We would meet there most every weekend night and we'd enjoy watching all the people shaking their stuff out on that dance floor. I actually met my current and forever husband at that bar, if you recall. Ladies, there are good men in bars, though I'd never have imagined meeting one there. I only went to hang out with Dianne.

Anyway, I admired the crowds of happy dancing patrons, even the truly goofy-looking ones, for they all shared the one thing I lacked —the courage to go out there and have a ball. I wished that I could be that brave. Of course, being that we were all in a bar, a bar that served alcohol, it maybe could've been that "liquid courage" working on those dancers. Coincidentally, I've yet to find the correct dosage of liquid courage that'll make me do it. Truth be told, I haven't tried very hard to find it either. Still, weekend after weekend, there I would sit, watching and sometimes envying the fun being had by all of those brave people. Oh, many times I'd have the urge to run out to that dance floor and join the party, but my overwhelming fear of making a complete fool of myself would always stamp out that urge and I'd remain seated. Then, one night there I was, elbows on the table, my chin resting on top of my folded hands, yet another night of watching everyone dance up a storm while I stayed put, motionless. I'd had enough. I braved up and…no, I didn't go out there and dance, but I did make myself a promise: "Before I turn 42, I'm going to go out there and shake my stuff!" Well…did I do it? Show of hands, do you think I did it? Did I? Why, of course not!! I'm well past 42 and I still haven't done it.

More recently, in 2017, I suffered from excruciating pain caused by a pinched nerve in my neck. I tell ya, I think I'd rather give birth ten times, without an epidural or any other type of pain medicine! It was relentless, constant, never easing, and nothing provided relief. Thankfully, I signed up with a wonderful physical therapist named Chad. During our sessions, we'd always talk and share a lot of laughs. I can laugh through pain, I'm tough like that. I got that from my father. That clinic sure was a fun environment to work the kinks out of your body. In one of my sessions, I shared with Chad the details of my anti-dance plight, of being too big of a chicken to just go do it and how I'd broken a promise to myself several years earlier. I don't remember how many therapy sessions I had before I was released and virtually pain-free. I continued the exercises at home and they finally stopped that last little bit of discomfort.

I did miss seeing Chad and went back weeks later just to visit. We chatted a bit and I told him, "I still haven't gotten out on that dance floor." He said, "You just need to go sign up for dance lessons at Arthur Murray. Just do it." Hmm... "Yeah, okay," I thought while kind of mentally rolling my eyes. But, when I left the clinic, Chad's words were playing on a loop in my head. Arthur Murray. Arthur Murray! ARTHUR MURRAY!! As luck, or fate, would have it, I was driving through the fairly large city where Arthur Murray just happened to be located. It was a busy time of day and traffic was very heavy. I drove straight through the downtown area with no idea why because I usually avoid that area at all costs. Then, I saw it. There in the distance was the road which leads to the road that would take me to Arthur Murray. I was in the left lane of the very crowded two lanes leaving downtown. As that right turn was approaching, getting closer and closer, cars bumper to bumper in both lanes, I said, "Okay, fine! If this crazy traffic opens up and allows me to get over in the right lane, I'll make that right turn and go sign up at Arthur Murray." I'll have you know, that the traffic in the right lane literally opened up at least two car lengths long. The universe was like, "Here's your sign!! Come on over!" I was stunned. I'm sure my mouth gaped open in disbelief. Well, this is sometimes what happens when you challenge the universe.

I arrived at the dance studio, walked in all brave (ha ha) and actually signed up for lessons. You don't want to irritate the universe, after all, especially when it opened a door of opportunity for you that was two whole car lengths long. I scheduled my first lesson for the very next day. I was so nervous. When you hear "private lessons," you picture you and the instructor in a room or studio alone, don't you? I know I did. But, you're in a large studio with other students who are with their own instructors. There are a lot of eyes in there. I made it through that lesson and drove home with the rhythm and count from my first dance still playing in my head. When I first started, my lessons were only once a month and it's a bit more difficult to learn dancing with that interval.

After several lessons, my instructor suggested that I "start coming to the group classes" so I could get more practice. I was nervous enough toying with the perimeter of my comfort zone with just the private lessons and he wanted me to join a group?! Then I decided, "I'm just going to do it! I'm going to the group lesson for the hustle dance." It was an advanced class for the hustle, too, but it was the only one available for me to jump on while I was feeling so fearless. Something pushed me to do it anyway. I was all courageous and daring when I asked the instructor if I could attend regardless of my current abilities and coordination. Surprisingly, she allowed me to stay. Well, you remember when I said my fear of making a fool of myself overpowered all my urges to shake it on a dance floor? Going to this advanced hustle group class was the very best thing I could've done for myself because making a fool of myself was exactly what I did in that class. I'd spin the wrong direction, step on toes, miss the cue to rotate to the next dance partner (you change partners frequently in group classes), and I'd sometimes hold my partner's hands too tightly. I looked like I'd been spun around about a 100 times and then unleashed onto the dance floor. I totally made a fool of myself. But, you know what? I survived. I wasn't thrown out of the class. I wasn't banned from Arthur Murray. Perhaps I could've been dancing all my life if I'd only gone out there and made a fool of myself sooner.

So, if there is something you really want to do in this life, but you are being held back by the fear of looking foolish, I say to you: Do it anyway! Do it now!! Go to the next higher level class like I did, dance like a buffoon, look that fear right in the face and say, "You don't scare me any more. I faced you and I survived." It's liberating! You may be wondering if I have yet to shake my booty or my groove thing out there all by myself. Not quite yet. But, I am getting closer! I'm currently learning how to shake my hips in couples dances. I didn't know mine would or could even move that way. I'd always thought it had to do with being limber or flexible. Did you know, that truly has nothing to do with it? It has everything to do with your knees. Your knees control your hips. Wow! Kaboom! Mind blown.

After a routine lesson, my instructor gave me homework. To prepare for upcoming events at the studio, I was to compile a list of songs that meant something to me along with the dance I'd like to perform to each song. Although Sleeping Beauty by Tchaikovsky is my very favorite, beloved waltz, it would have posed an unnecessary choreographic challenge for my instructor. I told him not to worry and that I would find another waltz, no problem.

After I got home, I started looking through the songs on my Prime Music playlist. It was very easy to find my very favorite disco song, Fantastic Voyage by Lakeside, that I would be dancing the hustle to, oh yeah. Maybe not the advanced hustle, just yet, but the hustle. The real deep disco beat in that song just revs me up. The foxtrot would most definitely be to the musical genius of Glenn Miller and/or Mills Brothers. After all, they are truly the best. My parents would agree!

But, now, the waltz...which waltz? I didn't have a second favorite, nor could I even name another one. Along with the 40's, 50's, and waltz music stations on Pandora, I would often listen to solo piano. It was so relaxing, soul-calming, and reminded me of my mother playing her piano which was also located in their basement. I did a lot of this type of thing while I stayed with Dad in order to remain calm, present and to lessen the stress of being away from my husband and my family back in Kentucky. I searched waltzes on Prime Music and the name of one of my favorite solo pianists caught my eye. His name is Brian Crain and the waltz listed, Butterfly Waltz. It's a piano and cello duet and has a lovely album cover, too. Of course, I had to play it right then and there!

I didn't recognize it as one I'd ever heard, but it immediately touched something inside of me. Something very deep in my soul and completely unexpected. Within mere seconds of listening to this beautiful waltz, I felt the welling up of emotions in my chest which grew and grew until they were bursting out of my eyes. Streams of tears were soon cascading down my face faster than I could wipe them with a tissue, and I let them. You see, I hadn't fully processed my grief after losing Dad (which I will tell you more about a little further on in this chapter). Oh, since my father died, I would allow some tears to fall here and there, but only in small, metered increments which I felt I could withstand. You see,

I'd still had a job to do and was determined to see it through and, hopefully, make my parents proud: I had to clean out their house, their memories and personal items, and sell their house. The house they'd lived in since 1965. The house was built in 1949, the year they got married. So, not realizing it, I'd put my personal grieving on hold. A serious hold. The task of selling their house was completed last October. I still haven't been back to see it, though I know it is being truly loved and well taken care of by my niece and her little family. There's new life in my parents' home now and I'm very thankful. It, too, had mourned my parents' passing and its grief was much more evident than my own.

I had found my waltz. It felt as though Butterfly Waltz narrated my entire life, playing it back for me in 3:43 minutes of beautiful music. It represented the sacrifices I made in order to take care of my parents, no matter the inconvenience or the cost. "Doing the right thing isn't always convenient," I would often say. It's putting myself on the back burner for one reason or another and the many decades of *maybe somedays*. But, most of all, it is me saying, "I did it, Mom and Dad! I took care of everything the way you wanted me to. And, look at me! I'm dancing to some of your favorite music now! Can you believe it?! It has been very hard, but I think I can let go of you now, feel my sorrow, and move forward with my life—my life without you here on earth. I hope I've made you proud. I love you both and will miss you every day—for always."

I imagined myself at the next Arthur Murray event, looking like one of the celebrities on Dancing With the Stars, dancing under the mirrored ball to a personally meaningful song with tears streaming down their face as the camera zooms in to get a serious closeup like they're trying to count each tear that falls. I may be a blubbering, floor-soaking mess. But, I'd be out on that ballroom floor—waltzing.

P.S. I still fully intend to master that advanced hustle dance, too, daggonit!!

. . .

A very wise old man, obviously nearing the great exodus, said to me, "Enjoy life all you can. You won't regret it." Gonna try to live up to that statement! Especially after experiencing such regret. One summer, years ago, while we were enjoying our annual vacation with my Florida relatives, we made the two-hour trip to Niceville to see my aunt. My mother's baby sister, Naomi. I had promised my brother and his family that I would make them a special dinner that evening after our visit because, I believe we were heading home the next day. Then, Naomi's husband, our Uncle Bob, invited us to go to dinner with them, his treat, at his favorite restaurant. Since I'd made a prior commitment for dinner, I declined this invitation.

I felt horribly, because he was obviously very pleased and excited to be able to take us out and share that time with us. Maybe on our next visit. I regret not going now, because, though I didn't think it at the time, that was our last opportunity to go out to dinner with Uncle Bob and Aunt Naomi. Uncle Bob became ill with cancer and died. I'm very sorry that we did not accept the invitation to have a lovely dinner together. I regret that.

. . .

After I'd been in Ohio for five months, taking care of my father, and having gone through almost all of my savings (which I amassed for the sole purpose of helping my husband cover expenses in my expected absence and inability to work), I needed to have a talk with my father explaining the circumstances. I had to tell him that I needed to get back to work, but yet, I had promised him that I would keep him in his home until the end. There was no way we would have even considered putting my father (or any of our four parents) in a nursing home. Not a chance. Remember, I made the commitment to care for them without regard to the inconvenience or cost. I asked my father —well, actually, I had his home health nurse ask him —if he would consider moving to Kentucky with us. I could not muster enough courage to ask him myself, feeling so ashamed that I could not keep up my part of the bargain. I was in the kitchen of my childhood home while the nurse spoke with my father. I felt sick. What if he refuses? What would I do? What if he agrees? Then, I'd feel bad for uprooting him from his home of 52 years, and breaking my promise to him. I heard the nurse's footsteps as she made her way into the kitchen, where I was waiting, nervously. She said, "He agreed to move to Kentucky with you." I was surprised, happy, nervous, elated, scared all at the same time.

At this point in time, my father was a hospice patient. It was in early June when we'd gotten everything set up for his move to Kentucky. It was not feasible to transport him in a car. It would have been extremely uncomfortable for him, and he was on continual oxygen at the time. So, we arranged for an ambulance to transport him to our Kentucky home. We all left Ohio about the same time, but I arrived home a couple hours before the ambulance because they had some mechanical issues and had to transfer to another vehicle. I remember standing outside as the ambulance was backing up to our driveway and hearing the "beep beep beep" warning. I could see my father through the back windows and I waved at him. He waved back at me. That is a sweet memory that always brings a smile to my face. He had told the driver that, "This isn't where my daughter lives." In his defense, he'd only been here during the winter months, once for our February wedding and then later for a Thanksgiving gathering. To see the pin oak trees that line our driveway full of leaves and the grass so green and healthy, it must've looked quite different than he'd remembered.

Now, while he was here with us, my brother was here, too, to help with Dad. While he was extremely helpful, always willing to do whatever was needed (well, anything except anything to do with cleaning our father) I was grateful to have him here to help with the muscle part of taking care of Dad. However, as much as I really appreciated his help, he got on my nerves equally as much. My father asked how I was doing with my brother here, and I told him, "As much as he is a help, he equally gets on my nerves, but I'm dealing with it." Dad grinned knowingly, understanding.

While I'd stayed in Ohio those months, I had a lot of one-on-one time with my father wherein he would share some family stories and history, much of which I preserved via audio recordings. However, when we transferred Dad to Kentucky, he and I had less of that special time. This was partly because my brother was always present (and, honestly, I would rather he'd not been there at all, but it was for Dad's care and he was the priority) and partly because I had so missed my home life that I wanted to simply enjoy some of it once again. So, I allowed my brother to help as much as he desired.

Anyway, during one rare occasion that I had Dad all to myself, my brother was off keeping our grandchildren entertained when Dad said to me, "If there is anything you want to know, you should ask me now, while you have the chance." I couldn't think of a thing. I could not think of a single question I wanted to ask him. I was totally dumbfounded. He added, "...any secrets?" I stood there kind of stunned, looking at him and said, "I can't think of anything, but I'll keep thinking on it." I never did think of any questions, nor did I delve deeper into his offer to share the "secrets" he was holding. This I regret now, very deeply.

. . .

It was three weeks to the day of his Kentucky arrival that my father died. He had stopped eating several days prior and his only intake was small sips of water scattered sporadically throughout the day. He had stopped those sips a couple days before he passed on. Being a nurse, I knew that without any fluid intake, his days would be very limited. The night before his departure, I remember checking on him, lying there in the hospital bed, in one of our spare bedrooms. He didn't move. He didn't make any noise. I could see his chest rising with every breath. He was still alive. He looked very peaceful. I wish now that I'd made a makeshift bed on the floor beside him, so I could be at his side during his last breath. But, I was exhausted. I'd spent weeks sleeping on a miserable air mattress in the basement of his Ohio home so I could hear him adjusting his motorized chair, and run up the steps at any moment. I had been very homesick. I also had what they referred to in nursing school when we learned about care plans as "caregiver role strain."

While I do not regret the personal sacrifices I made to take care of each of my parents during their last days, I do regret not being beside Dad the morning he died, holding this hand like I'd done with my mother. My husband had checked on Dad early that morning, before sunrise after he'd gotten up for work. Dad was alive. He was lying on his back, comfortable. Quiet. Before my husband left the house to head to work, he checked on Dad again. This time, however, he was rolled over on his right side, facing the window, with his left arm hanging off the side of the bed. Had he been reaching for something? Someone? Was Mom there, waiting to guide him to the other side? Did he call out and no one heard him? Was he needing something? Was he in pain? Did he have one last moment of lucidity wherein I could've spoken with him for the last time, and maybe heard a few of those secrets, or another,

"I love you, Vonda"? Somewhere between 5 and 6:30 a.m., Dad took his final breath.

This, too, has weighed heavily on my mind, keeping me awake at night. I'm so sorry, Dad, that I didn't just say, "Tell me everything!! I want to know all the secrets you have, and please, let me record them so I won't miss a thing." And, I'm truly sorry I did not stay with you during your final night in our Kentucky home. You died alone, 130 miles from where I promised you would die, and I always said, "No one should ever die alone."

Months later, while in the process of cleaning out my parents' home, I found diaries that each of them had written, many decades earlier. I read a few passages, but closed them, as I felt I was invading their privacy. Perhaps, just maybe, some of those family secrets are contained in those diaries, in their handwriting. Etched in time. I haven't found the courage to read through them just yet. But, I must, and soon, lest that be another entry in this chapter entitled Regrets.

If you are ever faced with having nearly 100 years of knowledge and experience shared with you, do not miss that opportunity. Ask questions! Listen to every story. Take notes. I don't wish this regret upon anyone.

· · ·

The hardest thing I've ever had to do, and how I got through it
The hardest thing I've had to handle was the sale of my childhood home. The house my parents lived in for 52 years. The only childhood home I remember, where we moved when I was four years old.

My mother died in 2013, and my father four years later. After Dad's passing, I would routinely travel to Ohio to check on the house, clean a little, etc. I whole-heartedly intended to work on the sorting of their personal items throughout those many months and multiple trips north, but I was paralyzed when actually faced with physically doing it. I would open their bedroom door, look around the room and see everything just as they'd left it. I'd sigh and close the door. This continued for more than a year.

In 1987, I moved to Kentucky, 2 hours, and 15 minutes from my parents' home. Since then, I had made that 280-mile round trip drive more times than I could possibly count. The frequency of my visits increased over the years as my parents aged, of course. For every serious illness, every surgery, I would put my life on hold to take care of them, or stay in the hospital by their side, whatever they needed. I missed quite a bit of work over the years, and I would do it all again. I vowed never to put my parents in a home, and I kept that promise. I can be proud of that. It gives me some peace.

My mother died in October 2013 due to Parkinson's complications, and my father died in June 2017 of interstitial lung disease. None of us expected Dad to last very long without his lovely bride. "Maybe six months" is what I predicted. He amazed us all and lasted 3 years and 8 months.

For six months after my father died, I continued to pay his bundled cable, internet, and telephone bill. It was silly, wasteful, and illogical. Every time I thought of discontinuing it, I felt like I was taking his entertainment and livelihood away from him, and that anguish was palpable and halting. It was almost a year later that I actually started working on cleaning out the house. Before that, I would drive up periodically just to check on it. I'd unlock the door that opens from the garage to the kitchen, step inside and smell that familiar smell of their home. Everything was so quiet. No news on the TV. No piano playing in the basement. Dad wasn't in "the little room," reading his email or listening to ragtime music with Kokie Poo perched on the folding chair beside him. I'd always go right to my parents' bedroom, open the door and look all around the room, which remained as Dad left it. I'd look at his dresser and the pictures on the wall. The bed where I used to kiss my parents good night during my visits years ago. Where I would tuck Dad in when he was all alone and finally stopped sleeping in the living room recliner. My chest would feel very heavy, and then I'd close the door and walk away. I simply could not disturb anything, not even the dust collecting on the furniture.

Everything happens for a reason. I've always believed that, but others do not. I mean it in the sense that every event in our lives is a stepping stone to the next event in our lives. Surely the non-believers can get on board with that description. The time to seriously work on cleaning out the house came when my niece's home sold at an unprecedented speed. I was not ready. At all. Although I had a sick feeling in the pit of my stomach, my brain told me it could take months or even years for their house to sell. Everything happens for a reason, remember. Having had some time to reflect on it, I would likely still be working on trying to start clearing out that house today if their home hadn't sold so quickly. In the big scheme of things, the bandage was ripped off, and I was left with nothing else to do but tend to the wound, get the job I was enlisted to perform done, and move on. My parents' house was also saved from devastation. Every time I'd gone up to check on it, something else was broken or falling apart. The paneling was coming loose from the wall upstairs. The garage door was decaying, pieces scattered on the garage floor. The house was experiencing some grieving of its own and needed a family to love it back to life again. I'm thankful to my niece and her family for doing just that. I wish I could have done a more thorough job of gutting the house for her, but at the time, what I did was my absolute best and all I could do.

I am still dealing with this, the hardest thing in my life for me to handle. We filled the sizable U-Haul truck, packed to the gills with boxes full of my parents' lives, and hauled it to our home in Kentucky. There, it was then transferred to one of our spare bedrooms—where it remains today. Oh, I've shuffled some boxes around and have emptied a couple of them. A couple I knew would be quick, easy, and not so sentimentally heart-wrenching.

It's been years since we drove that U-haul away, and my heart still feels the same. My very sweet niece and her family have made their home in the house now. It's very well taken care of, full of love, and I know my parents are smiling. That thought makes me smile, too. However, I still can't bring myself to go see the house, all different from how I remember it: The basement, which was their entertainment center. The two recliners positioned in the front of the TV with a large, brown braided rug on the floor. The fireplace with gas logs. The little black stool beside Dad's chair where all the remotes lay in a row. I can still see him sitting there, selecting our movie for the night. The last movie Dad and I watched was Savannah Sunrise the day after Mom's birthday in February 2017. I suppose he didn't want to spend any more of her birthdays without her, so we didn't watch any movies together for the rest of Dad's life, which ended on June 27, 2017. The nappy brown blanket covering Dad's recliner, along with a towel placed on the left arm-rest so Kokie Poo could sit with him and enjoy the nightly movies with us. The John Wayne blanket we'd given him for Christmas years before that he'd cover up with when the basement was chilly. Mom's piano against the wall behind the recliners. The surround sound speaker taped to the steel pole by the stairs. The stairlift, still attached and operational, collecting dust. Those and so many more memories.

Though I love the residents very much, and even though I know my parents lived their lives, their lives are done now, the house has become "the house my parents used to live in" instead of being "my parents' house…" My logical brain understands that. My heart, however, just…can't…see it looking differently. Not yet. Once again, I never ever could've imagined how emotionally difficult the task of being Executor would be for me, or how profoundly grief would have affected me. I'm not a very emotional person. I mean, I have emotions, don't get me wrong. It's just that I don't cry easily at all. Well, those AT&T commercials always made me tear up, but the tears don't drip from my eyes. My heart is not on my sleeve, that's for sure. I'm actually a little envious of those who can feel and freely express their heartbreaking emotions while they're happening. But, that's not me. I'm more of a get-the-job-done-and-be-sad-later kind of girl.

I have no idea when or if I will make that 2 hours and 15 minute drive again. Right now, today, the way I feel at this moment, honestly, it may be many more years. Yes, my parents' gravesites are up there, wherein their ashes were placed in their urns and sealed inside their vaults, then buried beneath the soil. But that's not where they are. They reside in my heart, and I can visit them there at any time.

So, that is the hardest thing I've had to handle in my life, and how did I get through it? The short answer is, "One day at a time." The long and ongoing answer follows.

My parents entrusted me with the incredible duty of handling their estate. My father instilled in me, by his example, that you always do the right thing, no matter the cost, the inconvenience or sacrifice required. To the best of my ability, I followed my parents' wishes as they were set out in writing and verbally expressed to me, regardless of my personal feelings about it. Regardless of others' not liking certain aspects of it, I did the right thing as they set forth, period. I put my grieving on hold so that I could focus on carrying out the tasks I needed to complete.

For several months after my Dad's passing, I was in a funk, a state of limbo. I merely functioned on autopilot. I didn't watch anything new on TV. I didn't watch any movies because that reminded me so much of my time with Dad. I watched nothing but reruns of my favorite sitcoms, over and over. Sometimes, I would just sit in our living room in complete silence. I don't recall if I did any kind of socializing during those months. I didn't have any type of "meltdown," as my friends and loved ones expected me to experience at any given moment. Like I was an emotional time-bomb waiting for 3, 2, 1 countdown. Honestly, I still really haven't, not what I would consider a meltdown anyway. I feel sadness while missing my parents very much, and at times, I've had a little crying spell, but a meltdown, no. Maybe it won't happen. It's been several years since my father died, after all. It actually makes me feel like I'm a failure at grieving. I haven't heard of anyone else having an experience like mine.

I began talking to a therapist to work through my complicated grieving process (that's what I call it) and to further heal the wounds of my past. Our first session was the get-to-know-each-other session. I told my therapist about my regrets regarding my parents' deaths and how I didn't feel my grief was progressing or even healthy. She asked me to share one of my self-disappointments with her, and I said, "I should've deep cleaned." She looked at me blankly from my computer screen, you know, since we're doing this social distancing thing. For a second or two, I thought my computer had frozen, but she was simply a little stunned and speechless. She said, "I've been doing this for a very long time, and this is the first time that someone said they should have deep cleaned." That made me chuckle.

Through therapy, I learned that grief does not have an expiration date. There is no Best If Expressed By date. It takes the time it takes, and that's all there is to it. There's no accelerator pedal, no fast forward button, no speed-grieving course. No one has the right to tell you, "Shouldn't you be over that by now?" If someone asks that, they clearly have not experienced grief themselves or are stuck in their own state of denial. Grief is personal. There's no right or wrong way to grieve, although some methods could be more destructive than others. For me, one day at a time, I "get through it" a bit more.

. . .

Once I'd finally cleared out the house and it was sold, I had nothing left to do but rejoin my life, already in progress. What was I going to do first?

It's a strange feeling when all the excuses you've given yourself, or deluded yourself with, for decades, are suddenly, well, gone. Your kids are now adults with kids of their own. Your parents are now deceased. You don't have to be ready to drop everything and drive the two-and-a-half hours to their house to take care of them during an illness or surgery, as you have dutifully done since you made a promise to be there for them at all costs and/or personal sacrifice.

You've fulfilled your promise and commitment to care for each of them during their last weeks/months on this earth. You've completed the long, daunting, anxiety-filled job as executor of their estate. Your life is yours. You CAN now do whatever YOU want. When the constant sense of duty to others, pressure you put on yourself, and dedication to fulfilling your commitments and keeping your promises that had been driving you for decades are no longer in the drivers' seat of your life, it takes you a while to learn how to drive your own life again. This is something I had not anticipated. I figured once all that was taken care of, I'd feel as though I'd been shot from a slingshot, finally released into endless possibilities. But, it didn't work that way at all. For those months leading up to the sale of my parents' house, I was basically numb, lost, frozen in time.

Where had my passion gone? Where was my creativity that I'd put on the back burner for so long? Had I lost it forever? Why didn't I feel like doing any of the things I'd longed to do while I was performing all my other duties?

By the way, I have recently completed a drawing of a woman's face. It was very good albeit not "perfect" in my eyes. But, that's OK. My creative passion is slowly returning to me. I'm thrilled.

• • •

My parents' had a cabin built on 72 acres in Brookville, Indiana. They always called it "The Farm." There's a half-mile gravel lane that leads back to their little cabin and another stretch that goes to the pond. We all spent a lot of time out there. We'd walk those lanes with Mom and our kids and we'd get so excited when we found one of these fossil "horns." We seemed to find them a lot. Then, they'd get harder and harder to find ... til the next time we visited, when they would seem to have returned. My sweet, sneaky, little mother would drop those horns along those lanes so we'd have the joy of finding them again. I didn't realize this until an old margarine container filled with those horns was found in my parents' house.

• • •

One night a little after 1 a.m., I'm in my parents' kitchen in the glow of the nightlight. Standing by the counter where my cell phone is charging, I unplug it and turn to leave the kitchen. All of a sudden, I hear a loud ruckus and a big splat on the floor! THIS CRAZY BIRD shoots and crash-lands outta her cage like a freakin' cannonball and crash-landed! I rush over to see if she's alright and she's just frozen, feathers all fluffed out, huddled on the floor. I pick her up and look at her. Still no response. Start to pet her and she's just shaking all over. Then, a miracle happens. Something that has NEVER happened with me and the 28-year history with this bird. She lets me HUG HER! Yes. Hug her. She seems to calm down a bit so I raise her up to put her back in her cage. She is not having it and bolts off my hand like a cannonball again. At this point, I realize this bird is not returning to her cage so I take her to the living room where she has a perch. Reluctantly, she leaves my hand and slowly grasps her perch. Still in shock.

Motionless and not blinking, she watches me get comfy on the loveseat. And, that is how we spend the rest of the night. I don't know if she had an exorcism through the night or her cage was cleansed with sage, but she's since returned to it and all is normal again. And, she's been friendlier to me ever since! The End.

* * *

Inspiration returns!

On a cool, late autumn morning in 2018, I was enjoying my ritual morning cup of coffee while reading posts on Facebook. A few weeks earlier, a dear friend, whom I now refer to as "my direct link to the universe," had suggested I join a private writers group on Facebook. I checked it out, sent my request to join and was accepted. I would get notifications of posts, but had not truly invested in the group, nor had I completely read any of the posts.

That morning, however, something caught my eye. In the comments to one particular post, a member suggested the book: "Big Magic," by Elizabeth Gilbert. I read the comment completely. Then, I read it again. It inspired me to check out the book on Amazon. I read the book's description as well as a few reviews which contained the exact words I needed to hear on that day. I purchased the audiobook and started listening. Within 15 minutes, my inspiration resurfaced and grew, along with the goosebumps on my body, and I had to pause the audiobook so I could write two full pages in my own book before they vanished from my mind. I had been asking the universe for direction, a clue, even a subtle hint about what I should be doing with my creative desires. Asked. Answered.

My good friend, Linda, has been instrumental in connecting me with the universe, and leading me to the messages I've needed to receive. A mere 24 hours later, I had typed 6,878 words!

. . .

Fear—Prison for your dreams

Fear. It's a peculiar thing. It's not something you can see. You can't touch it. It makes no noise. Yet, it can be quite a powerful and debilitating presence in your life.

For years, I've wanted to be involved in community theater and for a short period of time I attended acting classes. It was fun and I really enjoyed it. However, when it came time to actually "act" or "speak" on camera, I stopped going to class. Throughout my life, this has been my modus operandi. I will enthusiastically pursue an interest and then only take it so far. My progress stalls. Something inevitably stops me from going to the next level, from being the best that I can possibly be, living full-out, going for it full-bore and unabashedly, pedal-to-the-metal, lettin' r rip and reaching for the stars! I've done it with my artwork and drawing. I've done it with my love of photography. I've even done it with my ballroom dance lessons. And, I've been doing it with my book.

I'm not sure whether to dub this book my memoir(s) or my autobiography. An autobiographical memoir? I don't know. The definitions via my Google search were not clear enough for me to decide. Or, is the sneaky fear mongrel throwing another cleverly disguised slow bump down to impede the release of my creativity unto the world?

Recently, the universe graciously responded to my request of bringing a book editor into my life: a very kind man who has offered to read my manuscript and edit it as needed. Or, in the alternative, he will direct me to an editor-type person better suited to my written works. I was supposed to have sent him several pages of my manuscript this past weekend. I have not done that—yet.

I've typed nearly 100,000 words in my book draft and it's not far from its completion. Although, it has become apparent to me that I may be looking at a series of books. You know, since it's based on my life and all. It's funny. It's heartbreaking. And, sometimes jaw-dropping. It contains many details of my life that I'd never told another living soul. Well, that is, until recently when I opened up to my loving husband, sharing some of those long-kept secrets.

I dream of my book's completion as well as its publication and release into the world for others to read, enjoy, scrutinize and even judge. What an unnerving feeling! Yet, it is one of my deepest desires. My story, my true story, may hold that single passage that helps another human being with their internal struggle, perhaps the one which no living soul knows about. I love this quote, "What people think of you is none of your business." Then, why do we care so much about something that is none of our business and allow it to hold us steadfast, merely one step away from realizing our dreams?

One morning it occurred to me: I can do this once, rip off that bandaid and say, "To heck with this fear," and ultimately silence it for good; or, I can live with this feeling every day—for the rest of my life—and continue to be held back, stuck, basically trapped by this invisible force, never growing, changing, or learning. Do you get that? I could live with it every day, that's 525,949.2 minutes each year—FOR THE REST OF MY LIFE—or, I could take that one freaking step, or a jump, just one single action that takes a whole millisecond and which could ultimately obliterate this fear-based barrier. There's only one first leap, and it is the hardest one. I believed that once I took that leap, opportunities and blessings would spring forth with as much force as a breaking dam. I would essentially be breaking the damn barrier, and be on my way to realizing my dreams.

I knew there was a good chance I'd look back at that hurdle and think to myself, Hmm, that wasn't so scary after all.

CHAPTER SIX

"Hey Ruby!"

"Your fear is like a mall cop who thinks he's a Navy Seal."
—THE BOOK *BIG MAGIC*

The bipolarity of nursing

You may have that one patient who is so lovable, so pleasant, and with whom you have such an amazing instant connection, you want to take them home with you. You think to yourself, "I'd happily take care of 20 patients just like her. She's just awesome!" You go home from your shift smiling. Content. For this is what nursing should be...always.

Tomorrow, you may have that one patient who's outrageously needy, constantly uses the call bell, and incessantly whines, making you think, "What in the HELL was I thinking?!!! I went to school... FOR THIS?!!! I must've been out of my mind!" Then, you drive home after your shift in silence. No radio. Nothing. The only thing you hear is the sound of the engine and your inner voice desperately contemplating a new career! Any career! Dairy Queen, perhaps!!

Last night I had that one DQ patient and tonight I'm blessed with the one I'd really love to take home with me. I'll be smiling on my way home in the morning. Awww, this is what nursing should be...always.

. . .

Memorable patients

Once, I had the privilege of taking care of a very elderly woman who was a breast cancer survivor. She told me that after she had her breast removed, she didn't look at her chest for a long time. She just couldn't. Then, one day, she finally got up the nerve to do it. She looked at the space where her breast used to be, and then looked at the remaining breast, just hanging there all lonely. But, instead of getting all torn up and crying over it, she decided to go another way. She said she grabbed a hold of that lone, saggy boobie and "twirled it in circles" as if it were a celebratory tassel!! I almost peed my pants! As if that wasn't funny enough, when I was helping her get dressed, she twirled that one remaining, lonnng, saggy boob—at me! I don't know if I'm scarred or blessed to have had that moment with her. Maybe it's 50-50. It did take me a while to finally write about it. She sure was a treasure of a woman with an amazing spirit.

. . .

A patient once told me, "For every minute you spend angry, you lose a minute of happiness."

. . .

I took care of an 85-year-old woman who did NOT look 85. She was just beautiful. She told me she'd been married six times. She divorced the first one, who was the father of her children, because he was a cheater throughout their 20-year marriage. After that she decided, "I will only marry men with prostate cancer, emphysema and (something else I can't remember) because they won't cheat on me." I got so tickled at that—we were both laughing. But, she was successful! She buried them all after caring for them at home and wasn't cheated on again.

. . .

One night, after I handed a sweet, elderly woman her cupful of pills to take, she looked up at me and asked, "Now, which one of these is going to cure me?" How can you not wanna hug her?!

. . .

Flashback to nursing school. In the first semester, you spend a lot of time in nursing homes getting hands-on patient care experience. I remember sitting in the lobby of this particular home beside an elderly woman who was obviously suffering from a bit of dementia. I'd watched her quite a bit that day so I decided to start a conversation. "What's your name?" I asked, and she responded, "Why do you wanna know my name?" I said, "So I don't have to say 'Hey you' when I see you." She said, "Oh. My name is Ruby." I smiled at her. Then after a pause she said, "But you can call me "Hey, Ruby." That'll stay with me forever. Hey, Ruby, I remember you! I hope you remember me.

. . .

Irony in nursing: A patient whose body is at least 50% covered in tattoos asking if you can "numb the site" before you start an IV. SMHWTTS (Shaking my head with tilt to side).

. . .

You KNOW you're a nurse when you can sand your own fingertips with an emery board (because you wash your hands a gazillion times a day) AND gauze pads or cotton balls cling to your fingers like they're Velcro!! Yes, I know *lotion lotion lotion*...a fat lot of good it does when you have to wash it off five minutes later. Just sayin. I do gob it on before bed though. Splitting fingertips are no fun.

• • •

A patient gave me the sweetest quote related to grieving the loss of a loved one. She heard it from a hospice nurse. "The greater the pain, the sweeter the memories."

• • •

A dear nurse friend of mine was called an asshole by an 80-year-old man for no apparent reason. Well, you know I had to add that to my own bucket list!

• • •

Note to self: I have now officially dug shit out of a constipated ass. My nursing career has reached its peak. Or maybe its deepest depth.

• • •

During one night shift, I was suffering from a severe case of constipation. I was literally "full of it," and my gut was quite unhappy with its tight quarters. I had complained quite a bit about my predicament to my co-workers, so much so I decided to put it to music. I sang this little ditty to the tune of Linda Ronstadt's song, "When Will I Be Loved":

"I've been cheated, been mistreated.
When will I take a dump?
I've been packed tight, just can't poop right.
When will I take a dump?"

. . .

Every now and then, you get that patient who, the very millisecond the anesthesia wears off, begins talking. And, they continue talking throughout their stay. They're still talking as they are being wheeled out the front door. I *LOVE* those patients!

. . .

My favorite question from patients: Do you know what time the doctor will be here?

Why, yes, we do. All of our doctors have a set schedule which they stringently adhere to ALL the time. And, they will be here, in your room, within five minutes of our paging them, every single time.

I totally understand their asking that question, but it's impossible to answer like 99.99999% of the time!

. . .

My dream job was out there and it found its way to me—I am a fart coach!

Did I tell you that I get paid to listen to people fart all day AND I get to cheer them on? Well, today there were two male patients in the recovery room with an empty bed and curtains between them. Bed 1 would fire off a round and then Bed 3 would immediately answer and best him, every single time. I'd say, "OK, what do you have to say about that?" Then, the other guy would fire back, trying his hardest to best the last guy. This went on for several minutes. Then, a new patient entered in Bed 2 who happened to be a woman. At first, she remained sleepy and quiet as the anesthesia was wearing off. But then, she awakened to the sounds of dueling butt trumpets firing back and forth in stereo around her. Being that I'd previously informed her that "releasing air" was her job and knowing that she was smack dab in the middle of these two men, I said, "OK, ma'am, what do you have to say to that?" Without missing a beat, she fired off her little blip and we all four enjoyed some uproarious laughter!! And, the three of them never saw each other the whole time. It was seriously the Budweiser frogs but with farts instead of burps!

Now, I ask you. Have I found my perfect job? Ya think?

Speaking of farts, they have always been funny in my family. I literally bonded with my dearly departed father-in-law over a fart. Yes. It's true! When we'd be visiting, he'd always ask me to "pull" his finger. Of course I'd do it and he'd reward me with an explosion. After some time, I started asking him to "pull my finger," but sadly, I never seemed to have one in the chamber. Then, one day, we were standing in my in-laws' kitchen. I was against the fridge beside my husband and my in-laws were in front of us. I felt a little something in my belly and I put my hand out towards my father-in-law and said, "Pull my finger." He pulled my finger and to my delight, I was able to reciprocate—finally! We had the longest and most robust round of laughter, and I don't think he could've been more proud of me! And, from that day, we grew closer. It was like I was one of them, at last. I'll never forget that day.

My father-in-law has been gone for years now and we still routinely dedicate our flatulence to him. We miss him dearly.

• • •

On Christmas Eve Eve, my husband inspired me to write this poem, because of a fart. Yes, inspiration via natural methane gas. I hope you enjoy it. I know my father-in-law would love it! Although this was before my fart coach career, I thought it pertinent to this section of the book as it relates to my long-time inflatuation, I mean infatuation with farts.

An Aromatic Christmas in Salvisa

It's the night before the night before Christmas
and in our country house
It's just me here with Papa and that sneaky pooping mouse

There are holiday tunes a playin' on the SiriusXM
Our Christmas tree just a twinklin' like the stars in Bethlehem

It's sixty-four degrees outside and I hear the thunder rumblin'
This is just too weird for me, the snow's supposed to be tumblin'

I'm a present wrappin' fool atop our cozy queen-size bed
Papa's makin' sausage balls 'cause our peoples gotta be fed

The house fills with the aroma of Papa's yummy creation
Then, he visits me in our bedroom to share his flatulation

I can no longer smell that wonderful aroma
Because his nasty garbage ass has put me in a coma

I manage to revive myself despite my recent plight
Amazingly, with just two hour's sleep since my shift last night

All in all, I cannot complain, though the
lingering smell's quite gruesome
For this is just an average day in this family we call Newsome

I hope this silly goofy thing brings a smile to your face
For some of you have lost what you simply can't replace

This is the first Christmas with your loved one no longer here
But, trust in your heart and know fully that they are always near

They wouldn't want you crying or missing the festivities
So go on out, go carolin' and look at some nativities

If you find the tears, well, they just won't stay at bay
Then, reread the first eight verses about my smelly day

Though the tears may still flow, it'll be for a different reason
Just think of me here in fartland through another holiday season

. . .

One special dinner spent with my family

My husband, our three kids and all five grandchildren. During our dessert, I looked around the table at all the people I love most in the world, my heart overflowing with warmth and devotion, when a thought occurred to me. You know one of those that comes charging out of your mouth like a t-shirt out of those cannons at ballgames. While I made eye contact with each of those precious people, I said, "You know, other than my son-in-law, all of this was made possible because of my vagina." Kyler was a young teenager at the time and I don't think I've ever seen him laugh so hard since that day.

CHAPTER SEVEN

FIVE NICE ASS FRIENDS?

"The 3 Cs of life: Choices. Chances. Changes. You must make a choice to take a chance or your life will never change."
—UNKNOWN

We all have a cross to bear

Yes, we all have a particular something, be it an ailment or imperfection, that we carry with us throughout our day-to-day lives. It could be asthma, color blindness, flat feet, eczema, poor vision, or a mental disorder (not talking about me). Well, you get the picture. Or, maybe you are perfect in every way in which case that would serve as your cross to bear: superior perfection. Hey, I didn't want to leave anyone out of that "We all" statement I typed at the beginning. I have a few crosses. I'll pause for just a moment while you compose yourself. Right there at the top of my list of crosses to bear is—hearing impairment. Frankly, hearing impairment seriously SUCKS!! I mean, it sucks through a tiny, tiny straw—which means it sucks extra, EXTRA extraordinarily super hard!

Speech contains a lot of high-frequency sounds and, lucky me, that's precisely the portion of the auditory system that I don't possess at all. If you look at my hearing test graph, the section for those high pitches is blank. No hearing ability was found there. What did you say? I can't hear you! And, while I do have hearing aids, they do not, let me repeat that—DO NOT—bring your hearing to the "normal" range or enable one to hear as if they had no impairment.

Yes, hearing aids do make speech louder and much easier to understand. Along with speech, however, they increase the volume of the wind, birds, humming fluorescent lights, the rustling of chip bags, tapping of pens, the squeaky wheels of stretchers moving down the hall, and the like. Those sounds, along with my favorite, the popping of gum, can be at such levels of audible annoyance, I want to take the aids out of my ears and stomp them into a pulp! What was I saying? Oh! If one more person asks me after I didn't hear what they just said to me, "Do you have your hearing aids in?" Aargh!! They are not a cure for hearing impairment, they're only a tool to help us cope as best we can, and some days I don't cope very well.

If someone is speaking to me, they must be facing me so I can watch their mouth move during our conversation. I can't communicate by reading lips alone, mind you, but seeing a mouth move during speech does help me to understand better. If you are talking to me, then turn around and walk away while you continue speaking, don't expect me to hear what you say. It's not happening. I envy people with normal hearing, primarily how they can be engaged in one conversation and hear something in another discussion and respond to it. I literally can only hear one speaker at a time.

It takes an incredible amount of mental energy to focus on hearing people speak to me or around me. It's exhausting. I used to fake it, years ago, and nod my head and hope it was appropriate to the conversation. Then, I graduated to telling them, "I don't have good hearing, so you'll need to face me and speak up if you want me to hear your words." Nowadays, I may do a little of both, or I may employ my third tactic—not listening. Honestly, I very likely miss out on 40-50% of what's being said to me or around me. And, whispers, I can't make out a single word of that noise. I tell people all the time, "Go ahead and whisper about me; I can't hear it anyway."

This cross has been with me, well, probably my entire life. Like, I've always had a hard time understanding song lyrics. While I know all the words to several songs, most often, I only know the chorus parts. Since the invention of the internet and YouTube videos "with lyrics," I've been able to sing along to a lot more songs. So, that's nice.

It's not all horrible—not being able to hear like a person with good, healthy hearing. Sometimes, it's a blessing. It's like on the Netflix series "Grace and Frankie," one of my favorite shows, when the hearing-impaired Frankie tells Grace, "I'm never getting a hearing device. I think I'm better off missing most of what you say." That, and as you can probably imagine, the things that I hear incorrectly are plentiful, daily, and at times, quite entertaining. Once, while watching TV with my husband, he quoted a commercial by saying, "Another day, another scratch." I responded, "Something's digging in the trash?" This man truly deserves a medal, a statue, or a holiday named after him. Most likely, all three! He deals with this cross of mine every stinkin' day of his life. Bless his heart.

Our granddaughter, Emily, once asked me, "Do you remember the [blah blah blah—words that I don't understand] Internet channel?" Okay, I thought, I've got this one. I questioned her with, "Daisy—does the Internet?" Surely she wasn't seriously talking about internet porn! Emily, being very used to Gammaw's mishearing her, said with a smile, "The Daily Dose of Internet channel." Shwoo…thank goodness it wasn't porn.

But, my favorite episode of "I can't hear you" would have to be a conversation I had with one of our grandson's while we were swimming. I knew Conner's birthday was coming up, so I asked him, "What kind of birthday [party] do you want?" He said something that I couldn't hear (shocking), and I said, "What?" He repeated his answer, which I still didn't fully understand, but I asked him, "Five—friends?" He again told me his full, entire answer (he was so patient), and I still didn't catch it. He repeated his answer, but just a little bit louder for his hearing-impaired grandmother. Not believing what I'd heard and being semi-reluctant to inquire further, I asked him, "Did you—just say—'Five nice ass friends?'" Visibly tickled, and through his giggles, he answered me, with extra enunciation and volume, "Five. Nights. At. Freddy's!" In my defense, all that could've been avoided if grandma could wear her hearing aids while swimming!

Yeah, hearing impairment SUCKS. It sucks through a teeny, tiny, minuscule straw!!

· · ·

Have you ever watched those videos of young children hearing their mother speak for the first time after getting cochlear implants? I've watched several and could not stop the tears from flowing each and every time. I hadn't imagined going through such an experience, but here I am, going through it. Well, not cochlear implants, but being hearing-impaired.

On March 9, 2021, I had an appointment with Miracle Ear. The hearing aids I have are 13 years old and they have never provided me with enough hearing improvement. I still struggled to hear what people were saying to me. Add in some background noise, music or others talking—forget it.

Of course, they gathered my history and asked questions about my current hearing aids. Then came the hearing test. I was placed in a tiny, soundproof room with a window and the technician sat on the other side of it next to the controls. He'd placed some tight-fitting headphones on my ears. He began the three-beep series of tones and I pushed the button as soon as I heard any of them. I already knew that I'd proven my hearing loss. I didn't expect it to magically get better.

After the hearing test was complete, the female technician performed this test: she covered her face with a folder as she spoke words and I was to tell her what I heard. The first time, with no hearing aids, I got 30% correct. With my old HA's, I got 40% correct. Then, with the new hearing aids in my ears, we did the test again. As she spoke and I quickly repeated the correct words back to her, I glanced at my husband who was visibly affected by what he was witnessing, and I got choked up and couldn't speak for a moment. It hit me just how much I haven't been able to hear throughout my life. We continued the test. When we were done, she tossed the folder on the desk in astonishment. I heard 90% of the words —I had only misheard one word —and that one word could have been during my momentary lack of speech.

They went over the results and selected a hearing aid for me to try. With both securely placed in each of my ears, I was amazed at how much clearer everything sounded.

She walked into the hall and spoke to me to see if I could hear her. I heard every word and responded to her.

Then came time to go over the big issue: cost. Of course, there are several tiers of hearing aids: okay, better, best, with best being the most expensive. She explained the different channels that the aids had in each tier. After going through all of the prices and features of each one, it came time to make a decision. Then, Greg said, "Honey..." and proceeded, "the way I see it, you want the best

—I want you to hear everything." My emotions overtook me as I placed my hands over my face and wept, unable to speak.

Note: They had to take back the test hearing aids and I had to put my old ones back in my ears when our appointment was over. We picked up the new aids the following Tuesday! A little known fact by the general population is that hearing aids do not give the wearer "normal" hearing. They enable the hearing-impaired, but never to the level of perfect hearing.

• • •

Daily life with hearing impairment

I was feeling a bit antisocial one particular afternoon when the Fedex guy knocked on our door, so I just didn't answer it. About 15 minutes later, I retrieved the customary sticky note regarding his attempted delivery from our door. Then, I felt bad for causing him a wasted trip and called FedEx customer service to see if they could possibly have him come back, if he wasn't already too far away. The kind woman on the phone said that she can only "request" that the driver come back to our house but could not "guarantee" that he would make it back today. I was okay with that and stated that if he can't come back, we'd just get the package tomorrow. While I had her on the phone, though, I asked if she could tell me who was sending me this mystery package, to which the kind woman on the phone said, "It's from out of the country. Glenmount." What the...?! Is that a country or a company name? Or maybe it's the name of my distant relative, Glen Mount, who's left me $1 million!! That'd be okay, right? After the call, I texted my hubby to inquire as to any online purchases he may have made recently. Nothing. I then immediately Googled the Glenmount name in hopes of finding a clue as to who sent me this mystery package and why. Nothing. So...I went back to my sorting and cleaning while waiting to see if the delivery guy would make it back to our house. A few hours went by and my curiosity and concern were now increasing by the minute. WHO is it from ANOTHER COUNTRY that is sending ME something? So weird! Before my concern morphed into a full-on hyperventilating panic, I decided to call FedEx one more time and get more information. I talked to a very nice woman named Tasha who was most pleasant and helpful. I said, "I called earlier today about a delivery attempt and they told me it's coming from out of the country? Can you tell me who sent it?" She said she could only tell me the company name and did just that. I immediately busted out laughing and said, "Oh my gosh! I was afraid it might be a bomb or something! Now I know where it's coming from, it all makes sense!!" She chuckled right along with me. I had misunderstood what the woman told me earlier. I heard, "Glenmount" when what she said was, "GelMoment." It's the nail polish I ordered from my daughter, Amber, to help her reach her sales goal and it ships from out of the country—Canada!!!

When hearing impairment and a lil paranoia meet, this is what you get!!!!

• • •

Phone conversation one night with my wacky Aunt Mary:

Mary: Do you go to bed pretty early?

Me: It varies. Last night I was up til 1:00 a.m. because I couldn't sleep. But, I got a nap today.

Mary: You took a laxative?!

YES, hearing impairment does, in fact, run in this family! What? Did you say something?

. . .

Me: When's your appointment?

Cassandra: Lol. 2:39

Me: 2:39??

Cassandra: 2:30. Didn't feel like correcting the stupid 9. But since I have to explain myself...in hindsight I should have taken the extra second to correct the 9 instead of taking a minute or two explaining that the 9 was a typo and I meant 0 so the appointment is 2:30 and I am still using my old-fashioned thumbs and not the keyboard so I will still occasionally have typos.

Me: What a timesaver!

Both: LOL!

. . .

Autocorrect fail!

Apparently, my Bluetooth earbud voice text has an even harder time understanding speech. What I said was, "He is where he needs to be." What showed up was, "He is risen and pooping."

. . .

Is it time for new glasses?

On my way home from work this afternoon, I drove by a church and read its billboard. It said, "Jesus is our reindeer." Huh? I thought that was a little strange. But, perhaps it's a metaphor for the Christmas season. Like Rudolph leading Santa through the darkness, maybe Jesus is the reindeer leading us through our darkness. I thought it was kind of a nice thought though. When I got closer to the sign, however, and could see it more clearly, I found that it said "Jesus is our redeemer." That makes a bit more sense, doesn't it?

• • •

One night I was bored with whatever I'd been watching and started channel surfing. I came across a show called, "The Foreskin," Wait, what?! I paged back up and reread the listing again. It was, "The Forsaken."

• • •

You know how when you're sitting at a traffic light in a busy inter-section you see those little handwritten signs stuck in the dirt, like for jobs, houses for sale, etc.? Well, I was sitting at such a light and saw a sign that said, "Massage the rapists." I was like, *what the heck kind of crap is that?!* Took me a few seconds to realize the sign said, "Massage Therapists." The proper spacing of words and letters is critical!

• • •

Colonoscopies: Well, lemme just tell you. That Suprep stuff is no joke. It'll definitely put your digestive system in fast-forward gear. The end result left my body with such force and determination, a powerful vortex was formed which caused all the toilets in our county to flush—simultaneously!!

• • •

WOMEN!!! This is what they don't tell you about getting older!

Your bladder becomes weaker and it is much, much harder to hold your urine! My smooth maneuver is when I'm in a store and get the sudden, emergent urge to pee. The restroom is, without fail, a good distance from me and I generally have about a 15 second window of time to walk as quickly as I can in its direction before I lose all control. What do I do while I'm speed walking through the aisles en route to the nearest potty and the bladder spasms return before I reach it? Well, obviously, I think, "OOOOHHH NO! I'm about to pee my pants!" But, that thought is immediately followed by, "Oooh, look at that item on the very bottom shelf that I simply MUST look at more closely." In those several seconds that I'm stooped down studying this irresistible product, my heel is strategically placed in hopes that it'll be a strong enough dam to prevent the peeing of my pants while I'm focused on regaining another 15 second window of time that I can, hopefully successfully, race to the restroom. All along with struggling to maintain my balance, as well as my dignity. And, let me tell you, I've looked very closely at some very strange products in these moments. Oh, and add in a few full-body shudders in there, too. Ladies, you know what I'm talking about, when you've held your pee for too long, your body starts to shiver, shudder and shake. What I must look like at these times! I suppose it's less embarrassing than wet pants and a puddle. Desperate times!

. . .

Your vagina dries out. You know how when you were young it was always moist and uh—ready? It was like having an open wound that drained continually, not to be gross or anything, but it stayed sufficiently moist, at all times. Well, when you're older than 50, those days are gone! That sucker is dry. I'm not talking you-may-need-a-little-help-with-lubrication dry. I mean it is so dry, you could use it to draw chalk outlines!

. . .

There is a restroom within our break room and one morning I failed to lock the door behind me after I'd entered it. One of my nurse coworkers opened the door while I was standing there, facing the toilet, with my pants down around my ankles. Now, obviously, this is not a normal thing to find a woman doing in a restroom, right? Well, she was shocked, to say the least, and quickly closed the door while exclaiming, "Wh—what are you doing?!!!" I didn't mutter a word in response and remained kind of embarrassed for the rest of the morning, avoiding eye contact with her whenever possible. Then lunchtime rolled around. I had to go to the restroom, again. This time, there were six nurses dining at the break room table, including the traumatized one. I jokingly said to her, "I'm going to the restroom. Don't come in this time." She giggled sheepishly and again asked, "What *were* you doing in there?" I didn't answer and continued into the restroom. When I came back out, I said, "Well, if you really want to know, I'll tell you." All eyes were on me and all ears were poised to hear what I'd say. I continued, "I had gone to the bathroom and was all done, but then my PT cream started coming out and I had to wipe it away." One of the nurses asked, "PT cream?" I replied, "Pussy Therapy. Mine doesn't do what it's supposed to do anymore." Well, I almost had to administer the Heimlich to a few of them as they nearly choked on their lunches. One nurse was so red I thought her face may actually bleed, and the others almost needed the crash cart because the force of their laughter stopped their breathing! Through my own laughter, I said, "Well, now it's coming out again," and I went back into the restroom.

. . .

Another thing that is never discussed is this, which you may have already surmised from my PT story. When you place cream inside of your vagina, it does not get absorbed into oblivion up there. No! It stays a while, does its duty, then it starts trickling back out.

Very slowly, over several hours. This is not a pleasant sensation! You know. Just FYI.

. . .

You will shrink. Not your body weight. That'll be a serious struggle that begins around age 40. I mean your height will decrease. One year, I had gone to my annual womanly exam where I was told I'd shrunk half an inch. What the...?! Next stop, the mammogram. "If they tell me I've shrunk a cup size, I'm gonna be pissed!"

. . .

The chemistry in your body changes. For years, more like decades, I used Secret powder fresh deodorant. I loved the subtle scent of baby powder when I'd raise my arms up. Ah, nice. Fresh. Well...I guess it was in my early 50s that all changed. Quite suddenly, too. You wake up one day, take your shower and don your favorite smells-so-fresh Secret deodorant and go about your day. You start to get little whiffs of something that doesn't smell quite right. You check your shoes. Did I step in something? You check your bloomers. Did I pee myself? Nope. Then, you figure it out. It's your pits!! That delightful, fresh, baby powder scent has now been replaced with Eau De CAT PISS!!

. . .

Oooh, I forgot to tell you. When the PT cream starts coming out, it does not like your body chemistry either so, oftentimes, it comes out with a funky smell, too. YAY! This aging woman's body thing just keeps getting funner, doesn't it?!

. . .

You won't only get hot flashes. Oh no. We've got to mix some cold flashes in there, too. Oh my gosh, I'm freezing cold to the point of shivering! I get cramps in my muscles from it. No wait ... just give it five or 10 minutes. There it is! There's the fever. Here comes the sweat. I'm not cold any more. Would someone please get me a %$&@#&'ing ice pack?!!!! And, No. I'M NOT HORMONAL NEITHER!!!!!!!! I'm sorry. Didn't mean to be so gruff. I can't stop crying!!!!! DAMN it really sucks to drive in Lexington!!!!! Nobody knows how to fucking drive!! Has anyone ever died from hot flashes? Now where's that freakin' blanket when I need it! How's your day going? Shit, it's freezing in here!

· · ·

To cope with my EXTREME hot and cold flashes, I've been driving with both my air conditioning and heated seats on full throttle. It's like baked Alaska in this car, but at least I'm comfortable, for now!

· · ·

Then, my hot flashes that went on a vacation sent in the night fevers and sweats to fill in for them. HOW VERY THOUGHTFUL!! Seriously, I could pop corn on the back of my neck! Anybody up for a movie?!

· · ·

Since my hysterectomy, at every annual visit my groin-o-cologist (what Dad called them) asks how my bladder control is doing. I guess it's common to have issues once the uterus is gone because it helps hold all your innards in place up there. I told him I have occasional leakage when I cough, sneeze or laugh hard or if I have to pee really badly. He asked if I knew what kegels were and I, of course, said I was aware of them. He suggested I do 30 a day in sets of 10 repetitions and said, "You can do them anywhere.

You could be doing them right now." I said, "I am doing them." He looked at me and I said, "I'm not really. I don't wanna make your job harder."

. . .

I drove through Starbucks yesterday to get a nice, icy caramel frappuccino. The young, friendly guy at the window, of course asked how I was doing today, etc. I said, "I'm hot. It's very nice outside, but for a menopausal woman, it's hot." He kinda had a blank gaze and I asked him, "You won't ask that again, will you?"

. . .

The joys of getting older AND all the things that NO ONE tells you you're gonna face! Things like sneak farts! Yes, those sneaky lil SOB's that come out of nowhere—well, they do come outta somewhere, but you know what I mean ... unannounced, with no warning whatsoever! Like, you're standing there, just having a normal conversation, and "BLIP" that sucker just pops on outta your rear! "Backblast area not all clear!!" Sorry, flashback to the army. Sometimes these sneaky emissions go unnoticed by others, but other times, you know they heard it, too. Around the right people, it becomes group laughter! Around others, a very awkward moment. So, what do I do in those cases? I just keep talking. Like Dory would say, "Just keep talking. Just keep talking. Just keep talking, talking, talking. What do we do? We talk, talk." I'm just waiting for the moment when this happens in front of a doctor. I've decided I'm just gonna steer right into that skid! After all, these sneaky SOBs will likely become more frequent. I'll just say, "Ooooh, excuse me, sir! That's just my motor starting without me again."

• • •

You may look in the mirror and suddenly notice things like—Was my nose always connected to my face this crookedly?!

• • •

You know you're getting older when you lay face down on the chiropractor's table and a little blip of a fart escapes your backside without your permission! Yep! The sneak fart escaped during a doctor visit. Oh joy! He didn't say a word. Neither did I. Let's see now. What's next on my bucket list of the embarrassing joys of getting older?

• • •

I was out shopping for a new swimsuit one day. I was getting increasingly frustrated because all I saw were walls and racks full of teeny tiny swimsuits that would barely (I mean barely) cover a real human body. This young guy was sweeping the floor near me and I asked him, "Do y'all have any swimsuits for people who aren't 17-year-olds with perfect bodies?" He was stunned for a moment, but then started to chuckle and look around the store as if he was going to help me. I said, "This really isn't your area, is it?" Though he seemed a bit uncomfortably twitchy, he replied, "No ... not really." I left him to ponder my dilemma and continued looking through the aisles. Finally, I found the older lady section where the swimsuits either have skirts or would otherwise respectfully and appropriately cover the body. I saw the young guy again and yelled, "Found 'em!!" He seemed so thrilled for my success in locating them! I tried on six different suits and one actually fit AND looked decent!! As I walked toward the checkout with my acceptable swimming garment, I saw the young guy again. I held up my swimsuit with pride and presented it like Vanna White uncovering the letters on Wheel of Fortune. I got a thumbs up! I bet he was glad to see me leave the store. Maybe I should go back and model my new swimsuit. That'd surely push him over the edge.

. . .

When something feels not quite right in your chestal region and you realize it's your nipple sticking out of your bra.

. . .

Note to my lovely daughters

In the future, when you are shopping for my Christmas, birthday, Mother's Day, or any other gift(s), please keep this in mind:

Any gift you give me of the knickknack sort, though they will be appreciated, treasured and displayed by me on a shelf, collecting dust for decades (because it is a gift; you thought of me; and, therefore, I MUST keep this trinket until I die), YOU TWO will be sorting through ALL those little pretties one day.

Think before you buy!

That is all. I love you both VERRRRRRY MUCH!

. . .

Daily life with ADD—Oh, look! SQUIRREL!!

I've now made two trips to the kitchen with the sole intention of taking my daily meds. So far, I've vacuumed the kitchen floor and rugs, loaded and started the dishwasher, washed some eggs and cucumbers before putting them in the refrigerator, wiped off the countertops and put some things in the closet for storage. Do you think I've taken my meds yet? Anyone??

FYI: When I become a millionaire, I'm hiring myself a personal assistant. All serious candidates are invited to submit applications to me!! Thank you.

• • •

Well, on the bright side—when you forget where you put things "for safe keeping" then later, you're looking for another thing and come across this other thing you'd forgotten you even had, it's like Christmas every day!! Today's find? A brand new pair of snow boots! Woohoo! GO, ME!!

• • •

If I could bank all the hours I've spent looking for things that I'd put away in my lifetime (often in "a safe place"), and use that time later in life, I'd live to be a freakin' 125 years old. Seeeeeriously!

• • •

How an ADD brain makes life interesting:
While sitting at my desk, enjoying my coffee and Facebook time one morning, I got up from my chair three separate times with the intention of retrieving a bag from my car. The first attempt, I ended up feeding the cats. Back to my chair. Second attempt, I started a load of vacation clothes laundry. Back to chair. Third time up, I was actually going to poop. Pooped. Remembered to retrieve the bag. Got the bag. Back to my chair. Nuttin like a good poop to clear your head!

• • •

I'm beginning to think that ADD and lack of gracefulness go hand-in-hand. One day, in a matter of a few hours, I'd managed to char some turkey innards, fall backwards and land on my back in the flower bed (Greg wishes he'd videoed that), and empty a whole folder of owner's manuals on the man cave floor. Think I'll chill here on the patio swing, play with my kitties and listen to the wind chimes. Seems pretty safe ... so far.

. . .

HOW A PERSON WITH ADD READS A BOOK IN 10 EASY STEPS:

1. Select a book. It can be paper or Kindle, matters not.

2. Find a comfortable, cozy place to sit down and read the book.

3. Read a chapter or two, then have the overwhelming feeling that you're missing something exciting somewhere else near you. Yes, you're definitely missing something during this reading time.

4. Put the book down and go investigate what you're sure you are missing.

5. Find that it's nothing.

6. Get distracted by any other thing on the way back to the comfortable seat and your book.

7. Hours, days, weeks, maybe even months go by and you still have not returned to your book.

8. Realize that you really do have the desire to finish the book you'd started. But, your comfortable seat is like the repelling pole of a magnet, preventing you from relaxing enough to sit still and focus.

9. Order the book on Audible so the author can read it to you through your Bluetooth earbuds while you do all the other things that distract you from sitting down to read an actual paper/Kindle book.

10. Actually finish a book, audibly. Happy girl!

. . .

I have an Olympus digital camera that I bought several years ago. It takes amazing pictures. However, when I started using it, I was immediately frustrated because it didn't have a built-in flash. No problem. I shopped on Amazon and ordered an external flash accessory. But, since I struggle to learn electronic things from printed instructions, I couldn't figure it out. Grrr! Frustrated that I could only use this camera in good, natural light, I bought a Canon camera that had a built-in flash mode. While this camera had a working flash, and it worked wonderfully, I wanted to learn all the ins and outs of the camera's capabilities. Yeah, those printed instructions are no help to me. Light bulb! I'll see if there is a Kindle book! Why I did that, I'll never know. It's more printed instructions. I didn't get very far and decided there must be YouTube how-to videos for this camera! Voila! I was ecstatic! In the first lesson, I learned things I had no idea the camera could do and I continued watching a few more videos. ADD strikes again. Squirrel?! No. Olympus camera. I decided to give it another try, only the battery was dead. Luckily, a few weeks prior, I'd ordered a new charging cord and extra batteries. I charged up a battery, put it in the camera and took a test shot out the window. Decent. Put it down, and finish my coffee. Picked up the Olympus again, turned it on and some setting selections popped up on the display. ARE. YOU. FREAKING. KIDDING. ME?! There it was, in front of my face, settings for FLASH MODE! I selected the setting while thinking, *I don't know how this'll work without the flash accessory attached, but I'll try it.* I looked around for a random item to photograph and push the shutter button. What the...? The BUILT-IN flash popped open and FLASHED when I took the picture! Apparently, it had a built-in flash which could be set to work automatically. THIS. IS. *MY.* LIFE.

• • •

I pulled up to the drive-thru window of Skyline Chili one afternoon to order my favorite treat. The girl who opened the sliding window had a confused look on her face and said quite blandly, "Yes...?" I thought to myself, well hmm, that's a little unfriendly. But, I proceeded to place my order anyway. She rang me up, took my payment then said, "Just so you know, there is a drive-thru over there," as she pointed behind me to where the menu and ordering speaker were located. Apparently, I was looking for a more personal, face-to-face kind of ordering experience that day.

• • •

I think a better name for opera would be "cornhole sonata," for it is the sound one makes when it goes in the wrong hole!

• • •

Note to self: When you paper-cut your lip while licking an envelope, your salad dressing will flat burn like fire in said cut.

• • •

When you have red ink on your fingers, because you're soooo very graceful with permanent markers, then you cough into your hand and think you're expelling blood!

• • •

Note to self: When you tilt your head back to put in eye drops, it helps to remove your glasses first. Need windshield wipers!

• • •

What the heck is a Vondonkey anyway?
Are you wondering where that funky name on my blog originated? Let me explain.

You remember way back in the late 1990's when "getting online" was all the rage and AOL seemed to be the most popularly chosen dial-up internet service? Dial-up, yeah, I can still hear that modem screeching like a cat being swung around by its tail. Well, it wasn't long before everyone in our family had purchased a computer, signed up with AOL, and in no time we were all enjoying the online chat feature. It was especially nice for me, being able to converse with my parents regularly without running up those pesky long-distance phone charges on the landline. We had push-button, corded telephones, too. Wow, so much has changed! And, you know, that "You've got mail" thing—it was pretty cool.

During this time period, I took a Florida vacation wherein I stayed with relatives who, of course, used AOL. I mean, why would they not? They invited me to set up a screen name under their account which allowed me to continue enjoying the daily chats with my parents during my stay. Wasn't that nice of them? Coming up with a screen name took me some time, though, because I wanted something really unusual. I don't remember why I didn't want to/couldn't use my regular screen name on their computer. Then it hit me. I'll use…"Bondon!" In the 1970's, when my nephew, Jeremy, was very young, he could not pronounce "Vonda" correctly. It would always come out "Bondon." So, there was my temporary screen name! I put the KY on the end to represent the great state of Kentucky where I've resided since 1987. Anyway, this Bondonky name, as it turned out, was not temporary at all. It stuck with me long after that vacation even though I no longer used it on AOL. Or anywhere else for that matter. However, through many subsequent online chats with my father, he slowly and very skillfully changed it to Vondonkey. I suppose he did it because it more closely resembled my real name, you know, with a V and all. My Dad did it! He was always doing silly things like that with names and words.

Now, thirty plus years later, I am still referred to as Vondonkey by many of my family members. However, these days it is more often said with a very heavy southern drawl, with higher pitch and major emphasis placed specifically on the "key" part. Like "Vondon-KEEEEEY!" Sounds like something from HeeHaw, doesn't it? Now you know the history of Vondonkey. Won't you sleep better tonight after having gained this knowledge? Ha ha!

• • •

My Train of Thought Done Left The Station
It's day thirteen, I need to blog
But my head seems in a fog
A power nap I tried indeed
And dreamed that I was smoking weed
I've not done that in 40 years
Though I can hear the hippies' cheers
It'll be legal one day you'll see
But don't you pass that roach to me
It made me restless years ago
And paranoid the cops would know
My train of thought done left the station
To an undisclosed location
Tomorrow is another day
Surely I'll have more to say
It could be funny or may be deep
Could be thoughts that rob your sleep
Regardless, you'll be entertained
My 10 plus readers who've remained

• • •

I'm a late bloomer

No, I'm not talking about the development of secondary sex characteristics, I was on time for that. I'm talking about current trends, popular movies, and the latest music, etc. For instance, ABBA was a huge sensation when I was in high school, yet I wasn't thrilled with their music at the time. Sure, I sang along when I knew the lyrics, but I'd do that with any song on the radio. Currently, I find myself in love with their music and the meaningful lyrics to each song. However, it could be connected to me attending two community theater productions of Mamma Mia last fall.

Y'all may want to sit down for this one: I have not seen the original Star Wars movie, or any of the sequels. Are you okay? Breathe!! Should I call 9-1-1? The movie premiered when I was in high school and I went on a drive-in movie date to see it. My boyfriend and I were lying on our stomachs with the hatchback open, our heads supported by our arms and our eyes glued to the big screen. We were ready to be completely mesmerized by this motion picture. Less than thirty minutes into it, I was completely bored, rolled over onto my back and proceeded to watch the real stars up in the sky until the movie was over. I'm pretty sure he forgot I was even in the car with him, he realllly liked the movie.

When Titanic was the motion picture of the moment, I didn't go to the theater to see it. I didn't watch it until a few years later on a VCR in the comfort of my living room. I knew one of the main characters died and I wouldn't watch it until someone told me which one. I don't normally want to hear any spoilers, but that time was different.

I haven't watched a single episode of Game of Thrones or The Walking Dead, or any crime drama series on primetime TV or Netflix. Pretty sure that's not going to change. No offense to anyone.

I guess it's that I'm not immediately interested in the next big thing or the most popular shows or movies. I march to my own drum in a state of sweet oblivion to the current trends, and may or may not catch up later. Can you visualize a comic strip of me doing that? I can. Ha ha. I suppose that's why the peer pressure in high school wasn't that effective on me. If I didn't want to "C'mon, just try it, you might like it," I simply wasn't going to do it. Maybe it's that I am a rebel—that is, according to an online personality quiz I took recently. Or, maybe it's procrastination, you know, those "I'll get around to sometime" and it may take a long while.

This is just me pondering on a Saturday morning, enjoying my daily cup of the juice of life, while swaying and singing along with ABBA on Apple Music.

"I believe in angels, something good in everything I see..."

• • •

Pet Peeves

If you are one of those people who stand in a checkout line for 10 to 15 minutes, while everything in your buggy (totaling 50+ items) is wrung up one item at a time, THEN you decide to go rumbling through your purse trying to find your money, please unfriend me on all social media. You people scare me!

• • •

Useless Amazon reviews!! I buy a lot of stuff from Amazon, I mean A LOT. With everything I consider purchasing, I will check the number of stars other purchasers have awarded the item and then decide on the best product to buy. I will always look through the 1 and 2 star reviews first because, most times, they're irrelevant a/k/a useless and can be disregarded. Now, let me tell you, reviews like, "It arrived quickly, but I haven't used it, it's still in the box," or, "I just started using it so I don't know how well it's going to work," and then giving the product 1, 2 or 3 stars is NOT helpful to anyone!! To review a product means, you know, you actually USED it and have an opinion based on your experience with it. Giving a product such a low rating without even trying it out first is not fair to the seller, the product or any future would-be purchasers and is 100% completely useless! STOP IT!

. . .

(This meme-making thing really gets under my skin!!)
Those who cannot spell or use proper words with punctuation should seriously STOP MAKING MEMES! So many messages are worthy of sharing, but I won't because it's against my grain to propagate this annihilation of the English language! Ugh!

. . .

Okay, let me just say, I love all my Facebook friends and I read as many of your posts as I possibly can on a daily basis. But, some of y'all really need to go back to English class. When I read through some of the run-on sentences, misspelled, misused and slang words, my brain feels like it's tripping down a flight of stairs! But, I still love you. That is all.

. . .

Memo!
TO: Meme makers around the globe

SUBJECT: Learn how to FREAKING SPELL!

High hopes for a productive day
When I woke up this morning, I had such high hopes for a

wonderfully productive day. As per usual, I started by brewing my one cup of coffee, placing it in the mug warmer on my desk and then I commenced checking in with my Facebook friends. All pretty standard stuff when I don't have to get up at 5:30 a.m. to go to work. Nice, peaceful morning. Ahh.

Before long, it was lunchtime and I made myself a keto pizza. It was delicious, but I only ate half of it. Then, I decided to go out into the big garage, where hubby was framing in his garage so it can be insulated and drywalled, to see if there was anything I could do to help him. There was not much I could do to help him in that department, so he suggested that I start clearing out the storage space above his man cave. I decided to have a look since I hadn't been up there yet this year. I climbed the steps to the storage area–the steps which have no railing for me to grasp onto–and proceeded to grab every board along my path so I could go evaluate the job that lay ahead of me. And, what a ginormous job it would be to clear out the space. Wow! Our crap had literally multiplied when we weren't looking. Where would I even throw the stuff that will be discarded? Should I throw it down below onto my hubby's current workspace? I think not. There's no empty space for anything up here, much less another pile. Heavy sigh. Feeling overwhelmed and totally defeated, I went back down the steps with no railing, again clinging onto anything I could along my path, and left the garage.

Back into the house I went. I know, I'll make our favorite desserts, I thought! We have two desserts which I make regularly–keto chocolate brownies and keto chocolate cheesecake, but now we have a newly added favorite–chocolate ice cream, also keto. All three of these desserts require baker's chocolate which is very difficult for me to break into small pieces with my hands. A couple of months ago, I came up with a wonderful idea. Eureka!! I can use my marble rolling pin to help me break apart the chocolate. I laid the unopened box of baker's chocolate along the crack between our stove and countertop. The stove is a bit taller than the counter, so it provides a perfect slope to the box of chocolate. Then I proceeded to whack it with the rolling pin in strategic places until the chocolate was in pieces. This method has worked absolutely fabulously every time and this time was no different. Then, I placed the rolling pin back on its designated hooks behind our stove.

Before long, the ice cream is in the freezer, to start its freezing process. The brownies are in the oven, doing their baking and now it's time for the cheesecake. This dessert calls for two boxes of baker's chocolate. I repeatedly whacked that first box of chocolate into crumbles, set it aside and started with the second one–the last box of chocolate that I have to whack today–then, BAM!!!! I missed the chocolate and hit my thumb instead, successfully flattening it between the rolling pin and our stove! While screaming obscenities in my head and in near tears from the pain, yet not willing to let the sumbitchin rolling pin defeat me, I finished whacking the chocolate into pieces before I slammed that rolling pin into its designated hooks behind our stove, secretly hoping it would be impaled, and assessed my injury.

My poor thumb had a nice, purple bruise on it. I felt it may have been broken, but I thought it was only deeply bruised and equally humiliated. It was a bit swollen and bending it was not an option at that point in time. It hurt to hold a plate, or my phone, and LORDY LORDY, I had to pull up my panties one-handedly when I went to the bathroom. But, by golly, those desserts were made and that there is proof that I was wonderfully albeit painfully productive that day!

. . .

Thinking about going keto, huh?

The first thing you need to know is that "eating keto" takes work! Real, physical labor type work, and I'm not talking about exercise. There are very, very few ready-to-eat foods in grocery stores that support this way of eating. Oh, there are several products claiming to be "keto-friendly" and they may contain fewer carbs than their regular versions; however, many of these products still contain too many carbs and sugars for the gung-ho keto enthusiast. You can't just walk down the aisles of the supermarket, pick things off the shelves, then toss them in your buggy. Keto-eating requires that you read the product labels to calculate sugars, fiber and net carbs, etc. There is a very high likelihood that you'll be required to do a lot of home cooking. I mean A LOT. It will take some truly dedicated effort to start and maintain this way of eating, but it is totally worth it, in my opinion.

My husband and I have been eating the "keto way" for a while now. He's lost 50 pounds and I've lost 20. Both of us have met and/or exceeded our ultimate weight loss goals and, with only minor, temporary fluctuations, we've kept our weight off. Keto works. It is not intended to be a "fad diet" that you'll follow just long enough to lose weight fast and then slowly return to your old way of eating. It is intended to be a lasting change in your diet, your new way of eating, your permanently adopted lifestyle. In time, the carb cravings fade away. The foods you eat are much more satisfying and you remain satisfied for longer periods of time between meals. We still enjoy all of our favorite foods such as pizzas, tacos, hamburgers, and even desserts, all of which would normally be loaded with carbs. Our foods are simply homemade, from keto-compliant recipes, and they are delicious!

Now, I have always loved sandwiches, and sandwiches require bread, right? Keto bread is not (was not at that time) available in any of our local grocery stores. But, for a month or two, I have noticed ads for cauliflower-based breads claiming to be suitable for keto. I've read the nutritional info as well as ingredients and they really do seem to pass the test for being keto-friendly. That's cool! However, they are ridiculously high-priced. Some flatbreads will cost you a whopping $2.00 per slice which would make for an extremely expensive loaf of bread, given the fact that the seller requires you to buy a minimum of four packages. Since I flat out refuse to pay $20 or more for a freaking loaf of bread—ANY bread—I was determined to find a recipe and make it myself.

There are hundreds of low-carb bread recipes on the internet and I've tried a few that call for coconut flour. Disgusting! I have two containers of this coconut flour that will not be used in this household again and are now free to a good home! Or, any home! I'm an almond flour fan, to the core. Months ago, I came across a recipe for Keto Cheddar Bay Biscuits, you know, like those yummy delights they serve you at Red Lobster. I make them on occasion and we've used them for tuna salad or turkey sandwiches, as well as for hamburgers. These biscuits are truly delicious and I think I like them even better than the traditional ones. Sorry, Red Lobster. Still, I wanted to find a bread recipe that was more like, you know, normal bread.

My internet search yielded two acceptable recipes for cauli-flower bread that I was willing to test. My first attempt is the one for which I already had all the ingredients. Have you ever chopped through a head of raw cauliflower with a knife? Little beads and clumps of this vegetable bounce and scatter everywhere. Well, except for the 10% that actually remain on your cutting board. Next comes the grinding, or ricing, of the vegetable in a food processor. Once the cauliflower is sufficiently pulverized to the consistency of mashed potatoes, it goes into the microwave for five minutes of cooking. After it cools enough so as to not burn you when you touch it, it's time to squeeze out as much moisture as you can by putting blobs of the minced cauliflower on tea towels, wrapping the blob, then twisting the towel as hard as you can. I'd prepared three tea towels for this twisting-squeezing fun and divided the cauliflower guts between them.

Tea towel #1: I molded the cauliflower guts into a nice ball in the center of the towel, twisted the ends around it and commenced the squeeze-and-twist while allowing the liquid to drip into the sink. Unbeknownst to me, this little tea towel had a lovely little hole in it. So, when I began twisting and squeezing the blob of cauliflower, its guts spat out of that hole like a giant, explosive zit, spraying all over the front of my shirt and then dripped onto the rug beneath my feet. Did I mention that the guts were still a bit hot because I'm too impatient to wait until they're thoroughly cooled off? I gathered up what I could save the hot guts from the clean part of the sink and returned it to the tea towel. I ignored the mess on the rug, to be dealt with later. Then, I grabbed a regular towel to reinforce the defective tea towel and continued my squeezing twisting fun. Once it was as dry as I could get it, I dumped it into the mixing bowl.

Tea towel #2: Twist. Squeeze. Cauliflower guts shot all over the front of the sink and my shirt—again. How on earth am I not seeing these holes?! Do I need new glasses already? Grab another regular towel to reinforce this mess, too. Squeeze. Dump in bowl.

Tea towel #3: Surprisingly, this one was in perfect shape and I had no issues with hot, explosive guts, whatsoever.

While I was cleaning up the mess from the cauliflower massacre, I rinsed out one of the tea towels so I could use it to wipe the counters. Forgetting about tea towel #1's explosion, I stepped right in the pile of cauliflower guts on the rug and proceeded to create little mashed potato looking footprints between the sink and the stove. Good times! Rinse out the 5 towels that I'd used to make this better-not-freaking-be-delicious bread.

I was secretly hoping this bread would suck so I wouldn't have to go through the tedious and very messy process of making it— EVER again. After the timer went off, I opened the oven door and poked a toothpick into the middle of the loaf which came out clean. I removed my masterpiece from the oven. I've got to say, this bread looked absolutely beautiful! The instructions said to let the bread cool completely before slicing. I actually followed this instruction. This properly cooled loaf of bread sliced perfectly. It is a denser bread and is more moist, similar to a pumpkin bread. I decided to toast a slice because the ultra-moistness kinda grossed me out, seeing as it was intended to be more like traditional white bread, for sandwiches. So, I browned a slice in a skillet. This extra heat changed the bread's texture to one resembling that of a pound cake. Though this bread is more dense overall, it was sturdy yet tender and, according to my carb-junky daughter, "It's really good! I can't believe it's keto!" I see some toasted tuna salad sandwiches in my future and maybe a grilled cheese sandwich, or two.

Moral of the story: It appears that I will be making this bread in the future. Dang it!! However, not before new tea towels have been purchased, I'll tell you that much.

. . .

I Hugged A Stranger Today

I saw her in the doorway
Tears streaming down her face
We were strangers to each other
Meant to meet here in this place

Others walked on past her
Without a word or glance
I simply could not do that
And decided to take a chance

I asked her politely
"Hello, are you okay?"
She said that she was fine
But, I couldn't walk away

Instead I walked up toward her
Around her my arms did go
I hugged her warm and gently
I cared and she should know

We didn't exchange a name
And went our separate ways
But my life felt much fuller
I hugged a stranger today

Occurred: 12-1-17
Written 12-10-17

CHAPTER EIGHT

WELL...WHY NOT?

"I needed to lose you to find me."
—SELENA GOMEZ

Today is the day—I'm the driver of this bus now

Selena Gomez, your song Lose You to Love Me has inspired me.

Today is the day that I give up resistance. Anxiety, I no longer resist you. I surrender the fight to keep you quiet. Fighting you has only proven to increase your strength and keep me stuck in a recurring, non-progressive pattern. You no longer have a front-row seat on this bus. I accept you. I see you. Yet, you no longer have the power to stop me in my tracks. Anxiety, you are welcome to come along with me, but today is the day you cease and desist your debilitating presence in my life. My life is mine. From now on, you must sit in the back of the bus. I have given your front-row seat to faith. I have faith that I can achieve my dreams.

Recurring, negative memories of the past which have haunted me for decades, kept me awake at night, and have been a roadblock to living my life fully, I surrender. I will no longer fight to quiet you. I accept you, all my negative memories. I see you and acknowledge your presence, observe you and let you pass on through me. You no longer have the ability to send me through a downward spiral of regret, shame, self-condemnation, sadness, heartbreak, and dread. My past will always be a part of me, of course. However, today is the day that my past relinquishes its ability to affect my day, my life, my future. Yesterday is gone. Reliving the same memories day after day only keeps me stuck in the past—a past that cannot be changed—no matter how many times I relive in my mind. You, too, have lost your front-row seat and must sit in the back of the bus. I have given your seat to acceptance. I accept myself for who I am, flaws and all. I accept that I am worthy and I am enough.

Today is the day that I let go of guilt and resentment, and practice forgiveness. Guilt has plagued my conscience through-out my life. I now see all events as opportunities and/or necessary building blocks for my personal growth. I forgive those who have treated me poorly and have left scars within me. The scars of the past are now my badges of survival, proof of my inner strength, and I am thankful for them all. Guilt and resentment, you must sit in the back of the bus now. I have given your seat to forgiveness. I forgive myself for my mistakes, my wrongdoings, and the pain I have caused others due to my poor choices. Today is the day that I forgive those who have hurt me, abused me, or otherwise dam-aged me. All is forgiven.

Today is the day that I acknowledge my fear and give up the lifelong fight to silence it. Fear will remain a passenger in my life's journey; however, it is no longer fighting for the driver's seat, shout-ing directions, demands, and "You can't" or "You're not worthy" into my ears. Fear, you are welcome to come along with me on my journey. However, today is the day you cease being the squeaky wheel that gets the grease, stopping my progress. You, too, must sit in the back of the bus. I have given your front-row seat to courage.

I have the courage to acknowledge my fear and continue to forge ahead anyway.

To my anxiety, memories of the past, guilt, resentment, and fear: You must know this. You are no longer in control of my life's journey, impeding the progress towards my dreams. You can scream, shout, stomp, and throw an absolute fit, but I am progressing anyway. If you insist on being present, you're going to have to hold on and prepare yourself for a ride. I am realizing my dreams, with or without you. Oh, I fully expect you to come at me with your hurricane force, fighting to stay alive and in control of me. No CEO or president wants to lose their ranking as head honcho, after all. I will hear you, but your message will flow right through me. Like a summer breeze through a screen door, no remnants of your messages will remain.

And, all those empty seats between the front rows and the back seats? Well, they will be filled with my realized dreams, my new adventures, and all the wonderful memories throughout the rest of my life. Faith, acceptance, forgiveness, and courage are my A-team and we've got a lot to accomplish.

I am the driver of this bus now!

· · ·

Passions and dreams: Are they the same?

When I'm writing, I get completely lost in it. It's like Calgon has truly taken me away. It's—it's...transcendent. There's the word! That's something else I've learned through television. With the help of the Netflix series, Grace and Frankie, I have learned a lot of new and exciting vocabulary words. Words like *transcendent* and *ubiquitous*. Now that latter one is a really cool word, isn't it? I was super proud of myself for spelling it correctly when I looked it up online because, of course, I had no freaking idea what it meant.

Did you stop reading so you could look up the meaning of it, too? I have a spiral-bound notebook where I log my newly discovered television words. At this moment, I'm not exactly sure where that notebook is, but I have it here—somewhere.

A dear friend once asked me, "How do you know when you found the right guy?" My answer to her was, "When you no longer have to ask that question." So it is, I've learned, with finding your life's passion. I'm not talking about romantic passion. I'm talking about the passion you feel when you're doing something you really, really enjoy doing…eh, I guess that could mean both kinds of passion. Let me clarify, when you're doing something that could be your life's work, your career. Umm, well that could be even clearer still. It's when you are doing what you are called to do, the greater purpose for your life, be it the job or creative endeavor that truly sparks the joy within your heart. That's better.

You would think that finding your life's passion would be very easy, a no-brainer, that you'd instinctively know the answer to the question, "What is your passion?" But for some, that is not the case. It's apparently such a common subject for our human brains to wrestle with that scads of books have been written on the subject. I personally have read and/or listened to such books while discovering my passion(s).

Photography is a passion of mine. Wherever I am, or whatever I'm doing, I continually frame pictures in my mind and think, *That would be a great picture*, while snapping the photo in my brain (sometimes blinking my eyes like Barbara Eden on the 60's show, I Dream of Jeannie). When I look back through the pictures I've taken over the years, and there are literally tens of thousands, maybe even more of them, everything around me fades away. It's just me and those precious fleeting moments, captured and frozen in time with the click of a shutter button. I just had a mental image of me sitting in a zen posture, floating up above the clouds, everything around me is white, and I'm flipping through stacks and stacks of pictures. What exactly is in this Starbucks vanilla coffee anyway?!

Paraphrasing definitions from the internet: A dream is a vision or goal that resides in your brain. Passion is doing something you love again and again with ease and without getting tired. A dream may be pure fantasy, but passion is always real. I think that the two can sometimes be melded together. In 1982, the first of two times that I was approached regarding the Amway multi-level marketing plan, the presenter asked me, "What is your dream?" I said, "I want to live in the country, in a house up on a hill, with bay windows, a long driveway, a pond and a barn full of cats." Do you know where I live now? I live in the country with a wonderful husband whom I've been with since 2002. Our house is up on a hill. We have bay windows. Our driveway is about 600 feet long. We have a pond between our house and the main road. I also have nine cats who have a cushy space in our pole barn which I've named "the kitty condo." Don't tell me that dreams are just in my head. I've lived it. It may have taken me 20 full years, and one hell of a wild ride, but by golly, it sure came true, and with exquisite detail.

I've also had the wild dream of having Ellen Degeneres and Chris Tucker teach me to club dance. My favorite part of Ellen's talk show is her dance intro and I've watched the movie "Rush Hour" more times than I can count, mostly for the musical scenes where Chris is jamming to tunes in his car and such, but I laugh throughout the movie every single time. A little voice may occasionally whisper to me saying, "Yeah, right, like that'll ever happen. Chris and Ellen teaching you to club dance? Dream on." I simply answer with, "Well..why not? Did I tell you about where I live? It can happen!" Dreams don't just reside in your brain. They can and do come true! I'm passionate about my dream of being a published author, and it's on its way to being a reality. See? The two do go together.

When you're doing something that is in alignment with your passion, you'll be thoroughly engrossed in it. It comes easily and you don't notice the passage of time. You may forget to eat. I always thought, how the heck can someone forget to eat? Do you just not get hungry? Well, I can now say that I've done it. I have forgotten to eat while I'm writing. I have a potentially embarrassing confession to share with you. I have spent entire weekends sitting at my computer, completely focused on writing my book, barely eating, only leaving the house to feed the cats and chickens, and totally without showering. Do you know where the bridal bouquet tradition originated? Brides would carry strong smelling flowers, in part, to help mask their body odor. Daily baths were not a common practice way back when. Hey, at least I didn't pee in mason jars and line them up against the wall, and since my hubby has a man cave, he did have an escape from my potentially pungent aroma.

I worked on one blog entry for five hours and it felt like 30 minutes. Although I spend a crapload of that time reading, rereading and editing what I've written, the whole process seems to flow from me quite naturally. It's like I'm the instrument for something much larger than me. That may sound super cheesy and/or flaky, but it's the best way I can describe how writing makes me feel. The joy I experience when I'm writing, well, there are no words. No pun intended. You know, no words for the words I'm typing. I know, I'm silly.

Every day I ask, "What will I write about on my blog today?" Every day, I am answered. It may be a fragmented answer, sometimes it's a single word, like passion, that pops into my head. I'll take it, sit down in front of my computer, and just start typing. A word here and there. The next paragraph may be just a few sentences followed by a string of equal signs, my cue that I need to fill it in later. I just keep typing, editing, and rearranging until I think it will make sense to my readers. It's been pretty cool, so far, this whole blogging thing.

Hey, guess what! While I was searching for something else, I found the spiral-bound notebook which contains my list of vocabulary words!! Life is good.

• • •

Live your truth.
During a December weekend, I watched two Dolly Parton Christmas specials. The first one was her movie, Coat of Many Colors, and the second was her singing Christmas songs for an hour. I'm generally not a crier, and do not cry easily, but each of these specials brought forth an unstoppable stream of tears that flooded my cheeks and soaked my t-shirt. Conversely, those tears seemed to have opened a new door in my journey toward self-discovery and spiritual growth.

After a therapy session, wherein I shared about my weekend sob-fest, I became very curious about this iconic woman named Dolly Parton. I wanted to learn more, so I listened to a podcast wherein Brené Brown interviewed Dolly Parton, her lifetime hero. During the interview, Dolly mentioned that women should "live their truth." That got me thinking, What is my truth? Am I living it? How do I know if I'm living it?" I assumed that if I were living it, I wouldn't have to ask that question. Right?

While composing a blog post on the subject, I googled, "what does it mean to live your truth." The top hit read, "To live in your truth simply means to live as your most authentic self, doing things daily that bring you happiness and joy, living as true to yourself as possible." (https://www.thejournallife.co.uk/blog/ live-in-your-truth-and-be-your-most-authentic-self)

Okay, then. How do you know that you're living true to yourself? Am I living my truth?

I asked Google, "how do you know you're living your truth," and this was the top hit: https://www.lifehack.org/articles/ communication/10-signs-that-youre-leading-life-that-true-your-self.html, which is a straight-forward list of signs that you are living your own truth. While I do identify with some of the things on this list, reading through the items has shown me the areas which could use some real improvement in living my truth, full out.

I kept thinking, "At my age, *shouldn't* I be further along in my awakening journey?" My therapist taught me that this "s" word is a no-no and only serves to make us feel unworthy and undeserving, as well as like a defeated failure because it focuses on our mistakes or shortcomings. Yet, that word still pops into my thoughts from time to time.

Do you ever feel that everything in your life is NOT what you thought it was? Like, those around you see something in you, know something, but no one ever tells you and that if they did, it could be the golden nugget of information that opens up a whole new world for you? Then, at times, you realize some of these things and wonder if everyone else knew all along and just never told you? I know that's a lot of run-on nonsensical words, but it's hard to put this thought/feeling into words. Okay, say you're in the process of self-discovery, have an epiphany or revelation and are completely blown away by it. However, those who know you best already knew that about you, all your life, and were waiting for you to see it for yourself? Like when Dorothy awakened from her dream and realized that her "over the rainbow" had existed all along, in her own backyard. <—It still doesn't sound the way it feels in my brain.

However, surely a few of you know precisely what I'm talking about, having experienced it yourself.

Earlier this year, I had a free 15-minute personal critique via Zoom with Cristian Mihas, a blogging expert whom I discovered on Medium.com. All I wanted from this session was to hear his opinion about my blog, along with his suggestions for its improvement. He told me I was the only participant who didn't ask how to make money from blogging. Then, he paid me the most profound and touching compliment. He told me, "You are unapologetically yourself." Maybe, just maybe, I'm living my truth a little more than I think/feel I am?

. . .

Even funny people have their struggles

Sometimes in life, our burdens, worries, past regrets and mistakes, secrets we've kept, the peace that we've strived to maintain, can join together into a massive boil that must eventually burst open like an explosive, volcano erupting—regardless of how hard you've tried to avoid it, block it, or totally deny its existence. The truth pours forth with such force that it can no longer be avoided. It says, "Here I am. Now, deal with me." It can catch you off guard, rearing its ugly head right in your face at an inopportune time. Or, you can search it out and face it in your own time. But, eventually—it's going to happen. Let it. It's messy. It's unpleasant. It hurts. It's nasty and it just plain sucks!! But, once the purging occurs and you accept the truth and finally let it go, there is a sense of peace. An inner peace that is just as powerful as the necessary eruption that preceded it.

The phrase, "What you resist persists," is 100% accurate.

This is not an attempt for sympathy. I have no need for it. If one person reads this and sees themselves in my words, I encourage you to face your own volcano so your inner peace may take its place.

My heart is full.

. . .

What if..you DO IT ANYWAY?!

I must tell you—when you decide to do something creative, and put it all out there for the entire world to see, it can create quite the uncomfortable sensation within you. It's like you are standing in the middle of a crowded, busy city street, totally naked. All of your flaws are just hanging there, or sagging there, as the case may be. Nothing is hidden any more, no longer cleverly concealed by your exterior camouflage of cute clothes, long t-shirt, pretty jewelry, shoes or makeup. Your every scar, mole, oddly shaped body part, your crooked toe, along with all the things that are beautiful about your body are all right there, totally exposed. Let the brutal scrutiny begin!

One thing I have learned in my 60 years on this earth is that no matter what you choose to do with your life, your job, what you say, wear, drive, think, feel, write, draw or cook, there will always be that someone who doesn't like it, doesn't support it, is totally against it, or who will seek only to rip you and your dreams apart because they cannot fathom anyone being happy or succeeding in life while they are so completely miserable in their own. Anything you do in life, your creative ventures included, will face this brutality. Some people will like what they see. Some will not. All you need to do is read a few posts on Facebook to see this is true. There's always that one, isn't there?

Yes, the positive feedback is much easier to digest and makes us feel good, appreciated and valued. Of course it does! This feedback is very comforting and can keep us plodding along when we've had thoughts of just giving up. The negative ones, of course, can make you feel like total crapola, a failure, a dud—if you let them. I've been writing in my blog for what, two months now? My purpose in writing it was and is to entertain, make people laugh, smile, or just think a little more deeply. All positive goals, right? Yet, I have received some very negative, non-constructive comments on my posts, such as, "We don't care," and "It's called life. Get over it."

Well, as I see it, a negative reaction is still a reaction, an acknowledgement that what I wrote affected another human being, right? I could take these comments to heart, close my blog, huddle in a dark corner, hugging my legs toward my chest, my knees supporting my chin, and vow never to write a blog, or even finish my book, never opening myself up to this type of harsh scrutiny and humiliation again. Yes, I could do that. What would that accomplish, really? Why would I allow the 2% of negative comments have more importance or power than the 98% positive ones when I also have the choice to use these acidic, razor sharp comments to spur me forward, continuing towards my dream without regard to these speed bumps and potholes and daggers that are spewed at me by unhappy, negative people.

When you've chosen a path in your life, something you have been called to do, your life's passion, you will know it, without a doubt. Then you will—I mean inevitably—be faced with snags, bumps, road blocks, negativity, and the like, and you may feel that maybe you're doing the wrong thing after all, pursuing your dream or goal. All of these seemingly dream-crushing things are merely concrete proof that you are on the right path and that you need to do it anyway! It's during these times that many will give up. Just think. Without those who have continued without regard to opposition or failure, imagine all of the inventions which wouldn't exist today. The light bulb comes to mind. 10,000 failed attempts.

One doggedly determined, and doggedly criticized, inventor who did it anyway.

I am very appreciative of those who have encouraged me to keep writing. My family, my friends, and the strangers who've responded to my blog and/or Facebook posts. I thank you all. But, now, I'm also appreciative of you nay-sayers out there, too. You, my non-supporters, also help to keep me reminded—I am on the right track—and, well you just pressed down on the accelerator for my writing, and I thank you!! I must be doing something right and I appreciate your reminders!

What if I write it anyway? Let's find out!

• • •

Hey, you. Yeah, you. Choose you!

Do you know what it's like to be chosen last in gym class? It's extremely humiliating to be the last student standing there, unchosen, knowing you're basically the leftover who'll be thrown in with the team whose turn it is to gain a player. That was me, a time or two. It's such a cruel way to divide into teams, don't you think? On the other hand, this could very well have been a lesson for life.

Do you know what it's like to have a "friend" snub you when they're in the company of a certain other friend? I do. When I was in elementary school, I had a great friendship with one of the neighborhood girls. She was a good friend and we had a lot of fun together. That is, until she had a certain other friend visit her. I remember walking down the sidewalk alone and they'd be walking down the sidewalk on the other side of our street. Oh, how I longed to be asked to join them. They were having such a good time smiling and laughing. But, no, that didn't happen. I didn't get chosen, on multiple occasions. You would think that this type of thing would be restricted to childhood, but I've experienced this same situation well into adulthood.

Do you know what it's like to not be asked to dance? It's basically the pick-a-team in gym class all over again. Except, this time, you don't end up on a team by default. You just end up not dancing.

Do you know what it's like to smile at someone and not have it returned? I can't imagine anyone not having had this experience. There are a lot of unhappy people in the world and some will actually get irritated when another person tries to rain a little bit of sunshine on them. Continue to smile anyway.

Did you answer "Yes" to any of these questions? Well, then I'm talking to you. Guess what. That was the other person's choice, not yours. But, it hurts your feelings at times, doesn't it? Just because they didn't choose you, doesn't mean you're not worth choosing, because you are. You are worth choosing.

When it comes down to it, we are born into this world alone, and we will leave this world alone. Think about it. We are the sole passenger in our life's journey. We're the only one we have with us from start to finish. Every second, minute, year, or decade. So, don't you think it's time we choose to be our own best friends, first? So, you choose you.

It is in our nature to seek out, and sometimes crave, human connection. Along with that, sadly, comes the possibility of rejection. I have certainly experienced my share of it throughout my life and I learned how to handle it long ago. It's quite simple: I just keep being me. Some folks will like me, some folks won't, and that's okay. It doesn't change who I am.

Although I possess a very outgoing and friendly personality, and I'm generally a likeable person, I am still often surprised when a new acquaintance really likes me. Isn't that strange? I've been thinking about this for some time now, trying to make sense of it. I've boiled it down to this: I am genuinely happy in my own company. There is no pretension. I am what I am. What you see is what you get. I will strike up a conversation or crack a joke with anyone, anywhere. I'm just being me.

I've been in a kind of solemn/inner-reflective mood lately and just wanted to share these thoughts with you. Maybe they will resonate with the someone(s) who needed to hear them. Enjoy your own company. Be your own best friend. Just keep being you. Be happy with yourself. This may lessen the sting of any future rejection you encounter.

And, of course, cherish the precious people in your life who chose you, too.

· · ·

When I looked into my younger eyes

Throughout the decades and my multiple failed marriages, I would still draw a little bit, now and then. I always loved to draw eyes, so there are countless pieces of scratch paper with a random, single eye drawn on them, scattered throughout my many boxes of accumulated life crap. But, I hadn't done much in the way of a complete drawing or sketch. Perhaps I'd lost the talent, or the desire to pursue it. I don't know. I'd often wondered what happened to it. Did I lose the inspiration or passion for art altogether?

At the time of writing this, I was working on emptying my parents' house so it could be sold, the final and most difficult task in handling my parents' estate. I was cleaning out the attic and came across a stack of artwork. I knew it was mine because I'd remembered my mother telling me I needed to retrieve it and take it home with me, many years prior. I'd never gotten around to it and had assumed that it had been disposed of and was long gone. Thus, it faded from my memory.

Needless to say, I was thoroughly elated to find that it had not been discarded and immediately pulled it from the attic. I started flipping through all the drawings and I was stunned. I didn't recognize any of these drawings. There were pencil sketches, paintings, and watercolor pieces. It felt like I was looking at someone else's work, yet my name was on every page. I had no memory of drawing the sketches I was seeing. Whose artwork is this anyway, I thought, it must not be mine.

Though disappointed, I kept looking through each piece when I came across a portrait of a young girl. I paused for a long time, staring at it and wondering just who the girl was who posed for this portrait. You could see the sadness in her eyes and she kind of resembled Amanda Bynes. Then, it hit me. It was me.

After I stared at my self-portrait for quite a while, I continued paging through one incomplete drawing after another, and then memories of art class began trickling back into my brain. I remembered doing this black and white painting of a pot of gold and how every time I showed my progress to my art teacher she had me change something. I ended up not liking the painting at all. Even though I received an "A" it wasn't the vision I had for my completed work. It wasn't my version of perfect.

I moved on to the next piece, and then I started to remember being that 17-year old aspiring artist in high school and how I felt that none of my drawings were good enough. If I couldn't make it look the way I wanted it to look, I just wouldn't complete the drawing. Instead, I would start a new one, hoping it would be a work worthy of my stamp of perfection. Looking at those incomplete drawings with my older eyes, I could see how much talent I truly possessed. These drawings were really good! Why was I so hard on myself back then? More importantly, do I still possess any of that talent today?

With all these memories having been reunited with my near 60-year old brain, I returned to that self-portrait for another glance. This time, however, as I looked into my younger eyes, I was completely consumed by an overwhelming and indescribable feeling. It was as if I'd gone back in time and was reunited with the 17-year old girl in the portrait. The girl I'd turned my back on, left behind and had long since forgotten about. I could almost see her reaching her hand out to me and saying, "Come on. We're not finished yet."

Tears filled my eyes as I realized how much of a detour my life had taken. Don't get me wrong; it was my own life choices and decisions that led me down a different road than was originally intended. And, it's OK. I'm not expressing regret or blame here. It's just that the 17-year old me, and today's me, well we have much more we want to accomplish in this life. My life. It's time for Vonda's life now.

And, I've learned something. Even though I'd read it several times, heard it in various movies, read it in books, etc., it just wasn't something I could accept and do: You've got to embrace your past. You've got to make friends with it. Accept it. Be proud of it. I had spent literally decades denying it, pushing my past back in the recesses of my mind, the whole ignore-it-and-it-will-go-away tactic. That does not work. "What you resist persists," as I'd read in one of my many self-help books years ago. But, once you do it, really do it, you are free!

Once I'd left my childhood home at 17, I left my 17-year-old self there, too. That wasn't me any more. Her secrets, her shame, and bad memories were hers and hers alone. They had nothing to do with me, so they stayed behind—in that attic, trapped in the many pages of unfinished artwork—forever. It doesn't work that way. The more you deny your past, the stronger it holds you back in life, keeping you from growing, progressing and realizing your dreams. It will follow you, stalk you, and haunt you until you turn around and proudly say to its face, "OK, past. I acknowledge your presence. You are a part of me. I accept you completely. When we walk together, you can do me no more harm. You are my friend. Let's move forward now. We are not finished yet. I love you."

. . .

I should. I need. I am.

I should write more, like every single day. I need to write every day. I'm just going to challenge myself to write every day for 30 days. Maybe that will get me into the habit.

I should attempt to increase the traffic to my blog. I need to find a way to share my blog with more people. With a helpful suggestion from my magical friend, Linda, I've joined several Facebook groups that allow the sharing of blog posts, which have significantly increased the daily number of visitors to my site. I am getting more traffic to my blog.

I should exercise during this shutdown since the "I don't have time" excuse is sufficiently null and void. I need to exercise; I'm getting so out of shape and out of breath more easily. I am going to exercise.

I should finish listening to that Audible book on figuring things out on the journey toward your dreams. I need to finish that book. I am going to finish that book.

I donned my walking shoes, strapped on my iWatch, and went out the door. I gave myself a goal of 30 minutes. First, I trekked up and down our hilly driveway. That felt so good, I continued my walk around our property, to the pond, and down our street. All the while, I was listening to my Audible book through my single earbud. When I made it back to the house, I had walked 1.54 miles and brought two passengers with me—ticks! Ick! Ick! Ick!!! But, I am exercising, and I am finishing my audiobook book.

When you say, "I should" to yourself, you've already accused yourself of not doing something you feel you ought to, and you've just called yourself a failure. "I need" gets you a little closer to the ultimate, "I am," and just doing it. You have to figure out the how part! Whatever it is. Or, maybe it's the why part that you need to figure out. Why? It will make you feel incredibly, amazingly, wonderful that you did the "something" that you thought you should and needed to do—that's why!

. . .

Patience...or, what I refer to as the "P" word

I'll start with this: My husband has told me many times, "Patience is a virtue." This is like telling a hysterical and emotionally unglued person to just calm down. Works great, am I right? Not! My typical response to my husband is, "Well, I never claimed to be virtuous." Patience is not one of my virtues although I strive to improve upon it every day–I really do. That being said, I have a few thoughts on the subject.

If you're driving 10-20 miles below the speed limit on a 2-lane road and there are cars lined up behind you as far as the eye can see, you are an inconsiderate jerk! Pull over and let others pass. Yes, you have the right to drive slowly if you choose, but we also have the right to do the actual speed limit–sometime today! To the elderly man who lives near us who routinely drives 25 mph on our country roads, I sincerely apologize. I'm striving to do better.

If you are one of those people who drives the exact same speed as the car in the other lane, right beside you, thereby blocking every other car behind you, both of you are jerks! I have no apology for you right now, but I'm striving to do better.

I have a confession. I am an impatient driver. I apologize right now if I've ever cut you off in traffic, honked or flipped you the bird. I'm striving to do better. Seriously, I am. There are days when I have the purest of intentions to drive only the posted speed limit, to not pass a single car, and to enjoy a nice peaceful drive to my destination. I have, I'm proud to say, actually achieved that goal- like 4 and 1/2 times.

If you are one of those people at the grocery store who waits until every one of your 124 items are scanned and placed in bags before you even begin to remove your payment method, you are a jerk! I apologize to those of you who must do things in a certain order for your emotional stability. I'm striving to do better.

If you're one of those people in the drive-thru line who pull forward 6 feet and then stop to check your food order, you are a jerk! I mean, seriously. You're too far from the window at that point to even attempt backing up if you find your order to be incomplete. That, and the car behind you is about 9 inches from your bumper, and the car behind me is 9 inches from my bumper, and so on and so on. Get out the way, park and check your freaking food! Deep breath. I'm striving to do better.

Is a lack of sufficient patience a character flaw or is it simply one's nature and, more importantly, is it something which can be learned? I'd sincerely like to know the answer to that while I'm striving to do better. Can anyone answer the question? Anyone?! Sometime today would be grrrreat!

Yeah, yeah, yeah. Patience is a virtue. Well, I got your virtue right here!

I'm striving to do better.

• • •

I Strived to, and I did better!
In Eckhart Tolle's book, *The Power of Now: A Guide to Spiritual Enlightenment,* he refers to life's difficulties as "situations" instead

of "problems." He explains that if any situation makes you unhappy, you have three options: remove yourself from it, change it, or accept it totally.

Remember, I mentioned that I'd been striving to do better with my impatience behind my car's wheel? Well, without being aware of it, I utilized Eckhart's method.

First, I realized I can't remove myself from driving. Well, that is, unless I get a chauffeur (which I'd be more than happy to accept). My life does not exist exclusively in my house, it's in many different cities. Therefore, driving is a requirement.

Second, the situation cannot be changed. The fact remains, there are many drivers on the road who insist on moving below the speed limit, thereby blocking numerous others who want to get to their destination. Others feel it is their divine duty to control every car lined up behind them.

So, that left me with one option: acceptance. At first, I felt like I would be admitting defeat, that impatience was the victor, and I was a failure. Then I realized it merely is what it is. I have totally and completely accepted the fact that I am an impatient driver. I've embraced the realization that if a car on the road is poking along and I can safely pass them, I'm going to continue to do just that.

Surprisingly, with this acceptance, my patience has improved. What?! Yes, it did. It filled me with a feeling of peace, and I've discovered that I don't rush quite as much. Of course, I still pass slow drivers when it's safe to do so and go my merry way. Overall, driving is now a less stressful task, and I'm on my way to actually enjoying it. Wow.

One Monday, on my way home on the 6-mile country road, I encountered three very slow driving vehicles. Of course, one by one, I passed them all. I drove a couple miles further, and as luck would have it, I spotted a turtle in the middle of the road. By the way, I need a bumper sticker that says, "I stop for turtles." Anyway, I stopped to save the little guy from imminent destruction. As I was carrying him to the side of the road he was heading toward, all three cars that I passed moments before came along, slowed down, and allowed me to finish my life-saving turtle placement. One guy, driving a small white pick-up, stopped and said, "So you were in such a hurry to pass everyone just to stop and get a turtle out of the road?" I could've used some choice words, ignored him, or flipped him the bird; however, with my newfound acceptance and inner peace, I responded, "I am what I am. I didn't hurt anybody," and he drove away. I smiled.

. . .

If you could give your younger self your best advice, what would you say?

While I wouldn't go back in time to change anything in this life because it may also change where I am today, that whole butterfly effect and all, if I had a new life in another time, I would say:

Save half of your money. I mean 50% of it. Even if your allowance is fifty cents per week like mine was as a child, save half of that, put it in your piggy bank and when the piggy bank is full, put that money in a bank account. When that bank account gets really fat, invest that money so it can continue to grow throughout your life. Now forget about that half. Use the other half of what you earn for what you want/need. If you start this young and stay with it, you'll always have a growing stockpile of money as you get older, you will live comfortably within your means, and you will avoid unnecessary financial debt. Also, you'll have one heck of a retirement and can travel the world, multiple times. Save 50%!

Don't let the fear of embarrassment or failure stop you from doing the things that you feel in your heart you really want to do.

Embarrassment lasts such a short time, but the wishing that you'd done something—for years thereafter—well, that's sheer torture. Make that speech. Learn that dance. Ask that impossibly gorgeous girl/boy on a date! Whatever it is, just do it. Fear is the antidote for joy, squashing it like a bug. Someone once told me, "If you don't take a chance, you won't have one." Very wise words. Take a chance! Just do it!!

You may as well make friends with your body and right now. Yeah, it may not be "perfect" like those anorexic supermodels, but it's your body. It's going to be with you your entire life. There are many things about your body that cannot be changed such as the shape of your feet and hands, the size of your skull, the color of your eyes (although you could wear colored contacts), along with many others. Learn to love and accept your body just as it is and see it for the vessel that it is—specially made for carrying your spirit around throughout this human experience. Make friends with your body!

If you can go to college right after high school for free, meaning via scholarship or your parents are willing to pay for it, go!! My parents offered to pay for me to go to college just before my high school graduation. I thought about it, but later told them, "I don't even know what I would go to college for, so I don't want to waste your money." Mistake! If you don't know what you want to do yet, go get some kind of basic degree which can be built upon later in life when you do make that decision. Go while you are young and your brain is used to learning on a daily basis. Go to college right out of high school!

Don't argue with someone who compliments you in any way. The only acceptable response to a compliment is, "Thank you." Don't roll your eyes, or say things like, "Whatever" or "Yeah, right" or "I wish." When you do that, you're calling the person who complimented you a liar. They meant what they said and just because you don't see it in yourself doesn't mean that what they've said is false. Thanking someone for a compliment doesn't mean you're conceited, stuck up or have an inflated ego, not at all. It's merely a common courtesy. Just say, "Thank you."

Thank you for reading. Thank you to my magical friend, Linda, for this question.

. . .

What are the 10 most valuable lessons you've learned in life?
Not everyone is going to like you. Be okay with that. Like yourself first, and be happy being you. Others may take you, or they may leave you, but you will still be you.

Be true to who you are. Don't try to fit into someone else's mold or idea of how you should be. There is a reason and/or purpose for your life on this earth, and it's not to be someone else's puppet.

If you don't take a chance, you won't have one. Put another way, if you don't ask for what you want in life, the answer will always be "No." Fear equals death to your dreams. Just go for it!

Worry gets you nowhere and will only devour your precious time. That's time wasted. It's time that you can't ever get back. Oh, and what a hard habit worrying is to break. But, it can be done, or at least minimized.

The old saying, "It's in the valleys we grow," is 100% true! Our greatest lessons and growth come from the most significant challenges in life. The valleys are what mold us into who we're going to be. Without them, we would stagnate.

We all have scars. Some things happen in life that will have a lasting emotional or physical impact on you. You can spend the rest of your life being angry, hating, blaming, and forever remaining a victim, or you can say, "Okay, this happened to me. It was a bad experience. It left this damage. Now, what am I going to do to help myself heal? How can I release the anger and hatred and live my life to the fullest?" If you stay in victim mode, you are allowing someone to continue to hurt you. Stop it! They've basically left you with a burden while they're off living their happy, care-free lives, never giving you a single millisecond of thought. Yes, it's horribly unfair because *they did this*…and they should be made to pay for their mistake! Karma needs to show up at their house and unleash its wrath, and it would be oh so very satisfying to see them get what they so richly deserve. But, the fact remains—you are left with the mess. You can wallow in it, or you can seek help for your own healing. It's entirely up to YOU. Stop giving your past the power to keep hurting you! You need to take care of you.

We've all heard the saying, "The older you get, the faster time goes." It really does seem to fly by faster and faster the older I get, but I don't think that time is literally moving faster. Sixty seconds is still only sixty seconds, after all. The clock ticks at the same speed it has up until now. My theory is that while our minds are continually playing life's memories like a non-stop film reel, it distracts us from what's currently happening. As little kids, we didn't have that many memories, so we were much more engaged in each and every minute we spent playing. Remember how long summers seemed to last when we were in grade school? It's because we were paying attention to what we were currently doing. Adults can relearn how to do that. It's called being in the present, in the now. When you do that, time really does seem to slow down, almost standing still at times, while you savor each moment in life. It's wonderful. I think that also explains why our long-term memories are often much more vivid than our short-term memories. Did we pay closer attention way back when?

There are controlling people in the world, and some of them may enter your life. They can be family, romantic interests, or micro-managing co-workers. In my experience, I've found that many of these types of people, let's call them "control freaks," are functioning out of their own fear, their fear of having no control. They were once or are currently being controlled and/or manipulated. Or, perhaps, they endured a traumatic experience against their will. Now, they feel they have to control everything to make up for that lack of control. You need to realize that this is the control freak's issue, try to have compassion, and work toward a relationship of mutual respect (this can be genuinely challenging). In general, humans will only tolerate control freaks for a time—until they've reached their limit. Then they're flat-out done, out the door, gone. If you can identify with being a control freak, please seek help. Controlling every aspect of your life and/or others' lives will not fix the hurt and fear you hide inside.

That it is okay to remove toxic people from your life. Those people who live in the vortex of their sob stories and will jump at every opportunity to regale a new listener with every last daunting detail of their "poor me" perpetual victimhood. Over and over and over. I...simply...cannot—plop. They're often referred to as energy vampires. Though you may feel deep compassion for their suffering and have a sincere desire to help, interactions with these people can leave you feeling mentally and emotionally drained. It's heartbreaking to see another suffer. However, you cannot fix them. It is up to them to do that. There is a hole in their spirit, soul, and heart that you cannot repair for them. Regardless of how much effort you put into helping them, only they can fill that emptiness. Sure, you can listen to their drama and offer them all the understanding and encouragement that you can muster. You will feel that you've filled their cup after you've poured all of yours into it and that you did a good deed. It was a good deed. Inevitably, however, all the love you poured into the energy vampire's cup will drip right back out of their spirit's hole. They'll come running back to you for another feeding. You are their host now, and they'll often return before you've even had a chance to refill your own cup. They've lured you in, you are their new source of emotional nourishment, and they will drain your cup, again and again. Life experience has taught me how to quickly identify these vampires and when I meet them, I think, "Oooh...you're one of those. So here's another at-arm's-length kind of friend/acquaintance." Not going there. No, but thank you. It's okay and necessary to protect yourself.

Always listen to your gut, that intuitive feeling or internal nudge. Call it what you want—your guardian angel, the spirit of a dearly departed loved one, or the Almighty. These intuitive feelings are real, and they serve as guidance and protection throughout our lives. In the past, I'm sure you've said, "I wish I'd followed my gut on that one," or "I'm so glad I followed my gut this time." When you don't follow your intuition, it'll undoubtedly teach you a lesson. It won't necessarily be a dramatic lesson, though there will be some of those, and you will learn to trust that nudge in the future.

· · ·

ANGER: *Punishment you give yourself for someone else's mistake.* Think about that, really think about it for a minute.

· · ·

Well...through this phase of utter frustration and seemingly infinite screaming, I've learned three major lessons:

- When everything seems to be going against you, remember that the airplane takes off against the wind, not with it.

- Notice that the stiffest tree is most easily cracked, while the bamboo or willow survives by bending with the wind.

- When you pray and pray and pray, you may not get exactly what you pray for, but He will give you exactly what you NEED.

"Seek and ye shall find."
If you seek something to be pissed about; you shall find it.
If you seek something to scare the shit out of you; you shall find it.
If you seek something to prove that the world is a
horrible and scary place; you shall find it.
If you seek to find and expose mistakes
made by others; you shall find it.
If you seek something to make you smile; you shall find it.
If you seek something to renew your faith
in mankind; you shall find it.
If you seek to find the beauty in this life; you shall find it.
If you seek something to be grateful for in
this very moment; you shall find it.
BE MINDFUL OF WHAT YOU ARE
SEEKING; FOR YOU WILL FIND IT!

CHAPTER NINE

WHAT DREAMS MAY COME

"I dreamed I was a butterfly, flitting around in the sky; then I awoke. Now I wonder: Am I a man who dreamt of being a butterfly, or am I a butterfly dreaming that I am a man?"
—ZHUANGZI

I dreamed what?

I dreamed that I was very late for work and had no clean scrubs. However, they had all been run through the washing machine, while still on wire hangers. When I go through all the hangers to find a scrub set to throw in the dryer, I find that all I have is summer clothing, and I could only find one sock. While I'm dealing with all of that, I'm trying to figure out when to get a shower, too. It's already 9:30 a.m. and work started hours ago. Then, I'm told that I have to drive the school bus today. Since when do nurses drive school busses? Isn't that out of my scope of practice? They don't teach you bus driving in nursing school.

· · ·

I dreamed I was at a public sink washing a few dishes. From the line behind me, I heard a little poot sound. When I turned around to identify the offender, I found a blushing woman right behind me who was almost in tears. She looked at me with apologetic eyes and said, "Never trust a chicken fart." Now, that makes me wonder if chickens can fart. Off to consult Google!!

. . .

I dreamed that I was late for work, got lost on the way, couldn't clock in because I didn't bring my badge, and forgot to put on scrub pants. Whoa, what a nightmare!

. . .

Two guys were rollerblading through a shopping center parking lot in the rain. They were apparently studying or rehearsing something and Guy 1 asks Guy 2, "Which two of four do you want to do now?" Guy 2 says, "Two and four." Guy 1 says, "Do one and three." No sooner had he gotten the words out, Guy 1 completely wipes out on the wet pavement. Splat!!! I screamed, through my laughter, "That's karma!" Guy 2 soon follows, splatting to the wet ground, laughing hysterically. Then I yell, "I'm glad it's raining because I'm going to pee my pants!"

. . .

Dream about a friend

Oh, my friend. You and two other friends were going skydiving. I was in a house with several other folks and we had just gotten word that you all had made the jump from the plane. I immediately ran for my camera so I could capture this monumental event, but I couldn't find the darn thing! A frantic search ensued and my heart was racing. People were rushing outside in a fury! *I surely don't wanna miss this event!* After what seemed like hours, I finally found the dang camera and rushed outside!

I saw 50-100 people running to the field to view the event. I ran out there, too, as fast as I could, just to find you three easily visible in the sky and that you'd would be on the ground in mere seconds! I make a mad spiral dive to the ground, landing on my back with my camera facing skyward at the ready. As I was surfing across the field on my back, I tried frantically to get my camera turned on, lens cap off, etc. and it was not cooperating with me at all. I was so frustrated! After sliding for several seconds, I stopped just at the moment you all reached ground. With my camera finally ready, the event was over. Disappointingly, I wasn't able to record ANY OF IT! Not one picture. Not one video. I slowly got up, brushed myself off and looked at the ground where I'd just been. Head hanging low, I walked to the house to join everyone in the celebration that you'd all made it back to Earth in one piece. Suddenly, I picked up my pace knowing that what I've got to tell you will surely make up for the disappointing news that the event wasn't captured on camera! "Oh, yes," I think. "My friend is just twisted enough that this will make up for it." I found you in the house and I began to regale everyone with my tale of epic photographic failure. As I finished the story of where I'd landed and how I'd missed it all, the look on your face told me that you'd never forgive me. Our friendship was over. I'd let you down to such a degree that it could never be mended. "But, my friend," I said. "While I was surfing across the ground trying to get my camera ready ... all the while, I was sliding through a field of cow patties." All was forgiven.

Sometimes, your dreams are shitty!

* * *

I dreamed I was traveling on a train. After arriving at the station, I was maneuvering the steps on the broken escalator when I suddenly realized I'd left all my possessions on the train. I had no idea which train it was, where it was going or where it had been before I got on board. I woke up well before sunrise, in the midst of my sheer panic, but was quickly relieved that it was only a dream. So, I foresee a nap in my future and I plan to get all my stuff back from that damn kleptomaniac train!! Oh, and I hope they've fixed the freakin' escalator by then, too.

•   •   •

If I dreamed all night that I was at work, can I charge for overtime or just stay home because I've already worked a shift?

•   •   •

I woke up hungry because I dreamed we were at a bed and breakfast and I'd ordered a western omelet with coffee which was never delivered. But, while I was waiting, I was trying to give a patient morphine and a sedative, but spilled the drugs on the floor because I didn't cap the syringe. Then, I went to get the drugs out again, and look for a witness so I could waste my blunder, a nice puddle on the floor. I mixed the second batch of drugs correctly, but left the ginormous syringe (don't know why I used that one) on a metal table. Once I realized I'd left it, I went back to retrieve it, with my wet hair in a towel. I'd squeezed a shower in there, too. When I had returned to the metal table, a patient was playing with the syringe and I took it from her. Through all this, we had a family reunion in progress, I hadn't gotten outside to see any of my family yet and they were already putting all the food away.

Yeah. Go ahead! Analyze THAT!

•   •   •

We were driving somewhere and there was a lot of traffic. There was a split in the road and I asked which route to take. I was told to go left and we ended up having to get out of our car and walk. The trail turned into a stone/concrete stairway leading up the side of a mountain. It was very narrow and the side which would have had a rail to keep you from falling off was short, like maybe up to mid-thigh level. On the other side of that was straight down the mountain. In front of us was a very large man, much like the guy on "Mike & Molly" and all I could think of was him giving out and rolling down the steps right over all of us. He was huffing and puffing and would stop every little bit. Then, there seemed to be a resting point, sort of a deck area. That's when I woke up.

• • •

You know that laughter is a major part of your life when you laugh so hard in a dream, it wakes you up! I dreamed that a very large (as in severely obese) woman broke into our house. She apparently was someone who I'd had a history with and I didn't like or want her around me. I immediately called 9-1-1. She then proceeded to go through the house and we had a few physical altercations. Finally, I ran outside with my cellphone. My intention was to take a picture of her license plate so I could call it in to the police. In the meantime, she's on the phone, too. Then, she comes after me just as her posse is pulling in the driveway! I'm like, really??! Her thugs got here quicker than the freakin' police?! Anyway ... she's chasing me through the yard and around the cars parked on our hilly driveway and I say to her, "If you fall down this hill, you'll roll all the way to Georgia!!"

• • •

I dreamed that I had Leonard Hofstadter from "Big Bang Theory" as a patient in recovery. I was about to take out his IV and get him up, but as he sat up in the bed, he vomited on my new shoes which have mesh tops. Gross! I called out on our headset in an attempt to see if the anesthesia nurse could give him some medicine to settle his stomach. No one could understand what I was saying. So, I left the area to go find the anesthesia nurse and saw them wheeling another patient down to recovery. When I got back to the recovery room, there was a heavy wooden desk in front of the door. I could've crawled through a small opening at the bottom, beside the desk, but I refused. I stood there contemplating my next move, then an automatic glass door opened for me to enter.

• • •

I woke up in a pure panic after this nightmare: We were in a city near the ocean. I was with my husband, an elderly man and a young child (not sure who he/she was). We could see a tidal wave coming from the ocean. It wasn't very high up, so I felt we would survive it. I instructed the elderly man to take a deep breath in anticipation of us all being under water, temporarily. Then, I looked back at the tidal wave to see how much closer it had gotten to shore and it was towering over a building, basically across the street from us and had the top of another building in its grasp. With terror, I wondered how we'd ever survive this! I was screaming for my husband who was 8-10 feet from me, holding the small child. I woke up, my heart racing.

In researching the possible meaning of this nightmare, I discovered that: "To see a tidal wave in your dream represents an overwhelming emotional issue that demands your attention. You may have been keeping your feelings and negative emotions bottled up inside for too long." On a positive note, the tidal wave symbolized the clearing away of old habits." Also, to dream about a tsunami, "that you are being overwhelmed by some repressed feeling or subconscious material that is rising up to the surface.

You are experiencing some unhappiness and emotional instability in a waking situation." (DreamMoods.com)

I think, in my case, it's a little of both: I'm still wrestling with/sorting some emotions from the past. Trying to let it all go. The symbolism of my dream seems to be screaming, "Turning your back on your emotions/issues only makes them grow larger." On the positive side, I am embarking on new adventures—such as learning to dance and writing this book. I suppose it's time to do some serious journaling so I may completely and freely move forward with my life. Vonda's life.

This makes so much sense to me right now. I liken it to Tarzan—effortlessly swinging through the jungle from vine to vine. If he doesn't let go of the vine he's clinging to and fully trust that the next vine will take him where he needs to go, he wouldn't let go of the vine that brought him to his future. He wouldn't progress through the jungle. He'd just hang there, in limbo. Stuck. Motionless. Never growing. Never moving forward.

CHAPTER TEN

ReaD THe PLaTe anD FIGURe IT OUT

"I have found out that there ain't no surer way to find out whether you like people or hate them than to travel with them."
—MARK TWAIN

Sister Trip to St. Louis

My big sister and I embarked on a "sister trip," out of town for two nights. So, after a six-hour drive, we arrived and checked into our hotel. We're given room 120. I use the keycard to enter. The room is dirty. Back to the front desk we go. OK, now we have room 121. Enter the room with the keycard. Room is immaculate, so we happily unload the luggage cart. Heat does not work. Back to the front desk we go. I leave Becky in this room to wait with all the luggage. Get key cards for our new room, 131. Use the keycard to enter. Room is dirty. At this point, I'm laughing hysterically as I knock on room 121 to tell my sister of my brilliant success and that I'm heading back to the front desk —again. Tears are forming in my eyes at this point! The very polite woman working the desk goes herself to check on three "potential rooms," as I sit in the lobby and my sister waits in the cold room, 121. Eureka!! We have room 215, it's clean AND the heat works!! Home sweet home!! The desk clerk apologized repeatedly and said she was going to "talk to" her manager about our "inconvenience," all while I'm still giggling. I say to her, "You don't understand. This kinda stuff happens to me ALL THE TIME. I'm used to it." So far, our "sister trip" has been educational, hilarious, and not a bit dull.

. . .

Our phrases for this trip are "Read the plate" and "Figure it out." My Gypsy (my nickname for my GPS) has FREQUENTLY steered us wrong. Therefore, multiple U-turns and really slow driving have been necessary in order to find our destinations—to the dismay of busy locals who just want us to get the hell outta their way. I've received dirty looks and have had a few heads shaken at me. So, as they pass, I just say, "From out of town. READ THE PLATE."

My sister tried repeatedly to text her husband and daughter while we were traveling on bumpy roads and this just does not work out well. She resorts to using her voice text which royally screws up her intended messages. A lot. Frustrated, she'll voice text "Figure it out" at the end of the messed up message, then hit send.

. . .

We had to use a pay parking lot to go into the Hard Rock Cafe. Pull in, collect a ticket from the dispenser. Park. After eating, we couldn't find the ticket. Told the booth lady I couldn't find my ticket. She says, "Oh, please find it, baby. It's $20 to park if you lose your ticket. See this sign?" So, we drove back to where we parked and looked around. No ticket. Tore the car up short of turning it upside down. No ticket. Went back to the booth lady and I said, "Oh, baby! I couldn't find my ticket." Needless to say, we split the $20 or we'd still be in that SOB'ing parking lot!!

• • •

So ... we're on vacation in sunny, hot and very hot Florida, right? Do a little shopping, etc., in my nice air-conditioned car. Go on a cruise to the Bahamas, come back to Florida and the a/c doesn't work in my car!! What the...??? Greg thinks, well, maybe it's just a fuse or something simple and takes it to a Ford dealership in Pensacola. Oooooh, but NOOOOOO, it's not a fuse!! We apparently hit a bird somewhere on the way down and its beak poked a hole in the compressor. OH YES! A BIRD!! So ... now, $879 poorer, the a/c works so well we can hang beef in the car! NOTHING in our lives has ever been something as simple as a "fuse."

• • •

A dear friend asked me to find a "special" shell for her while we were in Florida:

> *My friend's shell, just like all of us, is less than perfect.*
> *Been through some rough seas.*
> *Sustained some damage here and there. Scars to prove it.*
> *Carrying a little baggage (the little shell wedged inside).*
> *But, through the grace of God ...*
> *We ALL see the true beauty within her.*

• • •

New York City Adventures

The first time I went to New York City was in 2012, with my friend, Allison. It was quite a culture shock. Like, immediately after we'd landed.

We've landed in NYC and are looking for the baggage claim area. We see double doors for it, but the sign on them says "exit only. No re-entry." So, I politely ask the guard where "the entrance" would be. The guard says, "We only have exits." So again I repeat my question about an "entrance." Again, "We only have exits." Thoroughly confused, I rephrase it to, "Where do we enter." "We only have exits." Then, he looks at me and says, "What is so hard to understand?" I just shake my head and we enter the "exit only" doors as he holds them open.

. . .

As we're entering the shuttle van for the hotel, there's a funny contraption on the floorboard. Allison hesitates because she doesn't know what it is and isn't sure how to step over it. The driver says in a very foreign accent, "Don't worry. It's not a bomb." It was a vacuum that plugs into the cigarette lighter. We burst out laughing! So, he gets in the driver's seat and plugs in his little GPS or kindle looking thingy. And, I have to ask…"Is that a bomb?" After we paid our fare and were exiting the cab, he thanked us for making his job fun.

. . .

One night, Allison and I are having dinner at the Hard Rock Cafe. Toward the end of the meal she mentions wanting to look in the gift shop before leaving the restaurant. I simply ask, "Where is the gift shop?" A bewildered look consumes her face and she proceeds to tell me, "We walked right through it upon entering the restaurant." A look of utter cluelessness consumes my face, effectively expressing the fact that the gift shop was completely unnoticed by me. With deep seriousness in her eyes, and a heavy sigh, Allison tells me, "I think that when God was creating you…he got distracted." I'm not sure I've ever laughed that hard prior to or since that night.

. . .

The second time I went to NYC was in 2018, on a school trip with my eldest daughter.

Upon arriving in New Jersey—apparently, our bus driver had his GPS set to "shortest route" and not the "route most suitable for a BIG freakin' bus." So...here we go.

We'd been on this ginormous, big freakin' tour bus for about 87-and-a-half hours, a very long and torturous ride from Campbellsville University to North Bergen, New Jersey. As the bus was nearing our destination, finally, we saw the hotel—at long last. Our home sweet home. Our get-me-the-frick-off-this-bus-already haven. All passengers shared a collective sigh of relief. But, our relief was short-lived as the bus driver drove on past the hotel. Wait! What?!

Perhaps he didn't see the entrance in time and didn't think he could make the sharp turn into the hotel. Maybe he simply intended to drive around the block so he could tackle the hotel's entrance at a better angle. However, around the block was literally around the block. He drove us down a very tight street through a neighborhood where cars were parked on either side. I said, "We must be staying at someone's house!!" He turned on another street and we were soon passing by a little alley that veered off to the left and seemed to descend into darkness. The driver kept going straight down the narrow road. Very, very slowly. About 30 seconds later, we were stopped because there was nowhere else he could go at that point. There we were—35 extremely tired passengers on a bus, stuck at a dead end. What the...?!

With no other options, unless he wanted to take out some cars and maybe a house or two, he put that monster bus in reverse and commenced to inch that ginormous vessel back out of the street! You could hear the gritting of teeth and feel the nerves twitching throughout the entire bus. Surprisingly and quite impressively, he managed to back that monster vessel far enough to see the opening he needed. There it was—that little alley to the left. The one that goes who knows where. I suppose he decided to take that route instead of backing the bus around another corner and back onto the main road. This small and narrow alley was very dark and went straight down a slope, so it felt like we were going down into a dark and mysterious tunnel.

When we came to the bottom of the hill, he needed to turn left. However, the length of the bus and the sharp angle of the intersection would not allow that to happen. On his first attempt, he almost took out a guardrail. He backed up, maneuvered a little bit and tried again. He would miss the guardrail this time, but a telephone pole was mighty close to the bus window. Like right by the one from which I was watching this entire drama unfold. I said, "It's gonna hit!!" It was like that scene on Titanic when the ship hits the iceberg right after that guy said, "It's gonna hit!!" I ·swear I almost got splinters! Then, I heard a fellow passenger say, "Aw, look at that cat." He was a pretty black and white cat sitting on his human's porch. Just relaxing and enjoying the night air. So majestic.

Then, the bus was in motion again and seemed to be steered right for that porch—AND the cat. In the blink of an eye, that cat shot off the porch like it'd been sprayed with a garden hose! There I am, trying to contain my laughter over this absurd situation. But, at long last, the driver gets the bus repositioned and starts to turn left on the street. Not so fast Mr. Bus Driver. We hear a very loud and horrendous scraping noise as the bottom of the bus is being used to excavate that New Jersey street. The driver tried to motor on through it, with the loud screeching noise getting louder, but he just couldn't get the bus free. So, there we are. Stuck. Blocking traffic both ways and the bus was not moving either way at this point. The driver walked to the back of the bus. I mean, inside the bus, passing all the seats, to the back of the bus. We all thought, well that was odd. What could he do about this current situation from the back of the bus? Oooooh, okay. He needed a potty break!

After he was done with his business, he told all of us to go to the front of the bus in hopes that our weight would enable him to get the bus out of its motionless state. Nope. So, we all had to evacuate the bus and some of us are taking pictures of this hilarious scene. Within a few minutes, some local good samaritans started helping direct the bus driver so he could get the monster bus unstuck. Cars are honking and flashing their lights. Like, OK, what do you want us to do—levitate the bus for you?! It was nuts and I was cracking up! Thankfully, though, the driver was able to rescue our bus and we all loaded back on while giving him some well-earned applause.

After we're freed from the bus we pack our luggage to our room. The air conditioning won't work. It's a bit warm in our room and I had pushed the power button, tripped the little test button and clicked the other one. Nothing. Amber calls the operator to alert them of our dilemma and a very foreign gentleman answers the phone. She couldn't understand him and handed me the phone. (Yeah, like THAT'S gonna help!) I told him the situation and that I'd done my very skilled troubleshooting without success. He then asks me, "Did you try the unit on the wall? Because that's what controls the AC, not the main unit." Umm...no. I hadn't tried that. Works fabulously now!!!! I'm not used to these fancy wall controls in a hotel room.

. . .

Oh, the looks you get when you and your daughter, wearing very casual walking around clothes, step into the NYC Tiffany's!! So tempting to use the lines from Pretty Woman. "You work on commission, right?" "Yes." "Big mistake. HUGE. I must go shopping now!"

As a parting gift to the store, my daughter said, "Everything's so shiny!!"

...

Nosy bus driver—I was seated on the bus directly behind the driver waiting for Amber to join me for our last trip into Manhattan. She climbed onto the bus with a very shiny, small black bag which she'd just gotten from the hotel's front desk. Our bus driver asked, "What's in the bag?" I responded, "You don't want to know." He insisted, "Yes, I do want to know." Amber, who was clearly uncomfortable with revealing the bag's contents to this man, raised her eyebrows and clamped her lips. She wouldn't say a word. Coming to her rescue, I said, "Breath mints! They gave her breath mints." "Oh, I'll take a breath mint," he said. Amber's knuckles were now white from the tight grip she had on the shiny black bag and her face was redder than I don't know what. You see, the bag contained personal products used by women on certain days on a monthly basis. Now she wishes she'd have let him look in the bag. That'd teach him not to be so nosy.

...

On our last day in NYC —We had such high hopes for completing our list of things to do and see on our last day in NYC. First on the list was taking the subway to Brooklyn and walking back on the bridge, which we accomplished with ease. Next, we ended up in the financial district of NYC and thought we'd track down the infamous Merrill Lynch bull since we were so close to it. I planned to have Amber take a picture of me standing at the bull's butt with my hand cupped around my ear like I was waiting to hear something come out. You know, being a fart coach and all, it seemed appropriate. We'd spent more than an hour in our search for that bull. Although we'd enjoyed the sights along the way, while racking up the steps on our Fitbit and iWatch respectively, we accepted the fact that we were simply not going to find that stinkin' bull. It had apparently been moved to the theatre district!! Shortly thereafter, Amber hailed her first cab and we were on our way back to Brooklyn for our pizza lunch. We hadn't been in that cab a solid minute when, "Oh, look!! Over there!" What was it?! It's the freakin' bull. Well, its backside anyway. That there's what you call irony.

Lunch was fantastic at Juliana's. Authentic Italian pizza. Our next destination? Grand Central Station. However, I got us on the wrong subway train. I take FULL responsibility. These things happen, right? So, while we were supposed to be headed for Grand Central station, we were now headed for upstate New York!

Instead of getting off at the next stop in order to remedy our situation, we decided to just stay on the train and see where it would take us. We're so adventurous. We rode that thing to the very end of the subway route. I mean, it was parked, done for the day, and we had to get off and board the train that would take us back the opposite direction to NYC, you know, AWAY from the ocean.

After seeing all the sights for the second time, we finally arrived at the Fulton Street station, where we should've been about two hours prior and would, at last, be on to our next adventure—Grand Central Station! We were making our way through the terminal to our next train, but, for some unknown reason, we decided to take the elevator up to our next subway ride instead of the stairway route we'd been taking, for the exercise benefit, of course.

Now, this elevator was kinda small and a large number of people quickly piled into it. I was basically up against a wall and Amber was, too. I could feel someone beside me, very close, and just slightly behind my left shoulder. Subtly, I turned my head a tiny bit and there was an oddly quirky man with his eyes very close to my chin. OK...it's just an elevator ride, we should be out of here very soon, I hoped.

I was staring a hole into the side of Amber's head in hopes that she'd make eye contact with me so I could say, "HELP ME!" with my eyes. I could tell she was fully aware of my predicament from the suppressed grin on her face. Try as I might, however, I could not get her to look at me. This guy was sooooo close to me, I could feel my hair being pulled into his nostrils with every breath he took! I could not move. I'd turn my head just a tiny bit to look at him and then I'd look back at Amber, who was now visibly tickled over this situation. Amber and I locked eyes for a whole millisecond, neither one of us could contain ourselves any longer and we both started to giggle. At this point, I'm shaking from my giggles and trying so very hard to suppress my full laughter. Breathe hair into nostrils, exhale hair from nostrils. "Someone, open the elevator door already," I wanted to scream! By the time it finally opens, I am in tears and can't speak. Once out of the elevator, we both lost it. It had to have echoed throughout the entire terminal.

• • •

We survived Europe...or, did Europe survive us?!

I had been working on this blog post since we got back to the states in the latter part of May, 2019. Nearly five months and 12,650 words later, I'm still not sure I've covered everything that I wanted to share, so this may be edited a time or two...or thirty after it's posted! I hope you enjoy reading about our trip as much as we enjoyed our 13-day tour of Europe.

While it had been a long-time dream of mine to visit Europe, I neither knew when nor how I would ever make the trip a reality.

It was one of those "someday" goals and I imagined myself doing it later in life, with a tour group of senior citizens or perhaps with the Red Hat Society. Then late in 2018, the university where Amber was a student extended their group tour to family members. It was incredibly priced, much less than commercial tours that I'd researched, and we simply could not pass up this opportunity. We acquired the last two available spots for this tour.

Immediately, I had two major concerns regarding this adventure. The first was my claustrophobia and being in a small, cramped airplane seat for 10 straight hours. The second was my swelling feet and being in a small, cramped airplane seat for 10 straight hours. These thoughts went through my head starting from the moment we signed up for the tour. Amber had a front row seat to my claustrophobic restlessness during a 2,000+ hour bus ride from Kentucky to New Jersey last October. And, we even stopped for breaks fairly regularly. My anxiety over flying for so many hours and feeling caged/trapped made her a little bit anxious, too. She'd said, "I'm not sitting by you," several times throughout the months preceding our once in a lifetime European tour.

Sometime during the week of our scheduled departure, I acquired a monster head cold which, given my past history with colds, was expected to wind up in my chest as a lovely case of bronchitis. My co-workers urged me to seek medical attention before leaving the country to stay ahead of it. I followed their advice and made an appointment with my primary care nurse practitioner. I told her, "I know there is no cure for a common cold, but I need something to ease these symptoms." She definitely hooked me up with all I could possibly need, cough syrup, nasal sprays, and even prescribed "just in case" antibiotics for an infection should my symptoms worsen (which I did not need, thank goodness). During this visit, I told her about the European tour which was only a few days away and how I worried about managing my claustrophobia. She prescribed an antianxiety medication, which was not a controlled substance, to have with me should I need it.

Before we go further, I should explain that at age 15 (there's that eventful year again), I was diagnosed with lymphedema praecox. "Praecox" is merely a fancy word that means occurring early in life, which for me was adolescence. What this meant for me was that my feet were swelling, there was no cure, I'd have to wear supportive compression hosiery for the rest of my life (a sexy addition to any teenage girl's wardrobe), and that it could, and would likely, worsen over time. At first, it wasn't so bad—the swelling. Some days it was unrecognizable, or was only recognizable by me, and I could wear pretty shoes with straps, etc. But by age 20, after I had my first child, my feet were swollen to some degree every single day and, as warned, it has worsened with age. For over 40 years, I've dreamed of wearing any kind of shoe that I want to wear. Each day the shoes I choose to wear are based on which ones will be the most comfortable, given the current size of my feet. I've said many times, "If my swelling feet could be fixed, I'd wear high-heeled hooker shoes with my scrubs every single day." I would, too—just because I could! I've kept this plight to myself for decades, with only my family and close friends knowing about it. Something about nearing 60 years old—it's not such a big deal any more, and letting out what you perceive as your secret shame and/or source of embarrassment is actually kind of liberating. Recently, I told my husband, "If they come up with a trial surgery/treatment for this, I'm going to be first in line!!" Oh, to have my shoes fit the same way every day. To be able to spend all day on the beach without my feet increasing in size by the hour. It's been a real hindrance to the full enjoyment of my life. The hot summer months are the worst for this lymphedema sufferer. No amount of elevating my legs is enough and my feet and lower legs become very swollen, hot, painful, not to mention extremely embarrassing. Also, so very sexy—on the beach! Anyway, back to our trip.

We had two separate flights from Kentucky to Munich, Germany. The first flight which took us to Atlanta was less than an hour long and was quite pleasant. That is until we reached our maximum elevation. This is where my nasal congestion increased to epic proportions causing extreme pressure in my head. My ears were clogged and felt like they would explode. I could not breathe through my nose at all nor could I blow anything out and when I tried to, my ears would squeak. It was sheer misery and, as luck would have it, my nasal spray was in my checked luggage. You know, since we're only allowed a whopping two tablespoons of liquid with us inside the freakin' plane. As we began our descent into Atlanta, things began to change. Quickly and rather drastically, the pressure in my head lessened, my ears popped several times and opened up. Then snot basically began gushing out of every hole in my face as well as running down my throat causing me to cough as if I were drowning. I was a human hagfish and couldn't keep the flow of facial tissues coming fast enough to catch all the mucus. Perhaps an air sickness bag would've been more useful at this point. Ha ha! I eventually got it all under control and could breathe again. We landed in Atlanta and rushed through the airport to catch our next flight. The big 10-hour one, going over the ocean, to Munich, Germany. Breathe!! It was during our rush through the Atlanta airport that the large suitcase I had borrowed from my mother-in-law started to lose its retread tires. I think the first chunk was lost on an escalator. Thereafter, wherever I pulled this mammoth and very heavy suitcase, it would clunk clunk clunk as the wheels turned. Won't it be delightful hauling this thing around Europe? Let the fun begin! Step, clunk. Step, clunk. Step, clunk.

In our travel information and tips provided by the university, it mentioned that we should "sleep as much as possible during the flight." Yeah, okay. I am not even a car sleeper, how the heck will I sleep on an airplane? In those cramped seats? But, I remembered I had medication along, took some deep breaths and tried to remain calm by natural methods.

The seats on this long flight were very small. I mean tiny. The back of the seat in front of me, which had a little tv screen on it for my personal enjoyment, could not have been more than 16 inches from my face. This is not an exaggeration. I've been in coach seats with much more room. Once we were safely buckled in our seats, I looked at my daughter while trying to contain the apprehension I was feeling, which was steadily increasing and very near full-on panic. She didn't know whether to smack me or request a different seat! As calmly and assuringly as I could muster, I said, "It'll be okay." I repeated this over and over in my mind. As we took off, I prepared myself for the clogging of my entire head again, which, thankfully, didn't happen on this flight. I suppose I had been thoroughly emptied of mucus in Atlanta.

Delta international flights are pretty cool! They served us dinner, a meal that most would describe as a "TV dinner." I was pleasantly surprised and found it to be quite tasty and filling. After our meal, the flight attendants rolled the drink cart through the aisles. I saw wine! Wine is good. Wine won't give me restless leg syndrome (like Benadryl has in the past). I requested a glass, of course. As I sat there, happily clutching my deeply revered beverage, I waited for the flight attendant to tell me how much I owed her. She just smiled and proceeded down the aisle with her cart. What? FREE WINE?! Delta ROCKS! I was saved. Maybe, just maybe, I could actually sleep on this flight and I'd wake up when we landed safely in Germany. Yeah, right.

Since I didn't know how the anxiety medication would affect me, I was hesitant to try it. What if it made me even more anxious? Benadryl has been known to do that. If I take 1/2 a tablet, it helps, but a whole one gives me the symptoms of restless leg syndrome— all over my body. Wouldn't my daughter LOVE to be sitting next to that for 10 hours in these cramped, tiny airplane seats! On the flip side, what if it totally zonked me and I had to be carried off the plane? I decided to just wing it....er, wine it—on my own and hoped for the best.

Side note: I can pretty much guarantee that when I'm way up there in years and the nurse gives me medication in hopes of calming me down and helping me sleep through the night, it will have the total opposite effect. Yep! I'll be the one running the halls, climbing the curtains and dancing a jig on the dining room table. In my lifetime I've taken three medications that generally cause relaxation and/or drowsiness for most people: Marijuana in my teen years resulted in extreme paranoia. Morphine in my 40's after major surgery caused extreme restlessness with no sleep whatsoever. And, most currently, Benadryl —a whole tablet gives me a full-body restless leg, as already mentioned. Perhaps the substances meant to perk me up would knock me out? Maybe, but I have no intentions of finding out.

Oh, and in my preparation for our long and most comfortable flight, I'd purchased two foot sling thingies for me and my daughter. I'm so thoughtful, ain't I? This device hangs over your tray table and provides you with a little hammock where you can rest your feet keeping them several inches off the floor. The pictures on Amazon sure made it look comfy. Well...when you barely have room for your knees and your tray table is trying to give you the Heimlich maneuver, there is no way that this handy dandy comfort device is going to work. It requires actual leg room. Epic fail. It wasn't long after our dinner that we were asked to close the cover on our windows, the overhead lights were dimmed and it was apparently nighty night time. At least for those lucky travelers who are capable of sleeping in a moving vehicle.

I was able to get about an hour of sleep while, one at a time, I'd wedge each of my already puffy feet between the head rests of the seats in front of us in a desperate attempt to achieve some elevation. Any at all. Mind you, I had to work quite hard in order to get my leg up through the 16 inches of space and up high enough that it could even be considered elevation. Higher than your heart, that's what they tell you. I looked like a circus contortionist wannabe who couldn't quite nail the audition. Take that foot down; work hard to get the other foot up there in this attractive position. Desperate times, right?

Hours and a few glasses of wine later, after attempting to watch movies or play games on the screen in front of me while every other passenger slumbered away, we were allowed to uncover our windows and let in the morning sunshine. From my window seat, I gazed down at the multi-colored patchwork fields as we were descending into Munich. It was such a beautiful sight. Breathtaking.

Filing through airport security in Munich was an experience. Not being able to read the signs or understand the language is very unfamiliar territory, a tad intimidating even. But, the gentleman behind the plexiglass at the customs counter gave me a friendly "Dankeschön" as he stamped my passport and we were all loaded onto a bus where we met our tour guide. He was a handsome young man, I guessed about 28 years old. He was tall, slender, and had long dread locks of blondish hair wrapped around the top of his head all held in place by a headband and his voice sounded just like Arnold Schwarzeneggar's when he told us, "Goot'n morning!" We later found out he is from Austria. Makes sense. Our bus driver was the epitome of a mountain man. A full beard, blue jeans, a belly that protruded above his belt, suspenders and hiking shoes. I nicknamed our tour guide "Sven" and the bus driver "Mountain Bob." Sven gave us a rundown of what to expect for the day along with a very serious lecture on the importance of being on time. He referred to it as "German time," meaning no leeway, no flexibility, you show up on the dot, period. "German time," he would proclaim, pointing to his watch. I thought, *who is this mother fella anyway?!* My experience in Europe thus far was a bit cold, unnerving and felt far too similar to riding on the "cattle truck" with 50 other brand new and nervous recruits on that first day of army basic training. What had we gotten ourselves into here?

After sitting and waiting on the bus for almost two hours, due to other tour mates having unfortunate and unexpected flight delays, we were finally on our way to tour the city of Munich! It was on this our first bus ride that Sven introduced us to "The water song." He told us that whenever we heard this song that he would be selling bottled water for two euros each and would deliver it to us as he walked the aisle of the bus. The song he played was performed by a band from Puerto Rico, if memory serves. It's pretty amusing, riding on a bus tour through Germany being guided by an Austrian man while listening to Puerto Rican music.

I was looking forward to checking into our hotel, maybe getting a small nap, and most definitely a shower. The bus took us to the hotel, but only to drop off our luggage. No sleep. No shower. Ugh! Onward we went to see Munich, on foot. Now, Sven? He is no ordinary tour guide. He is an extreme speed-walking tour guide. I couldn't have walked any faster if my ass was on fire and I still lagged behind the group. After we speedily walked 9,346 miles through downtown Munich in just under 90 minutes, we had a little free time. It wasn't even 11:00 a.m. but we felt like it had to be at least 5:00 or 6:00 in the evening. Our entire first day in Europe was spent walking the city streets of Munich and it continually felt like the clock was not moving—at all. That jet lag stuff? It is for real.

We enjoyed our first authentic German lunch consisting of white sausage and sauerkraut at a small restaurant in the city where we learned our first lesson in Europe: public restrooms are not free. There was a tip plate on the sink and they used the honor system with the patrons of this restaurant. Not knowing what the going rate was for using the facilities, I put a 2 euro coin in the plate. We also learned that drink refills are not free as they are in the U.S., and that water is not free. Okay, then. There were, however, a few restaurants and stores that offered a fee-free restroom and for this reason, our motto for the rest of our tour was, "Never pass up a free restroom." Even if you'd just emptied your bladder, just empty it again while it's free.

After lunch, we met up with the group and walked another 27 miles to look at the next exciting site— a garden. Really?! I was like, *Okay, this blows! We haven't even been to our hotel to get a shower or take a smidgen of a nap. We're tired, feeling grungy and now they want us to hike all over Germany like a bootcamp road march? I just wanna go back home. I wonder if I can bump up my return flight to like right f'ing now!* Nevertheless, I pulled up my big girl panties and persevered. I have to admit, the garden was quite beautiful. Fine. I'll stop being a big whiney puss.

Munich is beautiful and absolutely the cleanest place I'd ever seen. There is a sweet smell throughout the city that I was never able to identify or find its source. We walked through miles of a very wide piazza lined with churches, street vendors, shops and restaurants. Much like New York City, there were street entertainers and pigeons, too, but there was no litter or bird poop on the ground. Amazing! Amber later said, "Pigeons probably hold it because you have to pay to poop here!" The restaurants and shops had no dust. Our hotel was immaculately clean and it too had that sweet, unidentified aroma. I believe it was Walt Disney who wanted to create a place that was so clean you could eat off the streets. Well, kudos to you, Munich, you've accomplished that feat. Incredible!

After getting some much needed sleep our first night in a lovely hotel, we had to wake up early for breakfast and more speed walking. Oh, in the lobby of this hotel, there is—are you ready for this? A wine vending machine!! Yes, it's true! You put your euros in the slot, press a button and a chilled, single-serve bottle of wine pops out the bottom. How amazing is that? Eureka! Hmm...I might have a problem.

Every morning, the hotel offered a vast breakfast buffet which included some odd items, at least for this American. There was a large selection of what I'd call cold cuts. Lunch meat? For breakfast? Some of those meats looked kind of undercooked to me, too. I don't remember what I ate that first morning, probably some scrambled eggs, but I later succumbed to partaking of the cold cuts with a slice of cheese and a pat of butter. It was surprisingly tasty and I repeated it for nearly every breakfast thereafter.

Odd fact: In Germany (well, in this hotel at least), there are no washcloths for bathing. There were none in our hotel room, so we asked the front desk lady if we could have a couple washcloths. It took several attempts to get her to understand what we were talking about, but once she understood she told us that they did not have them there. I asked, "Well, then how do you wash your back?" She said, "Well, you have a friend in the shower with you." Well, okay then. Germans are no fools!

We did a lot of browsing through shops in Munich and always looked through the home goods sections to see if we could find washcloths. We weren't finding any! So weird. About the moment we called off our search, voila! We were in TK Maxx, that's a German TJ Maxx, and there they were on a shelf. There was only one color, mind you, but it was indeed a washcloth, it said so right on the shelf label. We bought two of them and once we returned to the hotel we so desperately wanted to show the front desk lady what we'd been talking about, but she wasn't there at the time. Ironically, Amber only used her washcloth once, then resorted to bathing the German way. Well, minus the friend to help her. I used mine repeatedly, not willing to risk missing that spot in the middle of my back.

We spent a total of three days in Munich. The Glockenspiel was something to see. It's like the world's largest cuckoo clock. I don't know that it actually holds that title, it's just what I call it. Every day at 5:00 p.m., it would start its show with moving parts on several levels. Sadly, we were only able to witness it one time. We also toured the first concentration camp ever built—Dachau, about an hour bus ride from Munich. This was a harrowing experience to say the least. So many innocent lives lost due to ignorance and hatred. No words can describe how it feels to walk through the room where people were ordered to completely disrobe for their "disinfection," men, women and children alike. Then, led to the adjoining room where they would all take their last breaths—of deadly gas. In the adjoining room—the many cremation ovens.

My daughter and I managed to get separated from one another in the Dachau museum. To be fair, it is a very large museum and was flooded with tourists. I went outside to see if maybe she'd started walking back toward the designated "meeting place." I didn't see her or the group. A few minutes later, the group leader messaged us on WhatsApp, asking where we were and if we were on our way to the bus. Apparently, they were all aboard and waiting for us. I looked around again for Amber. Nowhere in sight.

Not wanting to hold up the tour bus, I messaged them to go on and head to our next site, a castle, and that we would get a cab and catch up with them. Less than 10 minutes later, my daughter and I were reunited and walked to the main entrance to call a cab. Our cab driver was a slender female with coal black hair. She was wearing super high-heeled stiletto shoes and was dressed in like—well, I describe it as a feminine tuxedo. Very ritzy. Her cab was a Mercedes and its leather interior was immaculate. I'd never ridden in a Mercedes. You just don't see things like that in Kentucky—a Mercedes taxi? Come to think of it, I'd never had a female cab driver either.

The ritzy cab driver dropped us off in downtown Munich and we started walking to find the bus for our next tourist attraction, a palace. GPS on my phone was not helping. I messaged the group through WhatsApp and asked for directions. We even asked people on the street for directions and still couldn't find the bus. Finally, we realized that where the bus was waiting would be quite a walk, we didn't make it in time, and missed our ride. Again. At this point, my right knee is buckling due to the stress of all the speed walking we'd done and I could barely walk at all due to the severe pain involved. We decided to hail another cab and catch up with the tour bus. Again. We managed to find one and asked the driver to take us to the place where our tour was headed. This time, our cab driver was a very friendly and talkative Greek man in his 60's, I imagined. We'll call him Nick. Well, Nick told us how he loved Americans, where his family originated, and he shared a few other stories with us. He mentioned that he wanted to buy us "a cream." He seemed genuinely thrilled and delighted to have us in his presence. I told him we really needed to catch up with our tour bus and that we had a schedule (not that that had mattered much to us since we kept missing the bus). "Ooooh, it will take no time," he said. At this point, we are Nick's unwilling passengers as he navigates his taxi through the narrow side streets of Munich, all the while I'm picturing the news story about us being kidnapped by a psychopathic cab driver from Greece! Nick parks in a very tight spot in front of a gelato shop and leads us inside. Oooh, so "cream" is really gelato. Got it. It really was a gelato shop, but I wondered if it was a front for some sort of illegal business. *Breathe.* He asked us what flavor we'd like, paid the bill, and we all sat down at a little round cafe table to enjoy our selections. We really needed to get back with our tour, but Nick had other plans. He left the gelato shop to go to the adjoining store and soon came back with two lottery play bills for my daughter and I to fill out for him. He seemed convinced that being American, and "pretty women," that we would surely select his winning numbers. Okay, we'll play along. We selected some numbers on our tickets and Nick took them next door to make the final purchase. When he returned with his "winning tickets," he rubbed them on top of our heads, you know, for extra good luck. Then, at last, we were back in the cab en route to the tour, already in progress. We arrived at the palace just 10 minutes before the bus was to depart for the next destination. At least we caught it this time!

During our free time, we spent much of it walking around that piazza in Munich, browsing through the shops and the beautiful churches. Wow, the churches, all exquisitely adorned with sculptures, paintings and ginormous pipe organs. There were a lot of people walking through Munich, at all times. We assumed they were all German and lived there because they seemed to all know exactly where they were going. They all walked very briskly, too, and good luck to you if you happen to be in their path. Bam! I got knocked in the shoulder so many times, and they just kept walking. Then, I realized what I was doing wrong. These native Germans would make no eye contact with passersby. None. At least not that we saw. Aha! Okay, got it. So, I started walking exactly as they had, keeping my eyes fixed on my destination, attempting no eye contact with any passerby. Eureka! That worked. I didn't get knocked sideways any more after that.

One afternoon in Munich, we happened upon a very friendly French man who was immediately enamored with Amber. He was dressed very finely, with a tan trench coat, nice shoes and a hat. So dapper. He took off his hat and commenced flipping his long bangs back and forth, with his hand, from the back of his head to the front of his face. Then, he'd put the hat back on his head and continue talking to us. He must've done this four or five times during our conversation on that street corner in Munich. Is that a mating ritual in France? He was some kind of doctor, gave us his card and allowed me to take a picture of him with Amber. The look on her face in one of the photos clearly screams, "HELP ME!!" I couldn't stop laughing. I'm such a supportive and loving mother.

On our last day in Germany, we went to see the Neuschwanstein Castle. It's the castle that inspired the one featured in the Sleeping Beauty movie. It was truly stunning and we wished we could've seen more of it. But, the best part of that attraction for me was waiting in line and killing time by singing the Fresh Prince theme song in a duet with Sven. He started it, I just joined in. He really was a lot of fun throughout our tour.

Our time in Munich having been completed, we were on our way to Venice, Italy. But first, we would visit Innsbruck, Austria. On the way to Innsbruck, Sven had the bus pull over for a short time so that we could get some pictures of the majestic countryside. Oh, what a magnificent sight Austria is to behold. The mammoth, snow-capped mountains make the houses look like miniature toys. I couldn't take enough pictures of the awe-inspiring scenery. Exquisite!

Alas, our pitstop was short and sweet and we were loaded back onto the bus, you now, still operating on German time. We were headed down a pretty steep hill when I heard a few passengers gasp loudly and one woman said, "Did we hit it?!!" We'd apparently almost hit a deer as we were coming down that mountain. Then, before we could reach the bottom of it, the bus was pulled over for speeding and Mountain Bob received a lovely ticket. I exclaimed, "Hide the pot!!" It just was not Mountain Bob's day. Once he received his citation for speeding (not for drugs, the cop didn't hear what I'd said), he resumed his position behind the wheel and yelled out the window toward that cop, "I hope your mother knows what you've done!!" You tell him, Mountain Bob! Several tour mates would enjoy naps during our bus rides. I was envious, yet didn't want to miss any of the sites either. When we'd be approaching our stops, Sven would pick up the microphone and we'd hear, "Wakey wakey" through the speakers.

An hour or two later, we stopped at a McDonald's so that we could get a snack while the bus driver had the bus refueled. "Wakey wakey," Sven announced to make sure we were all awake. Amber noticed an Aldi store right beside the McDonald's and since neither of us wanted anything from McD's, we decided to get our snack there instead. We went through every aisle, comparing all the different foods to what we have back home in the U.S. We selected our snacks and exited the store. After a few photo ops with the Austrian Aldi sign, we ate our cheese sticks while walking around until it was time to load onto the bus. Once we got comfortably adjusted in our seats, Amber rustled through her jacket to locate her cellphone. It wasn't there. She gutted her purse and it was not there. I looked through it, too, just to be sure. Nope. Mere minutes from the expected departure time, we quickly got off the bus and I let the tour guide know what was happening as I ran back to Aldi to see if anyone had turned in a lost cell phone. This, after Sven had given us another serious lecture about the importance of "being on time" and staying "on schedule" because we didn't want to hinder the enjoyment of our fellow tour mates.

I looked through the aisles of the Aldi store hoping to find the phone on the floor. No such luck. I did, however, find a group of three handsome young men and asked if they spoke English. The first one pointed to the next one and then he and the second one pointed to the third guy. The third guy said that he knew a little English, in a voice just like Arnold Schwarzeneggar's (he looked like him, too) while making the "lil bit" gesture with his hand. I asked if anyone had turned in a phone and after rephrasing it a time or two, he understood and asked a woman clerk who happened to be wearing a headset. She called another employee and soon shook her head. No phone had been turned in. Dang it!

I thanked Arnold for his help and headed back outside. Amber had retraced her steps through McD's. No luck. Back at the bus, Sven asked, "Can't you track it?" I tried to use the iPhone finder app on my phone, but it requires Wifi and there was none on our bus. "Does McDonald's have WiFi?" Why, yes, they do! We rushed over to McD's and after several attempts, it finally connected to the Wifi. We were ready to locate Amber's phone, at last. Amber wasn't sure if she even remembered her Apple password, but she guessed it correctly on the first try. She reported her phone as lost and entered a six digit code to be used for unlocking it once it was located. Now, let's track that phone. And...go! Phone cannot be traced because it is offline. It was offline because the battery was dead. Amber's phone battery was dead more than it was alive, it simply would not hold a charge. She really needed to get a new battery, or a new phone. Amber felt sure she'd put her phone in her jacket pocket and since it was warm and sunny that day, she carried the jacket and assumed the phone had simply fallen out.

Plan C: We retraced our steps around the parking lot, the Aldi sign and the grassy areas where we'd been earlier. Still no phone. With sick stomachs, we admitted defeat and returned to our seats on the bus. I decided to check her purse one more time, just to be sure we didn't miss it. No phone inside. Again, dang it! Then, I spotted a little pocket on the outside of her purse. Maybe, just maybe. I unzipped the pocket and peeked inside. Voila! Guess what was in there? You guessed it! It was in her "pocket," just not the one in her jacket! I announced that the phone had been found and we were finally on our way to Innsbruck, only 30 mins behind schedule. So sorry, Sven. Tsk tsk. Later, Amber received an email saying, "Amber's iPhone was found near Brennbichl 6463 Karrosten Austria at 3:20 AM PDT." That iPhone tracker thing really works!

Along with my puffy feet and claustrophobia, I am also plagued with TC—"traveler's constipation." Yep. I travel. The gates get locked up. At this point in our tour, it had been several days since I'd had any output in the poop department and I was getting worried, as well as uncomfortably bloated. We were in Innsbruck, Austria, enjoying our walk through the streets of this picturesque city and, as luck would have it, we spotted a pharmacy. Yay!! Relief was in sight. Green Cross was the name of it. (Later, a friend of mine who'd lived in Germany for several years told me, "Always trust the Green Cross.") We went inside as I prayed that the pharmacist could speak even a little English. She greeted us at the counter and I asked if she spoke English to which she answered yes and asked how she could help me. As subtle as I could, I conveyed my problem to her and requested suppositories. She said, "Ahh. Do you want fast acting or slow acting?" Of course, I chose the fast one. Who wants to take a slow one, not knowing when or where that sucker would activate the old poop chute? She turned toward the shelves behind her and selected a green box of Dulcolax suppositories. I paid for my prize and told her, "Thank you!! This is my souvenir from Austria." She chuckled as we went on our merry way. We had a few minutes before catching our bus so we decided to get a cappuccino. This cappuccino was the very best one I had during the entire 13-day tour! I could spend a whole vacation in Austria. Innsbruck, much like Munich, is extremely clean. No pigeon poop on their sidewalks either. Our short visit was nearing its end and all of us tourists were mingling at the designated meeting place, waiting for our bus to pick us up. Then, it's onward to Italy!

We were all standing on the corner waiting for our bus to pick us up, just watching the cars, busses and trolleys go by when a woman in our group shouted, "I left my wallet!" She'd had it in the restaurant where they'd eaten lunch and she felt she left it in the restroom. She and her husband ran like the wind back to the restaurant, but the wallet was long gone. The police were called, reports given, and all the proper channels followed to start the process of getting her a new passport. What a day! Narrowly missing a deer, speeding tickets, and a missing wallet. Maybe Sven should've skipped the importance-of-being-on-time lecture—it sure seemed to be biting him in the backside. I felt so badly for our tour mate. Such a sick and helpless feeling—in a foreign land and your money, passport and identification vanishes without a trace. I told her how sorry I was that this was happening and hugged her. There wasn't anything else I could do to help her.

Along with my swelling feet, claustrophobia and lack of good hearing, plus traveler's constipation (isn't my husband such a lucky man), I have also been blessed with an incredible smeller —I mean, I smell *everything*. I once sniffed out a small water leak in our house because the smell of mildew led me to its source and my husband couldn't smell it. This super olfactory system of mine can be a blessing, and it can be a curse. I must tell you, if you are a smoker, I am not against you. You have the right to smoke wherever and whenever you desire. That being said, my ultra-sensitive nose simply cannot endure secondhand smoke. It's more than just an unpleasant odor in the air. It causes me real physical discomfort, like pain and everything. Thankfully, within our tour group, there were very few smokers. However, the ones who did smoke always seemed to be upwind of me and I seemed to relentlessly wind up directly downwind of their exhaust as they puffed away at every opportunity, during the miles and miles of walking through Europe. Having had enough of my sinuses, eyes and throat burning, I resorted to trying my best to stay in front and/or upwind of them. Aw, fresh air. It felt so good. However, my attempts to breathe clean healthy air seemed to be taken as a confrontational afront aimed directly at these smokers, like I was trying to race them and I always wanted to be first. While it may have appeared to be the case, I was just trying to breathe, people! Thus ensued the uncoordinated tango-waltz-foxtrot of me trying to breathe clean air and them trying to stay in front of the entire tour crowd, mainly me, everywhere we went. I was, I'm semi-ashamed to admit, tempted more than once to trip them as they raced in front of me time and time again, sometimes rudely cutting me off while we were waiting in single-file, standstill lines. But, I refrained. (Pats self on back with a devious look that says, now I kinda wish I had done it! I'm so bad.)

Also, in the travel tips and information we received prior to this tour, it was suggested that we pack light and plan to "reuse" outfits. Of course, I still packed like I was going on a month long safari and "may need this or that." I packed 4 pairs of shoes, and tons of clothes. This makes for an extremely heavy suitcase, broken wheels or not.

Prior to entering the hotel in Jeselo, Italy, where we stayed while touring Venice, we were told there was no elevator. With luck, Amber and I were assigned a room on the fifth floor. Oh joy! We were so excited about the opportunity to lug our suitcases up five flights of stairs. To our surprise and delight, however, after we'd received our room keys we saw an elevator! Why would they tell us there wasn't one? Well, we soon discovered the answer to that. This elevator was more like a supersized dumbwaiter. We pressed the button to open the door and looked inside. It was either pack ourselves into this closet trolley and suffer severe panic, possible heart attack and death, or lug our heavy-ass suitcases up five flights of stairs and suffer heart attack and death. Okay, we can do this. We stepped into this elevator of death and had to stand side-by-side very closely, I mean shoulder to shoulder, and then stack our suitcases on top of one another for everything to fit. Breeeeeathe. Push the "5" button. Off we go. Twenty-three minutes later, we reached the fifth floor. Not really, but it sure felt like it and it was super hot and stuffy in that thing! We headed to our room, 508, dragging our luggage behind us, my huge suitcase shedding more pieces of its retread tires along the way. I handed the key to Amber who tried it on the door. Didn't work. She tried again. Entry denied. She said, "You try," and handed the key to me. I couldn't get it to work either. I looked at the key, like I can figure out why it's not working and said, "Oooh, it's for room 506!" We walked the two doors down to our room and were laughing so hard that I had to stop and squeeze my legs together to retain my urine. I had almost regained my composure when our luggage fell over one at a time like dominos, which caused us to laugh even harder—making it completely impossible to retain my urine any more. There's one pair of pants I wouldn't be able to "re-use." Sometimes it pays to over-pack!

Our bathroom was equipped with a bidet ("buh-day" is how we pronounced it). Now, I knew what it was and how it's used, though I've personally never used one, but my daughter didn't. She couldn't believe it when I explained it to her. As we got situated in our room and I changed into dry clothes, we giggled all the while as we relived the hilarity of our recent death-defying elevator adventure, luggage fiasco and the whole bidet discovery. At one point, I chuckled so hard that an air biscuit was released into the air. Disgusted, my daughter demanded, "You're sleeping on the other bed!!" I retorted, "I've been farting all day and you haven't smelled anything!" She said, "Yes, I did! I thought it was your breath! Do they have Tic Tacs for butts?" She's so fun!

Despite the near constant rain and having to wear our plastic rain ponchos everywhere, we had a nice boat ride to Venice the next day. Venice is very, very crowded. We had lunch at a lovely quaint Italian restaurant we'd found while walking through a narrow alleyway lined with various shops. There were fine white linen tablecloths and napkins, and water was served in pretty stemmed glasses. Seated at the table next to us were two young men and a young woman. I enjoyed hearing their conversation in Italian, though I understood none of it, and watching the young woman talk with her hands as Italians are notorious for doing. At one point, the young woman and I met each other's eyes and I gave her a friendly smile. My smile was reciprocated by a stone-cold, emotionless gaze. Okay, I thought. Back to my lasagna. In Italy, waiters/ servers do not automatically bring your check to you near the end of your meal. You must ask, no matter how long you stay seated at your table. Italians don't rush through meals like Americans often do. Mealtimes are to be relaxed, enjoyed and thoroughly experienced, even if all you order is a cup of coffee. By the way, there are no "to-go" cups in Italy. You are to sit down, relax and take your time as you enjoy your beverage. We're on Italian time now, Sven. When we finished our meal, I asked our waiter for the check. He nodded and went about his work. Minutes later, afraid we were about to miss our next scheduled group attraction, I asked another server if we may get our check. He immediately delivered the message to our waiter who immediately looked at us with a perturbed, scowling expression on his face. How do you say, "I'm very sorry for appearing rude. It's just that we have a schedule to keep on our tour" in flawless Italian?

We somehow managed to miss the gondola ride through Venice, but I wasn't too thrilled about riding around in an uncovered boat through the pouring rain anyway. Nevertheless, we walked up and down the peers to see if we could acquire a ride on our own and we found several options. But 80 euros—each? Nah, we'll pass. Maybe next time. Ironically, our day in Venice, which Amber called "Monsoon Day," was the rainiest day of our entire trip and the only day that she put on sunscreen.

We entered the Dogea Palace with no idea what we'd find inside. It was our free time and not part of a guided tour. We walked around a few hallways, saw some sculptures and thought, is this it? This is all there is to—a palace?? Well, turns out, there was A LOT more to this palace once we made a few more turns and it could easily fill a city block, or twelve. Somewhere along our meandering through it, we decided we'd had enough and wanted to get a cappuccino or something. (There seems to be a lot of coffee and wine consumption on this trip. Hmm, so be it.) Okay, which way is the exit to this mother? Umm…we'll try to follow the arrow signs. Apparently, those arrow signs were taking us deeper into the palace instead of leading us out of it and we ended up in the dungeon. Okay, so we'll backtrack a bit and find the way out. Yeah, right! Turn after turn, down this hallway and that hallway, passing countless tourists, sometimes so fast their hair blew in the breeze created by our whizzing past them, we found ourselves in the prison located beneath the palace. *You gotta be kidding me!* The halls were getting more narrow and I was getting hotter and hotter as the air seemed to become thicker and thicker with every step. *HOW THE HELL DO WE GET OUT OF THIS PALACE?!* We would pass tiny windows and pause to look outside at our ever-elusive freedom, I'd take pictures, then we'd regain the strength to motor through another hallway to who knows where. I was on the brink of losing it when we finally located the gift shop. The exit has to be near the gift shop. That's where they always are, you know, so you'll buy something before you make your departure. No more palaces/castles for me, thanks. Well, so I thought.

The rain finally stopped just as we were about to leave Venice. We had a lengthy walk to the boat dock and had to cross a narrow foot bridge in a very crowded area. There were people crossing it, standing on it, blocking every conceivable passageway we could have taken. Well, we had a boat to catch and even though we were on "Italian time" and it is much more relaxed, the boat was still on German time. So, I basically forced my way through the standstill crowd and a woman turned around and cussed at me in maybe 12 languages. I just looked at her and said, "You'll be okay," and kept walking. They may not let me back in this country.

The next day, we stopped in Como, Italy before making our way to Lucerne Switzerland and the Swiss Alps (a dream of mine for decades). We had lunch at an outdoor cafe and I ordered a veggie pizza. Being low-carb keto, I scraped the toppings off with my fork and left the crust. Out of the corner of my eye, I could see and feel the woman next to me sneering straight down her nose a time or two. Perhaps it was an insult to Italians if you don't eat the pizza in its entirety. My apologies, Italy. After lunch, we walked through the city and spotted a gelato shop. Nick was a bad influence. We were studying the various flavors offered by this quaint Italian shop and we had a question or two, you know, not knowing how to read Italian. The fella behind the counter was immediately annoyed, scooped out two random flavors on little sample spoons and shoved them towards our faces saying, "Here! Try pistachio!!!" At this point, I was getting the distinct impression that those folks who lived in Venice were tired of tourists, or Americans, or humans in general. Nevertheless, we ordered our gelato and continued on our merry way through Como.

It was a long bus ride through gorgeous countryside from Italy to Switzerland. We rode past vineyard after vineyard and picturesque towns built into the hills. We arrived at the hotel Ybrigerhof in Unteriberg just before suppertime. It was a lodge type hotel set in the base of the Swiss mountains. There were no other businesses around it, no gas stations, no convenience stores, just houses which were built all the way up the hills that had smoke gently billowing from their chimneys floating straight up towards the clouds. I marveled at one house that was five stories high.

Once settled in our room, I soon discovered that none of the devices in my multi-pack of voltage adaptors wouldn't work in this hotel. Apparently, Switzerland has its own unique outlet. Thankfully, our tour leader had the right adaptor and agreed to charge up my camera batteries overnight. The thought of being in Switzerland without my Canon camera was completely unfathomable.

This hotel/lodge was a one-man show. The owner was a super industrious Turkish man with dark brown eyes and black hair, probably in his late 40's, who was quite handsome, and oh so charming. He handled the check-ins, the cooking, much of the serving and running the bar later in the evening. I only saw one other person help him, a woman who helped serve food in the dining room. I suppose she helped with room cleaning, etc., at least I hope he had help with that aspect of running a lodge.

Along with our supper that evening, we were given complimentary wine, one bottle per 4 people. We were talking with some of our tour mates, one of whom was from New Orleans. She told us that she had survived the devastation of Katrina, but lost every picture she had of her dearly departed mother. After she shared this with us, I got up from my seat and walked over to give her a hug. When I sat back down, Amber asked if I was okay. I said, "I can't imagine not having a picture of my mother," then began sobbing. Must've been the wine. Before we left the dining room, the Turkish man, who was immediately enamored with my daughter, gave her his "favorite" cork screw as a gift. European men just love her!

The next morning, it was time to realize my longtime dreams of going up the Swiss Alps!! Yay! It had rained for most of our trip up to this point, but we had high hopes that it would stop on the day we got to see the Alps. Alas, it did not. It rained continually, and was snowing when we got to the top of that mountain. The 90-minute boat ride and the long tram ride up to the top of the mountain were both fun and we saw actual, real live mountain goats! Amber and I went out on the observation deck in the blowing snow, and walked through some tunneled pathways out there, too. I held my blue rain poncho up and let the blustery wind try to pull it out of my hands. We could not see anything but white in every direction, but I imagined how it must look on a clear day and it was still a wonderful experience. We will definitely have to go back again and take in that magnificent view. The tram ride back down the mountain was amazing. I sat on the floor in the very front, which was top-to-bottom glass, right beside Sven. We enjoyed this front row view as the town slowly came into focus through the rain and snow and by the time we reached the station, the rain had completely stopped. We simply didn't get to spend enough time in the gorgeous, mountainous countries of Austria and Switzerland.

Before heading to France, we spent a day in Heidelberg, Germany. This is where we enjoyed our truly authentic German meal which included wiener schnitzel, white spargel (asparagus), and for me, a warm beer. A serving of beer over there is much bigger than in the U.S. I mean, the mug holds about a liter of beer! I never thought I'd like warm beer, but I really didn't mind it. It was actually delicious, although I have no plans to drink my American beer at that temperature in the future. It wasn't easy, but I made sure I finished that mega-mug of beer, too. Heidelberg is another place I would love to return to and spend more time.

On to France!! We spent a few hours in Strasbourg, visited another castle/palace, without getting lost in a dungeon prison or missing our bus, and walked through the picturesque city lined with sidewalk cafes, street artists and such incredible architecture, with me snapping pictures at every opportunity. This place must be where movies are filmed. The entire area looked like an intricately designed movie set. Stunning! Next up, the mega-fast train ride from Strasbourg to Paris. This train station looked like a gigantic spaceship. If you've never seen it, I encourage you to Google an image and check it out. Of course, we had to pay to use the restroom in this bustling train station. This one was the most unique, for sure. To enter, you had to purchase a ticket and walk through a turnstile which was very much like those in subway stations. Pretty cool. We had heard that the train traveled at an incredible speed, and it sure did. I think it was going like 180 mph.

I was startled with the loud whoosh sound created every time a train going the opposite direction would zoom past us.

The rain completely stopped, at long last, the skies were clear, and it was a delightfully sunny day in Paris!! We gathered our luggage and exited the train. At this point, the wheels on my large suitcase had shed every bit of their retread and were riding on the rims. Thankfully, this meant that the clunk clunk clunk that followed me through Europe had been replaced by a smooth ride.

Of course our tour bus took us right to the Eiffel Tower, then later that night we toured around the city by boat as the sun was setting. Amber and I sat on the deck at the front of this boat with our incredible tour guide, Sven. Later, he would call me his "Kentucky momma," and Amber his "Kentucky sister." Their birthdates are only two days apart. Such awe-inspiring sights and sounds as we cruised around the city on the Seine river, seeing the Eiffel Tower all lit up in the distance and the fire damaged cathedral of Notre Dame. There were many bridges and whenever we would go under one Sven would lead us in a whooping and hollering chorus, which we were to perform just as loudly as we could muster, while people on those bridges and river banks echoed it back to us. Too fun!

Sven, the awesome tour guide that he was, wanted us to experience all that we could on this tour and led us back to the Eiffel Tower that night so we could see the twinkle lights display that occurred nightly at 11:00 p.m. We followed his speed-walking through the subways, navigating the bustling streets of Paris and up about 150 steps to reach our destination. It truly was a great place to view the twinkling tower. He said that we'd watch it for a few minutes, then would head back to the hotel. It was a busy day and we were all tired.

You know me, wanting to get the absolute best locale for my pics/videos, I spotted a bicycle rack that extended out toward the tower. With my goal in sight, I purposefully walked toward it and tripped over a peddler's display of mini Eiffel Tower replicas that he had arranged on a blanket, knocking several of them over. He screamed at me, "Madam! MADAM!!" I said, "I'm sorry! I'm sorry!" and kept walking towards my picture and video location. No one was in front of me. There was nothing to obstruct my view. It was perfect. I was the only one out there, which made me wonder if this was a no-no and was a restricted area. No matter. I took a look behind me, just to be sure where the rest of the group was before I started my video. All present. Once the twinkling started, I was mesmerized and got lost in it. *I'm in freaking Paris, France watching the twinkling lights of the Eiffel Tower! Wow!!* I was recording the event on my camera as well as my cell phone and before I knew it, several minutes had gone by. I stopped the videos, turned around to locate the group again, and saw no one! *WHAT? Right there! That's where we were supposed to meet to head back! That's where they were before the twinkle lights started! Maybe they walked a little bit over this way?* I made my way out of the bike racks, being careful not to trip over any displays this time, and looked over towards the steps that lead out of this place and started walking in that direction. I could not find the group. They must have already headed back towards the subway. I took off walking, went down the many, many steps, crossed the busy 5-way intersection and headed towards the subway station. I was getting a lil frantic because I couldn't even remember the name of our hotel, you know, just in case I decided to hail a cab. Then, I thought I should check to see where everyone went, so I sent a "Where is everyone?" message on WhatsApp. A fellow tour mate responded, "We're at the meeting place." I asked, "Where is that?" They answered, "Where you tripped over the sales display." Oooooh!! I guess there were witnesses to that. I swear I did not see one familiar face after making my videos. Not one.

Once again, I crossed the busy 5-way intersection, trekked up the many, many steps, and found my tour mates all right where they said they'd been the whole time. Did they just play a masterful practical joke on me?

While in Paris, Amber and I enjoyed one very unusual meal. We wanted to try something different and authentically French for our lunch. But, since we could not read a word on the menu, we chose an entree from the featured pictures and decided to share the meal. It was some kind of meat and cheese atop a piece of bread similar to ciabatta and there was a sunny-side-up egg as well, along with french fries and a small salad. Assuming we were eating some true French food, I tried to guess what kind of meat we were eating. It was extremely tender and amazingly delicious. I thought it was likely lamb, but I really didn't want to know what we were eating since ingesting a baby animal has never been on my bucket list. Amber thought it was duck meat. Finding out what animal we were eating was not possible without asking the waiter. I still didn't want to know, but Amber asked him anyway. "It's tuna," he said. Turns out it was a kosher French meal. So, If you know of such a restaurant in Kentucky, please let me know. I'd love to partake of that tuna meal again.

FYI: France has the best butter I have ever eaten!! It is truly incredible. And, Paris has the busiest subway system I have ever experienced, even worse than New York's!

On one trip, we were jam-packed in the car so tightly, like sardines as the saying goes, that I could feel another human being pressed up against every angle of my body. I said, "I think we're engaged." It was literally becoming difficult to breathe as my lungs were being squeezed. I was starting to sweat and was thinking this is how it ends—on a crowded subway car in Paris. Just as I could feel the panic bubbling up inside me, I looked at Amber who was also looking at me, likely wondering how long I could endure this full body mammogram without completely losing my shit. Once we caught each other's gaze, we were both instantaneously transported back to the NYC subway with the hair-snorting quirky dude and we started laughing, which quickly grew into uncontrollable can't-catch-your-breath laughter for me. I suppose it was laugh or pass out, you know, that whole fight for flight thing. Let's try laughing first. Tears were soaking my face then dripping off cheeks and other passengers were beginning to stare. Is this woman laughing or having an emotional meltdown over there? Yes! As this continued, a few of the other passengers started laughing along with us. I suppose it was quite a funny sight. There is generally not a lot of laughter on subways. Or conversation. Or eye contact between strangers. In the midst of my hysteria, a fine young fellow said to me, "There is more room over there," eyeballing and nodding toward the other side of the car where people were standing—all with a comfortable amount of space between them. Being called out, they all reluctantly scooted a bit closer together so that we sardines could enjoy our full lung capacity once again. Wasn't that so sweet of those nice people?

During another fulfilled subway ride in gay Paris, there were two handsome young men and a beautiful woman standing near us, holding on to the rails. One of the men clearly did not speak English very well and asked the other man to speak to me on his behalf. This man leaned toward me and said, with a very heavy French accent, "He would like a drink of your water," and nodded towards the bottle of water I held in my hand. With a bit of trepidation and hesitancy, I slowly handed my water to the dehydrated fella who requested it. He removed the cap, took a large gulp, replaced the cap and then politely handed the bottle back to me while nodding his head and smiling with gratitude. Yeah, some weird stuff happens in Paris!

I truly enjoyed riding the subways in New York City. I enjoyed them in Paris as well, despite having my lungs nearly deflated on the very crowded cars. But, from now on, when I enter a subway station I will hear Sven's voice shouting, "Take care for your belongings, guys" and, "Guys?! Take care for your belongings," with that Arnold Swarzeneggar accent as we heard every time we traveled by train.

In the USA, the French have often been portrayed as cowards, running away from conflicts, surrendering, etc. It's even mentioned in the movie Pirates of the Caribbean when it was asked who invented "parlay," the word used by pirates to evade their impending death upon their being captured. I certainly did not see that type of demeanor in France. We were on a guided tour through a palace (yes, another one) in Paris led by a 100% French woman who was extremely proud of her heritage. She repeatedly boasted, "French is best," throughout the tour. As we progressed through the palace, if our very proud French tour guide found that you were not looking in her direction as she spoke, she would make it a point to bring you back. "Eyes on me," she'd shout to the group as she pointed to herself with both hands. Heaven forbid you look around the room at the amazing art displayed on every wall. She demanded that other tour groups allow space between theirs and hers and she even shushed a very large room full of tourists (men, women and children alike) and other guided tours, demanding that they not be so loud as it was causing her to talk extremely loud so we would hear her. Wow!

This dictatorial...ahem, guided tour ended around noon and we were led to a quaint cafe where we were told to line up and "collect our lunch." Our meal had, apparently, been pre-ordered for us in order to save time and get us back on the bus as expeditiously as possible. What delicacy did we get? A hot ham and cheese sandwich on plain white bread. I'm not a historian or anything, but I really doubt that a ham and cheese sandwich is any kind of authentic French meal. I asked, "Who ordered this for us?" "The tour guide," a fellow tourmate answered. "Well, then, *she* should eat it," I responded.

I've really got to work on speaking my mind more freely. Several times during this eventful, fun-filled trip, my daughter would try to pawn me off on other people, be it fellow tourists or strangers, didn't matter. She'd ask them, "Will you babysit her for a while?" Or, "Do you need a new friend?" But, I think my favorite one is, "Isn't she fun??"

After we'd finished our delicious hot ham and cheese, authentic French sandwiches (eye roll), I noticed that my shoes seemed a bit looser. I thought that's great, my feet aren't as swollen today. Cool. I also noticed that my shoes seemed dirtier than I'd remembered from the night before. I assumed that I'd gotten them dirty during the evening boat ride through Paris. No biggie. But, there's a small hole in the mesh now, too. Well, we are doing a lot of walking. Makes sense. Then, my daughter asked, "Do your shoes feel… big?" "Yeah, they do!" "I think you're wearing mine." Yup!! Sure was! We had purchased identical shoes months before our trip and had put on each other's shoes that morning.

An added adventure to our tour of Paris was the catacombs. I opted out of that one, not because the site of millions of skulls and bones would freak me out, I could've touched them all without flinching. No, it was the thought of the underground, narrow passageways and the possibility of me not being able to see in front of or behind me due to large numbers of people—that's what freaked me out—being trapped. I must've been buried alive in a prior life—that would explain it. While Amber went on the bone tour along with my camera to chronicle her experience, I enjoyed a snack and glass of wine with two other non-joiners at a lovely outdoor cafe. We had a good time and great conversation while people-watching on that busy Paris street.

On our last day in France, and Europe, we visited the Louvre Museum and saw the world famous Mona Lisa painting. The museum was in the process of renovating and this painting was in a large room with only a few other works of art. My daughter and I were both surprised at how small this painting truly is, about 2.5 feet by 2 feet. It was displayed on a large wall, protected behind thick glass and perimeter ropes designed to keep the hundreds of tourists several feet away from it. We managed to make our way through the crowd and up to the ropes, snapped some photos along with some selfies with Mona and continued on through the museum.

Then, just like that, it was time to head back to the USA. The seats on the flight from Paris to Atlanta were great! They had a lot more leg room. I wondered why we couldn't have had a similar plane on the way *to* Munich. Nevertheless, I was feeling relaxed and confident that this flight would be nothing but pleasant. Well, with our European tour being anything but dull, we couldn't stop now, could we? We were almost to Atlanta when we heard the announcement, "Is there medical personnel or a doctor on this flight?" *What? Really?* It was like something out of a movie. I'm a nurse, but I don't advertise it. My daughter, on the other hand, who feels quite differently, raised up from her seat, pointed to me and shouted, "She's a nurse!!!" Thanks, Amber, I say via my most disapproving facial expression. The male flight attendant who was standing in the aisle near my seat asked me, "Can you deliver babies?" I quickly responded, "I'm out!" He was joking, of course, and sent me toward the front of the plane to offer my assistance. I walked as quickly as I could to see what I could do to help. There was another nurse on board (possibly outed by her daughter, too) already tending to a female flight attendant who was sitting just outside the cockpit. She had fallen and hit her head, acquiring a small cut in her hairline which was bleeding a little bit. She seemed to be much more emotionally traumatized than physically injured. The first trauma nurse at the gruesomely bloody scene was taking good care of the injured woman, but I hung around for a little while to reassure the emotionally rattled flight attendant that she would be okay as paramedics had been called to stand by while the plane landed at the busy Atlanta airport. I rubbed her shoulder, gave her a hug (I'm such a hugger!), and she thanked me before I headed back to my seat. A standing ovation of coach passengers was waiting for me back there! *What?! Am I a hero now?* No, I'm just kidding. All I got was a bunch of "What happened" questions from those who needed to hear the details surrounding this riveting in-flight drama.

Our short flight from Atlanta to Louisville was pleasant, with no drama or incidents. Ahhh, that was nice. What an eventful trip we'd had!

Now, what's my take on this once in a lifetime European tour? Firstly, the great thing about group tours is that they are group tours. All the planning, ticketing, hotels, certain meals, tourist attractions, and such is taken care of for you. All you have to do is pack your stuff, grab your passport and show up. It's fantastic! You meet new people and come home with new friendships, although most are via Facebook. Secondly, the worst thing about group tours is that they are group tours. Unless you want to fork out your own money for transportation instead of partaking of what is already provided and go your own way, you will go wherever and whenever the scheduled tour takes you, which occasionally includes a city tour where you remain on the bus (not so good), as well as endure the various unplanned mishaps and hiccups inherent when traveling in large groups. Personally, I am not a big crowd type person, at all, and when our tour started, it was quite large. I want to say there were 66 people. There's a lot of herding required with a group that big. However, when we went to Paris, that number was greatly reduced as not everyone opted to go on to France. It was a much more comfortable and relaxing tour. Bottom line, I would definitely sign up for another group tour, albeit a smaller one next time.

I wore my iWatch throughout our tour to track my steps and we walked a grand total 64.28 miles while in Europe. Going on a tour led by Sven is like having your own personal trainer. My stamina had greatly improved, that's for sure. Plus, I lost 3 pounds even though I was not 100% true to keto in my food selections.

Although I've poked a lot of fun at this once in a lifetime trip to Europe, I did truly enjoy it! My favorite places remain Austria and Switzerland. The breathtaking mountains, the clean city sidewalks, the friendly people. Everyone we encountered was very kind to us. Did I mention the mountains? So very lovely. We certainly learned a lot about different customs and cultures, and the hundreds of photographs I took will be treasured for many years to come.

IT'S OK NOT TO BE PERFECT; COMPLETION IS BETTER THAN PERFECTION

Confront the dark parts of yourself, and work to banish them with illumination and forgiveness. Your willingness to wrestle with your demons will cause your angels to sing. Use the pain as fuel, as a reminder of your strength.
—AUGUST WILSON

So, here it is. My book. It's finished. It may contain imperfections and that's OK. I completed it. It's OK to not be perfect. When I've strived for perfection in the past and didn't reach it, I simply wouldn't have completed the project at hand. I robbed myself of being me, being…good enough. I stunted my creativity as punishment for being less than perfect. I wish now that I had finished all those drawings 40 years ago and knew that even though they may have fallen short of my idea of perfection, they were good enough and it was OK.

If you caught typos in this book, it's OK. If I used the word "to" when I should have used "too," it's OK. If I used the word "OK" too much, that's OK, too. If I had a dangling participle, or four or 50, it's OK. So what if I used the word "just" 301 times (yes, I counted them out of curiosity because I noticed I use that word—a lot). If I varied the tense from past to present within a story, that's OK, I write the way I speak.

I didn't write this book for the purpose of allowing perfectionists to critique it. And, if you're a perfectionist, that's OK, too. Critique away! I won't try to stop you.

There is an incredible amount of vulnerability you feel when you share your life's story(ies)—the good, the bad, the ugly, the shameful, and hilarious. It's a metaphorical cliche, but it feels as if you're standing naked in Times Square. Well, maybe not Times Square. You can see just about anything there! More like standing naked in Amish country. There, that's a bit more descriptive.

My goal in making myself vulnerable and writing this book was, and is, merely to bring a little more levity to the world. To make people laugh at the bumps and ditches we encounter on this road called life. This is my completed work. It's exactly the way I want it to be. I chose to self-publish and not submit my creative efforts to that art teacher—*um*, publisher—who would ask me to change this or that to fit my book into his/her idea of how it should be written. It's my book and it's good enough. I hope you were able to look past any imperfections long enough to just enjoy a good laugh or two, or 99. Perhaps, I need to work through my perfectionism hangup a bit longer...ya think? Hmm.

My sincere hope is that it made you laugh until you cried, snorted, farted, snort-farted (obviously, that's a snort and a fart simultaneously escaping your body), or otherwise made it difficult for you to breathe. Well, not the medical emergency type of not breathing. You know what I mean. ← Is that a dangling participle?

Made in the USA
Coppell, TX
17 November 2021